DIAMONDS
IN THE ROUGH

DIAMONDS

IN THE ROUGH

Non-League Football's
Biggest Success Stories

JOSEPH POPE

pitch

First published by Pitch Publishing, 2025

1

Pitch Publishing
9 Donnington Park,
85 Birdham Road,
Chichester, West Sussex,
PO20 7AJ
www.pitchpublishing.co.uk
info@pitchpublishing.co.uk

A CIP catalogue record is available for this book
from the British Library.

ISBN 978 1 83680 154 2

Typesetting and origination by Pitch Publishing

MIX
Paper | Supporting
responsible forestry
FSC
www.fsc.org
FSC™ C016779

Printed and bound on FSC® certified paper in line with
our continuing commitment to ethical business practices,
sustainability and the environment.

Printed and bound in India by Replika Press Pvt. Ltd.

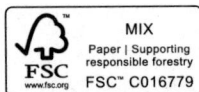

Contents

Introduction

NON-LEAGUE FOOTBALL. A cauldron of emotion – the sport stripped back to its roots in the rawest, most humble form – and an unrivalled product that continues to be the envy of football fraternities across the globe. There is something extra special about the non-league game. To the more infrequent, prawn sandwich brigade of football goers, non-league is seldom afforded the respect that it deserves. So often, fans at the top level of the sport look down their nose at non-league with the view that the fabricated construct that plays to the gallery of a monetised global audience – which they enjoy solely from the comfort of their sofa in front of Sky or TNT Sports – is in every way superior to the real-life humility of non-league.

The perception about non-league is that it is some sort of departure lounge for talent; an abandoned rumble strip where the once high-flying professionals ply their trade. And yet this couldn't be further from the truth. Indeed, for all of the 'glitz and glam' of the top flight and 'Premier' football, all of that would be irrelevant if it weren't for non-league, with so many players who are now – and have in the past – enjoyed the limelight at the very top having started out from the humble beginnings at the bottom. As George B. Hinckley once said, 'You can't build a great building on a weak foundation. You must have a solid foundation if you're going to have a strong superstructure.' Thus, the strength of the non-league scene is equally important, if not more so, as the quality of the leagues above it.

Indeed, while its 'non' prefix paints the picture of some sort of deficiency, non-league is rich with talent. The National League – England's fifth tier – is now very much viewed as League Three (albeit not officially) with an ever-diminishing disparity between the EFL's basement tier and the premier division of non-league. Many have also argued that the National League is as strong as League Two, with calls for 'three up, three down' as strong as they have ever been. This view is supported by the strong recent track record of teams promoted out of the fifth tier doing well in League Two and the wider EFL, with Luton Town having sealed promotion to the Premier League in 2023 having been in the Conference as recently as 2014.

Since the turn of the millennium, the record of sides promoted out of the National League to the EFL has been nothing short of superb. Indeed, since the start of the Football League as we know it today, not a single team has been relegated out of League Two into the National League at the first time of asking. In addition to Luton, there have been a further three sides to have got promoted all the way to the Championship following entry or return to the Football League: Yeovil Town, Doncaster Rovers and Burton Albion. Indeed, since 2004/05, of the 42 teams that have won promotion out of the National League, 26 have since then won promotion out of League Two, underlining the view that the National League – and as a consequence of this, the wider non-league pyramid – is more than capable of holding its own, owing to the quality within it.

And it is not just the three National League derivatives that act as the bottom barrier for talent; the depth and quality of non-league extends far beyond that. Be it a local playing field of a Sunday league side or a semi-professional setup with just one man and his dog watching on, so many of the players who have gone on to grace the biggest of stages in the EFL and indeed the top level in England and Scotland, as well as abroad, can count these humble beginnings as where their careers took flight. The title of this book – I feel – poignantly encapsulates non-league and what it stands for in all of its glory; the perfect environment in which players with undeniable talent can polish their skills, hone their craft and have a springboard for a successful career.

Having been a fan of Torquay United since 2008, and running a website – the Off The Line Blog – dedicated to showcasing the very best of non-league myself, I would like to think that the non-league scene is my bread and butter, having endured and enjoyed all of the trials and tribulations that it has to offer. It is through my support of the Gulls, and in my role as an aspiring pundit, that I have been able to first hand see the quality of players in the non-league pyramid and see the many 'diamonds' that it has to offer in the 'rough', so to speak. Be it watching a budding Kieffer Moore turn out for Torquay on loan in 2016, watching him start as a teenager with Truro City in 2012, or even prior to that kicking a bag of wind around on a local youth pitch in Paignton, I've had the privilege of seeing so many players come through and make a name for themselves before they were even 'household names' or in Moore's case the big cheese on the Welsh international stage. Moore is one of a long list of players I've seen start out right at the depths of the pyramid and go on to be a rip-roaring success in their own way at the top, be it simply playing in the EFL, tasting glory in the Premier League, or representing their country.

As a result, the hidden gems of the non-league scene have – to me – become the household names in the same way a Kevin De Bruyne or an Erling Haaland are to Manchester City; I raise your De Bruyne and Haaland and give you a Josh Stokes and an Alfie May.

This book aims to shine a light on some of the standout examples of players to have started out in non-league and then gone on to have successful careers; in reality, this merely scratches the surface. Indeed, there are so many more players who could have been included in this book to extend my exploration of non-league's many diamonds in the rough who have since become gems. For everyone discussed, I could have picked out four, five, six or even more who have trodden a similar path; the success of non-league really does extend to those great lengths. For example, I've not spoken about Tom Pett, formerly of Potters Bar Town and Wealdstone; Rob Atkinson of Basingstoke Town; Ryan Wintle of Alsager Town; Ebou Adams of Dartford; Connor Washington of St Ives Town; Joe Ward of Chelmsford City; Cauley Woodrow of then non-league Luton; Jacob Brown of Guiseley; Duncan Watmore of Altrincham; Ashley Barnes of Paulton Rovers; Dan Scarr of Causeway United, Redditch United and Stourbridge; Will Norris of Hatfield Town and Royston Town; Lee Gregory of Staveley Miners Welfare and FC Halifax Town; Josh Windass of Harrogate Railway Athletic; Marvin Johnson of Solihull Moors, Romulus and Kidderminster Harriers; Michael Smith of Darlington.

And that is merely 16 names; I could quite easily name another 200 on top of them.

This solely covers players to have started out in non-league; including those who have featured for non-league teams during the early years of their careers the number is even higher. While so many have been on the books of a top academy as a youngster, a large majority of those in fact took their first steps in first-team football out on loan in non-league. It underlines just how integral the non-league pyramid is as the bedrock of English football. Be it a local park pitch with a crowd of one man and his dog, a village team or a junior side, so many of the modern game's top professionals are indebted to their time on the lower rungs of the pyramid in giving them the foundations on which to kick-start a career.

For example, when England jetted out to Germany for Euro 2024, while the players prepared to represent their country at the very highest level it was nice to see the FA give a nod during the build-up to their humbler beginnings; murals were put on social media when the squad was announced detailing where each of Gareth Southgate's selections had started out their footballing journeys. It was refreshing to see the FA shine a light on where their careers had begun, even as low down as who they played for at Sunday league level: teams that many fans have never even heard of, yet have played an important part in producing some of England's finest players today. It almost makes me want to champion that the FA announce all future England squads in this manner, instead of mentioning your Manchester Citys and Arsenals of this world. I'd much rather see the limelight given to those smaller local youth clubs and Sunday league sides that are the epicentres of local footballing communities; the same youth clubs that when every major tournament comes around turn into a sort of shrine in championing their former players. So many of them are sterling champions in recognising the part they have played; Dickerage Lane Adventure Playground, for instance, still have an area dedicated to showcase former player Declan Rice. There are so many more clubs who can take similar pride in the part they have played – big or small – in unearthing the country's footballing diamonds, all wonderfully named: Reddish Vulcans; Leominster Minors; Epsom Eagles; Washington Envelopes; Whitehaven Miners; Ridgeway Rovers; to name but a few.

It is fair to say that non-league has been – and continues to be – vital in giving a platform for the best up-and-coming players that the country has to offer. I'm going to do my best to champion the standout alumni of non-league in this book. Some have gone on and achieved more than others, while some have simply reached the EFL and forged successful careers; all the while indebted to non-league. I aim to give the limelight to those more well-known, lower-league successes, as well as shine the focus on to players that you perhaps weren't even aware had started out as a non-league footballer.

1

1966

IF YOU ask any English football fan what the greatest achievement the country has ever seen is, while notable mentions may include Leicester City winning the Premier League title in 2015/16, Luton Town being promoted to the top flight in 2022/23, and Brian Clough's Nottingham Forest side winning the European Cup in 1979 and 1980, by far and away the one that eclipses those is England winning the World Cup in 1966.

At the absolute pinnacle of the sport, the team that lifted the Jules Rimet Trophy at Wembley against West Germany will rightly be regarded as the greatest that the country has ever produced. It is single-handedly responsible for some of the most revered players that the UK has seen, from a strong West Ham United core of captain Bobby Moore, final hat-trick hero Geoff Hurst and fellow goalscorer Martin Peters, to bastions of the English game in goalkeeper Gordon Banks and brothers Bobby and Jack Charlton.

Of the 22-man squad chosen by manager Alf Ramsey, two members deserve particular recognition: midfielder Alan Ball and forward Roger Hunt. While the contributions of everyone involved were equally as deserving of the praise that they received – recognised with the award of MBEs – Ball and Hunt share the added acclaim of having hailed from the humble beginnings of non-league. They both established themselves as household names for various clubs in the First Division in the late 60s and 70s, but equally count non-league as the roots of their illustrious careers that saw them amass a combined 106 international appearances, three First Division titles, an FA Cup winners' medal and two runners-up medals, four Charity Shields and around 1,300 professional appearances.

Alan Ball and Roger Hunt

When we talk about the greats of the English game, there aren't many better than Alan Ball. Inducted into the English Football Hall of Fame in 2003, he was also added to the Hall of Fame for Everton in 2001 and Blackpool in 2006. To be inducted into one is enough for most players to get a sense of the scale of success that they have tasted, let alone for two of English football's biggest clubs. These sorts of titles, which are bestowed on so few, make it clear that Alan Ball is one of the true greats of his own – and indeed, any – generation to have stepped on a football pitch. Ball sadly passed away at the age of just 61 in 2007, and he has continued to be remembered fondly.

Ball reached the peak of his powers in the formative years of his career, making a total of 380 appearances with Blackpool and Everton across a combined ten-year spell by the age of 26. Yet it was at non-league outfit Ashton United that he had started his career. Right from the outset, it was clear that Ball was going to try and pursue a career in football. After all, he left education without anything in the way of qualifications or degrees, and so it was very much 'all or nothing' on whether he would make it as a footballer. His dad – also called Alan – was also a player in his own right, albeit not even a patch on the one that Alan Jr became. It shouldn't have been a surprise that Alan Jr would try to pursue a football career.

It would come as little surprise as to where Alan Jr would make his mark in the men's game to begin with; Ashton's manager at the time was none other than Alan Ball Sr, so young Alan would juggle playing for the Robins with still studying at school. As you will read in this book, there have been various routes and reasons as to why the players discussed opted for football careers – from excellence in their youth, chance viewings, or because they were good at nothing else – and in the large part the latter is true for Alan Ball (I'm going to drop the Jr suffix; just know that I mean Jr and not Sr). Ball was – let's say – 'not a fan of school'; he left without a single qualification to his name. Thus he almost had no choice – other than to get a 'proper job' – to be good at football. Luckily, he was.

After featuring for Ashton in the first team at the age of just 15, Ball would get an opportunity with Wolverhampton Wanderers. At the time, Wanderers had some of the best players in the Midlands, including Norman Deeley, Eddie Stuart, Ron Flowers, Billy Slater and Eddie Clamp to name but a few. Ball wouldn't join up and play for the senior team, but would bunk off school to play for the Wanderers. Yet his chance of signing for Wolves would not come, as he was let go by them at the end of his education.

After Wolves, he briefly joined Bolton Wanderers, but they too released him. Apparently, their excuse was that he was a 'bit too small'. Take it from me as someone who is small myself – the best things come in small packages. And, if they had concerns over his size, they would most certainly live to regret that when they saw the player that he became.

Having suffered the rejection from the two clubs, Ball looked to try and reignite his playing aspirations and it was thanks to his dad that he landed an opportunity that he couldn't turn down; it's who you know, not what you know! One of the first-team coaches at Blackpool under then boss Ron Suart had played with Alan's dad back in the day, so Alan Sr managed to twist Suart's arm to get young Alan a trial with the Seasiders. Blackpool had some good players at the time, with forward Ray Charnley and future England international Emlyn Hughes, as well as the legendary one-club man Jimmy Armfield. And, as a young whippersnapper, Ball went on trial to try and earn a deal. Blackpool didn't have to wait long to come to a decision over whether Ball would get a deal, wasting little time in shoving a pen and paper under his nose.

While Ball would only spend four seasons with the Tangerines, that was enough for the midfielder to break into the England team and make his debut in 1965, in time to be included in the squad for the 1966 World Cup on home soil. Ball was perhaps helped by the fact that Blackpool at that time were not the strongest. Indeed, in the four seasons that Ball spent at Bloomfield Road, they finished 13th twice, 17th and 18th. As a result, Ball stuck out like a sore thumb, with clear individual quality befitting of the big stage. So much so that Alf Ramsey decided to make Ball the youngest member of the squad at the age of just 21.

In that same squad was Roger Hunt. This is where I pause our exploration of Ball's journey, parking it poignantly at the start of the 1966 World Cup in order to instead shine a light on his international team-mate Hunt and unearth where the forward started out.

Hunt was born in Glazebury, Lancashire. His route to the top was one of the more unconventional ones, so to speak, with many hurdles that he had to overcome in the process and it is perhaps a tad fortunate that he would indeed end up being plucked by a Liverpool side right at the peak of the English game. Certainly, in terms of what we come to know in the modern era with youth football and progressing through into the first team, Hunt's journey would take on a very different path.

He was described as having always been an avid football man, and got his first taste of football playing for Croft Youth Club; the equivalent of Wallsend Boys Club to Alan Shearer, albeit without the long list of successful alumni to show for it. He would initially have to prioritise working for a living over and above football aspirations. At the time, his family owned a business specialising in haulage, and Hunt juggled the demands of working full-time in that business with playing part-time for non-league side Stockton Heath. The business was based on the outskirts of Warrington in a place called Culcheth, and this was merely a convenient 20-minute drive for Hunt to Stockton Heath. Stockton Heath are – for the benefit of the younger readers – now known as Warrington Town, having been so since 1961, just a couple of years after Hunt signed for Liverpool.

At 18, his work would have to come first and his football a close – yet all the while prominent – second, as

Hunt was forced to join the army as part of his national service; he isn't the last player in this book to have had to swap grass for guns. Hunt wouldn't let joining the army curb his enthusiasm for football, though; if anything, it made his love for the game stronger. Hunt was stationed in Le Marchant Barracks in Devizes, Wiltshire, and split his time between his many exploits and playing for Devizes Town.

During that period, Hunt was allowed to go and sign for a second team closer to home, returning to Stockton Heath. When he was stationed in the barracks, he would play for Devizes.

Indeed, it was while playing for Stockton Heath that Hunt was spotted. For those of us who have played at a junior level, we have all wished that one Sunday morning there would be a scout in attendance and that you would have your best game in hope of keeping alive the distant dream of being a professional; we all have, haven't we? Hunt was scouted by one of the bastions of English football in Liverpool, who at the time were managed by Phil Taylor.

Taylor opted to sign Hunt, who would have to bide his time when it came to getting his opportunity in the first team; having joined in July 1958 and it was only in September the following year that he got his first run out. The game would turn out to be 'Textbook Hunt', as he went on to score. If you had told Liverpool fans that the goal would be the first of a club-record haul then even they would perhaps have been a tad surprised. Yet it was, and it was just the start of things to come. While Taylor was the one to sign Hunt, it was only under the manager's successor – the legendary Bob Paisley – that the young forward would go on to show his best qualities. In 1959, Paisley would take over after Taylor's failure to win promotion from the Second Division with Liverpool and his eventual resignation from the role; Paisley's arrival would turn out to be an inspired one for Hunt's form.

Despite only being 19 at the time, there was a lot of pressure on the shoulders of Hunt. Paisley's first act was an overhaul of the squad, after 24 players were let go by Taylor. Almost an entire overhaul, and yet one of the only players who did remain was Roger Hunt; a little feather in his cap. Looking back on it, Paisley would be pleased that he made that decision.

Liverpool would end up being promoted to the First Division under Paisley's leadership – winning the Second Division title in 1962 – and it was very much Hunt-inspired as the striker would score an astonishing 41 goals in 41 games; not a bad effort, that! As of the end of that campaign, Hunt had already amassed 77 league goals by the age of 22 in a Liverpool shirt, so very early on it was clear he was a hugely talented player that was going right to the top.

It wouldn't take long for Liverpool to leave their mark on the top flight, winning the First Division within two years of their promotion and the FA Cup within three. Hunt remained a central figure to that success; in his first four seasons in a Liverpool shirt in the First Division, he smashed through the 30-goal mark three times, scoring 128 times in all competitions. He would finish the 1965/66 campaign second in the club's all-time scoring charts – bearing in mind he still had another four campaigns with the Reds – and with his reputation as one of the leading lights of the English game firmly rubber-stamped.

It was because of talents such as Hunt that England went into the home-soil 1966 World Cup as one of the favourites to lift the Jules Rimet Trophy. This is where we bring Alan Ball back into the conversation as the pair were in the 22-strong England squad picked by Alf Ramsey. For Ball, it was completely new to him – having only gained his first call-up a year earlier – while Hunt was in his second World Cup having gone to, albeit not played in, the 1962 World Cup in Chile. The pair would quickly establish themselves as two of the standout performers, with Hunt leaving his mark on the group stages after a goal against Mexico, before grabbing the headlines with both of the Three Lions' goals in a 2-0 win against France to ensure that England finished top of the group.

The quarter-final against Argentina saw Ball and Hunt again feature as mainstays of Ramsey's team, with the latter particularly impressing in what is remembered as being a feisty affair at Wembley. Three days later, England were involved in a game remembered for all the right reasons, a classy clash hallmarked by skill, artistry and attacking flair. They beat Portugal 2-1 and they were in the final. Ball and Hunt had an opportunity to play on the biggest stage of them all. The Lancashire lads had gone from playing on the lower rungs of the ladder to facing the prospect of lining up in the World Cup Final against the likes of Franz Beckenbauer and the five-goal Helmut Haller to name just two. The 1966 World Cup hosted some of the best to have ever played the game in the likes of Pelé, Garrincha and Flórián Albert. Yet in the competition's showpiece were two players who were just five and eight seasons respectively out of non-league: Alan Ball and Roger Hunt.

The rest – as they say – is history; the one and only time it has ever *come home*. Alan Ball. Roger Hunt. World Cup winners. And, if you ever needed a bigger feather in the cap for Ball, he was regarded by many as the standout player in that final despite Geoff Hurst having scored a hat-trick. It was Bobby Moore who was voted by the press in attendance as the man of the match in that final, but according to many of his team-mates in the aftermath, Ball was credited as the key player for England. His performance was so good that even 50 years later, it was analysed in all its glory on Sky Sports' *Monday Night Football* by Jamie Carragher. How many World Cup winners can say that they have had that honour?

So, as England lifted the Jules Rimet Trophy and paraded it around Wembley, Ball and Hunt stood with their arms aloft in the knowledge that they had won the greatest prize of them all. Two lads from the humble roots of non-league had done it. Respect.

2

Rags to Riches

WHEN DISCUSSING players who have gone from non-league to football's top table, without a doubt the gold standard remains Jamie Vardy.

If you had floated the idea that at the age of 23 – by which time most players have often had their break – he would be playing in the seventh tier, outside of the Football League, and just six years later would be a Premier League title winner and goalscorer for England at a European Championship, it would have seemed barely believable. And yet Vardy has etched himself into recent legend as one of the biggest success stories, if not *the* biggest, to come out of non-league. As such, he gets a whole chapter dedicated to him.

His story is all the more remarkable given that Vardy decided to pack in football for eight months in his mid-teens, the age when players are often starting to get their ambitions of a successful career up and running. Indeed, if there was ever a player who encapsulates the definition of being a 'late bloomer', Vardy is that. Aptly, in the writing of this book, Vardy played a prominent role at the grand old age of 37 in helping Leicester City back to the Premier League in the 2023/24 season.

Right from an early age as a youngster, Vardy was a massive football fan. He grew up in Hillsborough, just a stone's throw from Sheffield Wednesday's ground. Thus, unsurprisingly, he was raised supporting the blue and white side of the city. He used to go and watch the games, and that intensified his ambition for one day becoming a professional, better still following in the footsteps of his footballing idol David Hirst. Hirst is one of the true greats in Wednesday folklore, spending nine years at Hillsborough and scoring 106 league goals. In terms of emulating his hero, Vardy would indeed go on to make a name for himself as a striker, albeit not in the Wednesday blue; it would be in a different shade of blue in the Midlands that he would make his mark.

It is fair to say that Vardy has had to go through his fair share of trials and tribulations to become the player he has, but in his youth it was seemingly – initially, at least – plain sailing. A football-mad lad, he ended up playing in the academy at his boyhood club, signing for the Owls as a schoolboy; he lived every young fan's dream. Yet, at the age of just 16, his world would come crashing down as his ambitions of going on to play for Wednesday would be stopped in their tracks. The club decided that Vardy wasn't up to the grade to be kept on with professional forms, and so would be released.

For many, receiving the rejection of being deemed not good enough and cast aside by your boyhood club would be enough to give up on their dreams of becoming a footballer; indeed, so many fail to recover after not making the grade in the ravine between the academy and first team. Vardy would initially struggle to come to terms with the news of his release, and in the wake of that he contemplated giving up football completely. Gone were the days of this young lad keen for the sport and dedicating every hour of the day to following his dream. Instead, he tried to do everything in his power to ensure that he *didn't* play football. But I'm one for the old adage of fate, and in 2003 he decided to indeed return to playing. Looking back, I think he will be glad that he did.

After his hiatus, Vardy rediscovered his love for the game at nearby non-league outfit Stocksbridge Park Steels. Originally going into the reserve team as a 'wee nipper', Vardy managed playing for the Steels alongside working 12-hour shifts at a local company making prosthetic limbs. In 2006, at just 19, Vardy made his debut for Stocksbridge, chucked in at the deep end by manager Peter Rinkcavage.

It was hardly the 'glitz and glam' of Sheffield Wednesday, but it was Vardy's chance of being a professional, and one he took with aplomb. Earning just £30 a week, and having to deal with the logistics of playing for six months with an electronic tag following conviction for assault, Vardy would not let that deter him. It was in the 2007/08 season – under new manager Gary Marrow – that he really flourished, scoring his first goal for the Steels in the FA Cup against Curzon Ashton in September 2007. Under Marrow, Vardy would go on to score 44 goals in all competitions, including a brace of sub-ten-minute hat-tricks in a league game against Grantham Town in September 2008 and in the FA Trophy against Mossley in the October of that same year; taking only six and three minutes respectively.

He continued to score under another new manager, Simon Collins, and such form attracted several higher-level clubs. In January 2009, Vardy was invited for a trial with Football League outfit Crewe Alexandra. It proved to be unsuccessful but there was no let-up in interest in the forward. Rotherham United later offered him the chance to sign for them but, as a Wednesday supporter, not even the offer of a short-term contract at a League One club was enough to persuade him to take the plunge. Instead he stayed put at Stocksbridge, albeit not for long.

In June 2010 Vardy was on the move as then Northern Premier League side FC Halifax Town secured his signature. Shaymen boss Neil Aspin managed to convince chairman David Bottomley to fork out £16,000 for the 23-year-old, landing him on a four-year deal. It was a large sum of money for a player untried at that level of football, but it proved to be a wise investment.

He made his debut for Halifax on 21 August 2010 in true 'Jamie Vardy fashion' – he scored the winner in a 2-1 victory against Buxton at The Shay. That goal would set the tone for an impressive first season and any fears that Shaymen fans would have of whether Vardy would succeed would be alleviated fairly quickly: he ended the campaign with an impressive 25 goals in 37 games to finish as the club's top scorer, his goals helping them to win the Northern Premier League Premier Division title by an impressive 21 points ahead of second-placed Colwyn Bay and finishing the campaign having scored 108 goals.

Vardy claimed particular recognition in March 2011, scoring eight goals in the space of three games: all three in a 3-2 win over Chasetown, a hat-trick in a 4-2 away win against Kendal Town, and a brace in a 3-1 home victory against Nantwich Town. He missed out on three consecutive hat-tricks by just a single goal. To score one hat-trick in a season was enough for some strikers, but to be so close to three consecutively in the same season is a crazy statistic. It is fair to say he was firing on all cylinders. His form earned him praise and he was voted as the supporters' player of the year for that stellar first campaign, one that would prove to be his only full one with Halifax.

Interest in the forward continued into the start of the 2011/12 season and as the Shaymen started life in National League North, there was no downturn in Vardy's form. If the step up was supposed to be a tough one, he certainly didn't get the memo; he scored three goals in his opening four league matches. Fleetwood Town lodged a bid, ahead of interest from several other Football League sides, including Preston North End, Burton Albion, Huddersfield Town (as a Wednesdayite, there were two hopes of that move happening), Crewe Alexandra and Stockport County. But, it was indeed the Cod Army – managed by Micky Mellon – who managed to land him, forking out £170,000 and taking him to the Conference Premier, the top level of non-league football.

Indeed, he made his debut for Fleetwood on the same day on which he signed his forms. It didn't take long for Vardy to announce himself in a Town shirt – only three games in and he was among the goals with a brace. At this point, Vardy had firmly rubber-stamped his reputation for being a goal machine, and one of the brightest hotshots in non-league. His early weeks at Fleetwood saw him regularly on the scoresheet, with a hat-trick of consecutive braces against Kettering Town, Gateshead and Ebbsfleet United. At the start of December, Vardy was named Conference Premier Player of the Month having scored in six straight matches.

Such was the way in which he adapted to life in the top division, Vardy was again attracting attention for his services despite only being five months into his deal with the Cod Army. His displays were so impressive that even in the wake of a 5-1 FA Cup defeat to then-Championship outfit Blackpool in January 2012, a bid of £750,000 was lodged for him by Seasiders boss Ian Holloway. For Fleetwood to be so convincingly beaten but for Vardy to score and stand out, it spoke volumes for his talents. A year earlier he had been playing away to Northwich Victoria in the Northern Premier League Premier Division; now he was the subject of a big bid from a club in the Championship. How time flies when you are a superstar sensation.

Fleetwood rejected the approach in what was arguably the first major realisation by the Cod Army – if they ever needed it – that they didn't just have a decent player on their hands, but one with the potential to play much higher. Opting against Vardy's sale in the 2012 January transfer window proved to be an astute decision as he would go on to score 31 league goals and in the process finish up as the divisional top scorer, helping Fleetwood Town to the Conference Premier title and earn a maiden Football League campaign.

Yet Vardy would ultimately not be sticking around to help them compete in League Two as he received interest from higher in the pyramid, such was the wave of attention he was getting from afar off the back of his accelerated rise and unmissable form. Leicester City came calling for Vardy during pre-season ahead of the 2012/13 campaign, as Foxes boss Nigel Pearson looked to assemble a squad capable of getting City promoted out of the Championship. Under new Thai ownership, the Foxes opted to shell out a remarkable £1m. That remains a record for any signing out of non-league, and would in the process put a metaphorical chain around Vardy's neck of being recognised as a million-pound player.

Vardy made his debut for Leicester in the League Cup in early August, and I was in attendance that day as Pearson's fantastic Foxes rolled into town to roll over Torquay United 4-0 with a dominant display. They had a star-studded team with players such as the mercurial Matty James and Danny Drinkwater in midfield, Wes Morgan, David Nugent, Lloyd 'Road Runner' Dyer, the immensely talented Ben Marshall and Jamie Vardy leading the line alongside experienced figure Jermaine Beckford. Instantly it was clear why the Foxes had paid out the fee they had for Vardy: he was unplayable. Granted, he wasn't up against a backline full of greyhounds and Jamaican sprinters, but Vardy's pace was electrifying and he'd go home with a goal for his troubles. My thoughts going away from that game were 'wow, they've got a proper player'. Little did I know, that was just the start.

Having finished ninth in the Championship that campaign, Vardy's arrival was part of the driving force behind the Foxes making the semi-final of the play-offs, where they were a Manuel Almunia save and *that* Troy Deeney goal away from a potential spot in the Championship play-off final. Vardy would not be a guaranteed starter in that first season, with experienced David Nugent and Martyn Waghorn still preferred to him. However, he would make a good impression at the King Power with a total of 26 appearances in all competitions and five goals. Considering that he not only had to compete with Nugent and Waghorn, but also a plethora of top strikers – Kiwi Chris Wood, Hungarian forward Márkó Futács, evergreen Jermaine Beckford and an on-loan youngster called Harry Kane – to feature as often as he did and show an ability to score should have been more than enough to vindicate City's decision that shelling out £1m was a good call. And, if anything, it provided Vardy with the confidence that he could handle the step up.

Yet what makes Vardy's story all the more amazing considering the career that was to follow was that his cameo in a Foxes shirt that season was not enough to convince him that he was ready and could be a success. Instead, Vardy considered packing in the game in favour of pursuing a rather different profession: becoming a club representative 'living it large' in sunny Ibiza. A mere five goals was not the level of return that he was used to and he felt that it was a sign that he was in fact not up to the level; patience, Jamie! Nigel Pearson stuck by his man and so did his team-mates, and former Foxes midfielder Ben Marshall spoke in an interview with the *Undr The Cosh* podcast about how they convinced Vardy to opt against shelving his football aspirations in favour of stacking shelves on the dancefloor in Ibiza. They would be glad they did.

After the disappointment of losing in the play-offs, the Foxes would go one better and win the Championship in 2014. Vardy would be a prominent figure of that side, scoring 16 league goals and being named as the players' player of the year. A ploy to ensure he didn't go signing deals with clubs in Ibiza maybe, but rest assured the forward had an outstanding second season and his exploits in front of goal helped City to smash through the 100-point barrier and finish with only six league defeats.

Their first season in the Premier League would be a tough one, however, and while he wasn't by any means prolific – again, only scoring five goals – it was the magnitude of those goals and better still the quality of his performances at the back end of the campaign that helped the Foxes pull off a great escape to ensure their top-flight status.

While their turnaround was very much a collective effort, Vardy is often credited as the one whose goal inspired their astounding twist of fate in the final months. The Foxes went to West Bromwich Albion at the start of April, and he scored a 91st-minute winner to seal a 3-2 victory on the road: remarkably only their sixth victory in the space of 31 league games. Surely, though, they wouldn't stay up, would they?

Vardy's goal was the catalyst for the Foxes and they would win seven of their remaining nine league matches. But if Leicester thought the finish to that campaign would be a show-stopper, little did they know what was around the corner. And, if they thought Vardy had played a key part in their great escape, it is fair to say that the following campaign would have Vardy's fingerprints all over it and then some.

Even now, when writing this, I get goosebumps thinking about it; and, that is as someone with no allegiance to Leicester. It is a sporting feat that very much goes down among the greatest that has ever been achieved. Better than Greece winning the Euros, or Luton Town getting to the Premier League; to go from relegation fodder one season to winning the best league in the world in the next was some turnaround. And Jamie Vardy was very much the poster boy of that.

Overall, 2015 was hugely successful for Vardy. He had finished the 2014/15 season strongly and managed to ensure he was still a Premier League footballer by the end of it. Then, in May 2015, Vardy would get the call that every football player dreams of: he was selected for his country. England boss Roy Hodgson chose him for his squad and in June Vardy would pull on a Three Lions shirt for the first time as he came on against the Republic of Ireland for Wayne Rooney.

In November of that year, Vardy also hit the target away from the field as he set up the V9 Academy. After his success clubs are always actively looking for 'the next Jamie Vardy' and so he decided that he would make use of his platform to try and assist clubs – and most importantly the players – in that search. The academy runs as week-long showcase events, in effect giving a stage for players from across non-league to demonstrate their talents in front of an audience of top-level scouts, agents and coaches. It has had its fair share of success, with several players landing professional deals off the back of it. Of the first intake, there were four who landed pro contracts, with two – Lamar Reynolds and Danny Newton – being budding young strikers looking to follow in Vardy's footsteps. In the main, the V9 alumni have not gone on to great heights – certainly not to the level of Jamie himself – but perhaps the biggest success story is Sam McCallum, who has since gone on to play in the Championship with Norwich City, Coventry City, Queens Park Rangers and Sheffield United.

But without a doubt, Vardy's biggest attraction in 2015 – and beyond that into the start of 2016 – was his performance on the field; think Neil Warnock telling Victor Moses that he has 'arrived'. That year, Vardy most certainly arrived, announcing himself on the big stage in the most emphatic of ways.

You don't need me to tell you what happened in the next bit of the story: Leicester City would achieve the unthinkable by winning the 2015/16 Premier League title. It would be a campaign hallmarked by Vardy's brilliance. That team had the likes of Riyad Mahrez, N'Golo Kanté and Danny Drinkwater in it, yet without doubt the standout was Vardy. He would go on to finish the campaign with 24 goals in the league, with only fellow Englishman Harry Kane scoring more with 25. On an individual front, Vardy was rewarded for his stellar campaign with being voted the Premier League Player of the Season. Add to that two Player of the Month awards, a Football Writers' Association Footballer of the Year trophy and a spot in the PFA Team of the Year, and there wasn't a great deal that Jamie Vardy *didn't* win during that campaign.

In a season full of highs, one of the highlights will no doubt have been his famous goal against Liverpool. A dipping strike from distance on one of the memorable nights for the Foxes, it was a strike befitting of his quality. But perhaps his best moment of the campaign would have been his goal at home against Manchester United on 28 November. That in itself was a good achievement – it is always nice to see sides score against the Red Devils – but that goal was particularly special for different reasons: it was the 11th straight Premier game in which he had got on the scoresheet, beating the record that was previously held by Manchester United frontman Ruud van Nistelrooy. It was a season that just kept on delivering, with records being smashed and accolades being waved his way.

Vardy's form that season earned interest from Arsenal. The Gunners have boasted some of the best forwards to have ever stepped foot on the pitch in English football – Ian Wright, Thierry Henry and Dennis Bergkamp to name just three – and Arsène Wenger decided to bid in excess of £20m for Vardy. Looking back on it now, to think that they only bid a little over £20m for someone who had just steered Leicester to a title win of epic proportions and been crowned the division's standout player of the season, it seems incredibly low; £20m wouldn't buy you half a top striker nowadays, let alone one of the best. Perhaps Wenger thought he would be able to persuade Vardy to join with his French charm. Whatever he thought, it didn't work, and Vardy opted against a move to the Emirates in favour of staying put at the King Power. Indeed, he remains with the Foxes at the time of writing.

The 2016/17 campaign would prove to be a tougher one for City as a collective, with league struggles in wake of their title win and manager Claudio Ranieri's departure. However, it would still be a hugely positive one for Vardy on an individual basis as he would help the Foxes to make the Champions League quarter-finals in their maiden campaign in the competition. He would only score once at that level during the season – at home against Atlético Madrid in the second leg of that quarter-final – but it is fair to say that the Champions League campaign was one in which he would get a realisation of just how well he had done, to go from non-league to the top level of club football in a matter of six years. During that time, he had gone from playing Cambridge United, Southport and AFC Telford United to coming up against Club Brugge, Sevilla and Atlético Madrid; it was quite the glow up.

The 2019/20 season would be one in which Vardy would really excel, with several personal achievements to help the Foxes finish fifth in the Premier League and qualify for the Europa League. They set a club record in October, as they ran out 9-0 winners against Southampton in the league; Vardy helped himself to a hat-trick that night. He would grab another slice of history the following July, reaching his landmark 100th goal in City colours, in the Covid-delayed season.

That wasn't the end of the accolades for Vardy as his form in front of goal was so strong that he finished the campaign as the Premier League's top scorer with 23 goals, joining a long list of greats in the competition's history: Alan Shearer, Cristiano Ronaldo, Thierry Henry, Luis Suárez and Sergio Agüero among them. And the individual feats would keep coming: that campaign, Vardy was 33 years of age, and in the process he managed to beat previous record holder Didier Drogba in being the oldest player to win the Golden Boot. His tally may have been fewer than he scored in 2015/16, and fewer than he scored for Fleetwood Town in the Conference, yet in terms of individual seasons that would have to be up there as his best.

Vardy has become less of a recognised starter for the Foxes in recent years, featuring just three times during the 2022/23 campaign as City were relegated out of the Premier League before bouncing back at the first time of asking. While in his late 30s, he has certainly not lost his pace and continues to be a threat with his ability to run in behind, and has maintained his strong goalscoring record; he hit 18 goals during their 2023/24 Championship campaign, meaning that in the 12 full seasons that Vardy has been in Foxes colours he has only failed to hit double figures in three of those. His exploits have seen him move into third place in the all-time goalscoring charts at Leicester City, behind only Arthur Chandler on 273 and Arthur Rowley on 265.

Jamie Vardy will without a doubt go down as one of the best that we have seen; the fact he has done so in Leicester City colours makes his achievements all the more impressive. We may well not see the likes of him again in English football and he is without a doubt the standard bearer for what can be achieved by players out of non-league. To have smashed through 300 career goals alone, with almost 150 in the Premier League, puts him in the pantheon of the greats, and he will continue to inspire others.

3

The Ultimate Elation

IN 2023 came one of the most fairy-tale moments in English football history, with Luton Town sealing promotion to the Premier League at Wembley. Ordinarily, promotion to the top flight is an achievement to be heralded, yet when you put into context that only nine years previously the Hatters had been plying their trade in non-league, there is something particularly impressive and indeed special about what they were able to achieve.

Their rise through the leagues has been meteoric by every imaginable metric to say the least, and the like of which we probably won't see for a long time – at least not in my lifetime. For Luton to be relegated out of the Football League in 2009, in effect dumped out of the league by way of a 30-point deduction due to transfer irregularities and administrative mishaps, and then rise their way back up the pyramid and seal a return to the Premier League 31 years after they dropped out of the old First Division the season prior to the new competition starting – puts into perspective that anything is possible.

Along the way, the Hatters have churned through six different managers and a lorry load of players, and yet there is something particularly poetic about the fact that the only real constant on the field during this time has been one player who stands alone in the club's recent history: Pelly Ruddock Mpanzu. Of the hundreds of players who have pulled on a Luton shirt between their first season back in the Football League in 2014 to their promotion at Wembley in May 2023, Mpanzu is the only one to have appeared for the club at every level and in every season along the way.

Indeed, in Luton's opening fixture of the 2023/24 Premier League campaign, a 4-1 defeat to Brighton & Hove Albion, Mpanzu became the only player in the history of English football to have played for the same club at every level from the Conference to the top flight.

Born in Hendon, Greater London, Mpanzu started out his career as a youngster with Boreham Wood: the same youth setup that has since been responsible for Sorba Thomas and Iliman Ndiaye, both of whom have gone on to play right at the top level and represent their countries. At the age of just 15, Mpanzu joined Wood's academy, before transitioning into the first team after two years in which he had excelled. He particularly caught the eye as their youth team made the first round of the FA Youth Cup, and would go on to make 13 appearances in the first team under legendary non-league manager Ian Allinson.

Allinson has a decent track record of developing players, with several having graduated under his leadership into the Football League; Mpanzu is the most notable of those. Indeed, despite only playing 13 times, his displays for Wood earned him the interest of Premier League outfit West Ham United, who at the time were managed by Sam Allardyce. It wasn't only the Hammers, however, who were interested in making a move for his signature: Queens

Park Rangers, Watford and Reading all followed suit with approaches.

West Ham would clinch Mpanzu's signing on a two-year deal. He was so set about signing for United that he repeatedly went out of his way to instruct Wood chairman Danny Hunter to reject any further approaches for him other than that from Sam Allardyce. In December 2011, Mpanzu was officially announced as a Hammer; as a 17-year-old he would have to bide his time for a chance in the first team, however. In October 2013 Allardyce opted to chuck Mpanzu in from the outset, playing the full 90 minutes as West Ham knocked out Burnley in the last 16 of the League Cup.

Coincidentally, defender Dan Potts also made his debut that night; Potts would go on to be a part of the same Luton side alongside Mpanzu that would seal promotion to the Premier League. The verdict of his debut in a Hammers shirt would be a positive one from a notoriously tough taskmaster in Allardyce; just the start of things to come, surely? Wrong. In fact, that would prove to be Mpanzu's one and only appearance for West Ham. After such an impressive debut and as a highly rated young prospect, it would seem – on the face of it – inconceivable that Mpanzu would not go on to play again for the Hammers.

Yet just a month after that game at Turf Moor he was back in non-league, albeit only on loan to begin with, at Luton – managed by none other than the Grand Master. John Still. During his loan spell, Mpanzu showed his versatility. He made his debut in the same week of his signature at Kenilworth Road, and was deployed at centre-back. Luton then drew 0-0 with Staines in the FA Trophy but won 2-0 in the replay with Mpanzu in midfield, bagging the man of the match award. He would quickly establish himself in midfield, and it is in the centre of the park for which his spell with Luton is best known, as a hard-working cog of their side.

Mpanzu would end up going back to West Ham; not because he didn't impress, but more so because of the Hammers' injury struggles. Yet he had got a taste for it during his time at Kenilworth Road, and in January 2014 the Hatters made a permanent move for him.

So often we see players try to make it at the top level and wait for a chance that so seldom comes; Pelly Ruddock Mpanzu was different. He just wanted to play so, at the age of 20, Mpanzu made the brave decision to leave Premier League West Ham and join non-league Luton. Looking back, I think he made the right decision. Just a tad.

Pelly had worked hard to forge an opportunity for a shot at the big time, progressing through the Boreham Wood academy and then having to prove himself on trial with West Ham. He had seemingly done the hard yards to 'open the door' and yet was prepared to give up all of what he had worked so hard for and chance his arm with a move back into non-league to a Luton team on the up. And it was right that he should; non-league is the oasis for aspiring footballers, providing so many with the platform to propel their careers, not least playing regularly and proving themselves. It was a big call, but one that – on reflection, at Wembley in May 2023 – had proved to be the right one. It also underlined that non-league provides the ideal environment for players to get regular minutes under their belt; the olive branch that it provides to those with talent in need of a chance.

Luton had been plagued by financial problems in the years prior to signing Mpanzu, having been deducted ten points for going into administration during the 2007/08 season; they knew first hand the value of financial stability. For them, therefore, to be splashing out undisclosed fees, especially as a Conference side, spoke volumes of how highly John Still rated Mpanzu. Still very rarely got it wrong in judging players' abilities, and this would turn out to be another of his success stories.

Just as he had done on loan, Mpanzu would impress after turning his deal permanent and would make 24 appearances – virtually an ever-present – as the Hatters would go on to win the Conference by a whopping 19 points ahead of Cambridge United.

Mpanzu would suffer a setback in the following season, limited to only ten starts; the latest hurdle he would have to overcome in his journey. Injuries would continue to plague him in 2015/16, making only 21 league appearances. But those setbacks would not deter the midfielder; he was steadfast in his mission to 'make it'. They would instead only propel him on with an even greater sense of desire to do well. He would thrive under new manager Nathan Jones, missing only four league games in 2016/17 and making a total of 52 appearances in all competitions. His performances were so good and his role so crucial to the Hatters that he was rewarded with a three-year deal to keep him at Kenilworth Road. There was no chance of him leaving; he was now part of the furniture.

During that spell, Luton would continue their rise up the leagues with back-to-back promotions under Jones, finishing second in League Two in 2017/18 and then going on to win League One the season after. The latter was Mpanzu's biggest bulk of work in a Hatters shirt as a lynchpin of their midfield; he was one of an elite club of only eight members in League One to start all 46 league games. The others were Jon McLaughlin (Sunderland), Danny Andrew (Doncaster Rovers), Tony Craig (Bristol Rovers), Lucas Akins (Burton Albion), Mark Hughes (Accrington Stanley), Tomas Holy (Gillingham) and Alex Cairns (Fleetwood Town). The fact that Mpanzu had suffered with injuries like he had and then went on to make more than 40 starts in three consecutive seasons – missing only four league games across those years – was indicative of his battling qualities, which have made him a firm favourite at Kenilworth Road.

After an ever-present 2018/19 campaign, Mpanzu would up his game a notch or two in 2019/20 as he was named the Hatters' player of the year in an uncharacteristic season for Town where they finished 19th in the Championship. It was by far and away their worst season as a collective during Mpanzu's time at the club, yet the no-nonsense midfielder was the pick of the players.

While the 2019/20 campaign was to be one of individual recognition at club level, 2020/21 was to end with the most fairy-tale moment for Mpanzu, as he received a call-up to the national team of the Democratic Republic of Congo. While he was born in Hendon, Mpanzu was eligible to play for the Leopards and he got his first taste of the international scene in June 2021 during a friendly against Tunisia. Ten years previous, Mpanzu had been playing against Tonbridge Angels and Truro City; how time flies.

* * *

In 2024, I had the absolute privilege of speaking to John Still about his time managing Pelly Ruddock Mpanzu, a player and person he still – to this day – takes a huge amount of pride in being able to springboard to the success he has had at a club he holds so close to his heart.

You have managed some top players over the years. Did you know that Pelly was going to go on and be as successful as he has been?

'To tell you the truth, no. I thought that he was always going to be a good footballer; I felt that in time he would come on and make a career for himself. But, if someone said to me, "Would he play in the Premier League?" then I wouldn't be sure as the level now required to play in the Premier League is so high and it's difficult to make it at that very top level. However, I knew that he would be a good player; how far he got with that ability was another thing altogether. Of the ones that I have had that have since gone on to play in the Premier League, there isn't one that I could look at and say for definite would go on to do so.'

Out of all the other players you signed at Luton, Pelly is the only one that remains at the club now having been at the club in non-league. Why do you feel he has been able to keep elevating his game?

'That's a difficult one, and there are a couple of reasons why I would say he's been able to do that. The first one is ability. If you haven't got the ability, you haven't got a chance. You have got to have dedication. You need to get up every day and want to be better, to work on your game, to improve, and that is the second thing; the mindset to want to get better. I think that if you have the dedication and commitment to work hard on your game, you will reach your potential. Everybody has a set potential that they can aspire to, and it is only when you work hard and apply yourself as Pelly did that allows you to reach that potential.

'So many players don't reach that potential as they don't have that dedication and mindset. You need to live right, eat right, train right, etc. If you give your all to all of those things, that gives you a good chance to be able to reach your potential whatever that may be. Players can look back at the end of their careers and say, "If I did this, could I have done this?" and yet Pelly can look back on his career and say he has given everything to achieve the utmost of what he is capable of. Pelly has reached his potential.'

You signed Pelly at Luton when they were in financial hardship. Despite those financial constraints and the outlay you paid for Pelly, did you know at the time that you just had to get the deal done to land a player of his ability?

'Absolutely. I'm a West Ham United fan, and he was at West Ham United at the time, and so I had seen Pelly play. I felt he had pace, power, strength and at West Ham United he was taught how to play properly. I thought that the ingredients he had would benefit us and if he worked on those then he would polish his attributes and become a good player. I had a feeling that if he could work on what he had and get better then he would go on to bigger and better things, and that would only benefit us in the long run.'

You have managed lots of players over the years. How does it make you feel to see a player like Pelly go on to achieve what he has done?

'It is absolutely brilliant. I look out for all of my former players, and follow their careers and speak to them when I can. Managing football clubs and winning cups is great, but watching players you have managed go on and have good careers is a great feeling. I met him in May when they got promoted; I was there at the final at Wembley. To see Pelly go from the National League to playing in the Premier League is so rewarding.'

Pelly Ruddock Mpanzu was a smart kid at the time of joining Luton, dropping down the divisions in order to join you. Does that just show how important it can be dropping into non-league so that players can get the game time and the chance to develop?

'One hundred per cent. I was talking to Matt Ritchie. I took him on loan from AFC Bournemouth at Dagenham & Redbridge. I took Matt Cash on loan from Nottingham Forest. They now both play in the Premier League. I took Joe Worrall on loan; he was captain for Nottingham Forest when they won promotion to the Premier League. Those players haven't dropped down the levels and thought "I don't fancy that", but have instead dropped down to the lower leagues and played games.

'When players are playing in the academy or reserves, there is no pressure. When they play in first-team football, that is people's livelihoods and there is more expectation and demands on you to perform, and I feel that going out and getting that game time and experiencing that is so important.'

* * *

Sorba Thomas and Iliman Ndiaye

Two more Boreham Wood alumni who have since gone on to hit great heights are Sorba Thomas and Iliman Ndiaye.

Thomas is in many ways Pelly Ruddock Mpanzu V2; not down to stylistic similarity, as Thomas is an out-and-out winger, but purely for the fact that Thomas has trodden a similar path into the professional game. Yet, all the while, Thomas's journey is rather unique in that he made the seldom seen jump from non-league's premier tier straight to the Championship, rather than the season-on-season progression of Mpanzu.

As far as a likeness to Mpanzu's rise goes, Thomas also played some of his youth football at West Ham United, a logical first step on his journey for a lad born in Newham.

While Mpanzu's time at Upton Park was brought to a halt aged 20, Thomas moved on to pastures new and shelved such ambitions of a pathway and potential career with the Hammers as early as 16. He would end up at Boreham Wood, in a reversal of Mpanzu's move.

Such was Thomas's reputation and impression as a youth player, he was given professional terms just a year later. It was in early 2016 in which the youngster particularly propelled himself into the headlines as an emerging talent as Boreham Wood beat the youth teams of Football League outfit Northampton Town and non-league sides Wealdstone and Hanwell Town to reach the second round of the FA Youth Cup. Granted, the FA Youth Cup was simply against players Thomas's age, but it acted as a good barometer to set him aside from his peers. It was clear: he was a high flyer.

A trend shared by so many of the players in this book is the importance of loans at a lower level and the benefit of game time in men's football at a young age, and Thomas's development was aided by a brief spell at Cheshunt; the 'dip your toe in the water' loan before being launched head-first into the deep end of Wood's first team. Under the guidance of manager Luke Garrard, Thomas quickly established himself as a regular; after only making eight appearances in 2017/18 in his breakthrough, Thomas became a fixture with back-to-back campaigns of 32 appearances each.

The 2019/20 campaign was cut short for Wood by way of the Covid pandemic – playing just 37 National League games, in which Thomas featured 32 times – but Garrard's side qualified for the play-offs by way of an average of 1.62 points per game. Despite their eventual shortcomings in the end-of-season eliminators, Boreham Wood went into the following campaign with a billing as being one of the contenders for the title; Thomas was deemed a constituent and prominent part of their squad. They would start 2020/21 in a somewhat inconsistent fashion, but one player who certainly began well was Thomas with ten appearances and not a single minute missed, scoring three goals including in his final game against Aldershot Town.

At the time of his transfer to Huddersfield Town, Thomas had received a call-up to the England C squad, albeit he never received a cap, due to the game's Covid cancellation. However, he was very much viewed as one of the stars in non-league and he was signed on almost a 'trial run' by the Terriers in January 2021, on a deal purely until the end of that campaign. Thomas was viewed as being the potential 'next big thing' to follow in the footsteps of Josh Koroma, who was on the books of Huddersfield at the time having earned his stripes in Leyton Orient's bid for promotion from the fifth tier, and so they had high hopes that Thomas could be a similar success.

Thomas would extend his deal beyond that season, outperforming initial expectations of just being a backup player to begin with as he made seven appearances in the Championship. Come the start of 2021/22, Thomas had made such an impression that boss Carlos Corberán made him a fixture of their side as they went on to make the Championship play-off final. Quite the glow-up for a player who a year earlier had been playing the likes of Woking and Bromley; a starter in the Championship's showpiece. Although born in Barking, Thomas has since gone on to play internationally for Wales after qualifying due to his Welsh mother. Looking back on his career, I think even he will admit he has surpassed initial expectations; not just to get the move, but to go from the fifth tier to the second tier with such seamless transition, to be 90 minutes away from being a Premier League player, and to gain flowers on the international stage.

Iliman Ndiaye's journey, meanwhile, is all the more intriguing, and certainly more chaotic in its route: as a youngster he played for more clubs in his youth, five, than the three he has appeared for as a professional.

The early years of Ndiaye's youth development would come in French football. He was born in Rouen on 6 March 2000 – just two days after my good self. I am not going to lie, but as someone who grew up with the very slim chance yet all the while desire to one day be a professional, to see Ndiaye – who is virtually the same age as me – reach the

Premier League, play for his country and line up in Ligue 1 alongside Pierre-Emerick Aubameyang and against Kylian Mbappé by the age of 23 does make me wonder where my own footballing career fell flat.

So, where were we? Rouen. Northern France. That was where Ndiaye's footballing career would start off, unsurprisingly playing for local side Rouen Sapins (Rouen Fir Trees, to us English folk). He'd spend time with them before moving on to the premier team in the city, FC Rouen, and then joining the youth academy at French giants Marseille. Little did they know at the time that the 11-year-old would one day return to the club on a permanent basis.

When Ndiaye was 14, he and his family moved to Senegal. Eager to continue his love for football, Ndiaye signed for youth club AS Dakar Sacré-Cœur – partner club of Ligue 1 side Lyon. His family would again be on the move after just two years, with Iliman's dad Abdoulaye moving to England. Iliman would join the Boreham Wood academy – like Sorba Thomas – as part of the Partnership for After School Education programme.

The youngster would make quite the impression on and off the field, as he would not only shine in a playing capacity but also show his love for the game in going above and beyond off it. During his downtime from playing, Ndiaye would volunteer in helping coach in the community; he was just desperate to consume football however he could get it. He was so eager to play as much football as he could that alongside playing in the academy with Boreham Wood during the weeks and on Saturdays that he spent time turning out for Sunday league side Rising Ballers. If that wasn't enough, Ndiaye also played for Atholl 1965. It was clear that he was football mad. If he could get a football fix, he'd find it.

Ndiaye would be a hit straight from the off with Boreham Wood in the academy, scoring on his debut, and he went on to play an integral part in reaching two national cup finals as well as helping the Wood to the second round of the FA Youth Cup. Boreham Wood would realise his potential and wouldn't waste time in attempting to tie down his future with the club, handing him a professional deal at the end of the 2016/17 campaign. Better still, despite being just 16 years of age, he was fast-tracked to the elite squad playing with lads years his senior. Yet such was the extent of Ndiaye's talent, he would actually not get the chance to play in the first team with Wood, as he would spend the next two years in the academy and would be sold to Sheffield United before he could make the step up.

Ndiaye would go on to get his first taste of men's football but with Hyde United back in non-league on a short-term loan in which he strengthened his growing and glowing reputation. Ndiaye would be hugely indebted to Blades manager Slaviša Jokanović; the Serb didn't do much of note during his time at Bramall Lane, but one thing he did do was hand a chance to a keen and budding youngster. It would be one that he would not regret as Ndiaye would not look back, quickly establishing himself as a first-team fixture and forging a reputation as being one of the standout young players in the EFL.

He was handed his debut for the Blades in the Premier League in 2021 as they lost to Leicester City; not the worst place to make your professional debut on the big stage. It was, however, in United colours during 2022/23 that Ndiaye would announce himself as not just a 'talented player out of non-league that the Blades took a chance on', but someone supremely talented and heading right to the top: player of the year; young player of the year; EFL Team of the Season; PFA Team of the Season. His haul of 14 league goals was enough to propel the Blades to promotion to the top flight, while early on in the campaign he was selected for Senegal's 2022 World Cup squad – qualifying because of his Senegalese father. Welcome to the big time.

Friday, 25 November 2022 will be etched into Ndiaye's memory for the rest of his career as the day he made his bow as a World Cup player, coming on as a substitute in Senegal's 3-1 victory over hosts Qatar. A young lad who had been rejected by Chelsea and Southampton yet all the while had remained steadfast in his belief that he would be a professional footballer had done it. Since that feat, Ndiaye left Sheffield United at the end of 2022/23 following their promotion to the Premier League to return to former club Marseille, then he returned to England with Everton in the summer of 2024. Ten years earlier, he had been playing on the streets of Dakar. It is fair to say that he has had quite the rise.

* * *

Cameron Mawer is an experienced coach in non-league football, and he was at Boreham Wood when Sorba Thomas and Iliman Ndiaye came through with the National League side. I spoke to him about what it was like managing both players and why they have gone on to have had successful careers in the game.

Iliman Ndiaye made it clear from an early age that he wanted to be a footballer. Why do you think he has

been able to achieve that when so many with similar ambitions don't?

'He was relentless from the first day that I met him and he had a work ethic and mentality the likes of which I've never come across before. I have worked with – and continue to work with – a lot of players who want to be footballers and make a career for themselves, but they are not prepared to live Monday to Friday as a footballer with dedication to the profession. Iliman was different; he was an unbelievable grafter. He didn't care what the situation was, he would find a way to be there on time and train with whatever group he could. He was the first in and the last out. He was always the best trainer and the hardest worker in every session that he went into; he just had that relentless work ethic to be successful and was willing to dedicate his time to do so. He was without a doubt incredibly gifted in terms of technical ability, but he grafted, listened and implemented, and if it wasn't for that he wouldn't be where he is now.'

Having coached Iliman, what do you think makes him such a top player?

'He is technically excellent, but everything comes very natural for him. The way that he handles the ball and the way he moves his body was the first thing I noticed; it really stood out as being that extra bit unique and better than the rest. He works hard off the ball and very much plays in the modern way of pressing hard and winning the ball back, and so he has everything.'

What were your first impressions of Iliman?

'He was a very quiet boy, but one that went about his football in a professional manner. Like I have always said about him, his love for football is beyond the norm. Players love the game and they think that talking about it is enough, but Iliman was prepared to work tirelessly from day one. I would even go as far as to say he was a little selfish in his ways, but in a good way.'

Iliman Ndiaye was rare in that he wanted to consume football as much as he did; not just playing, but also in a coaching capacity. How important was that mindset?
'You certainly do not see that mindset now in young players. There is often a lot of talk, but not a lot of action. Iliman was different; it was the other way round. His football would do the talking. He was – and is – so humble with all of his work, whether it was playing or coaching; nothing phased him. Setbacks weren't setbacks for him; it was all about taking everything in his stride to get to where he wanted to be, and it has certainly paid off.'

How difficult – and rewarding – was it to manage a talent like Iliman?
'Words cannot describe how proud I am of him, and to be able to say that I worked with him for three years day in, day out in helping him become the player he is today is something that I will always cherish in my coaching career. He wasn't an easy player to manage in many respects, as he was so hungry to win; he was on another level in terms of his will to win, and that sometimes spilled over the wrong way. I have worked with lots of players with talent, but you can always spot players who have a chance; they have that certain edge to them which sets them apart. I love it, because they challenge themselves and they challenge me, and Iliman certainly did that.'

Iliman struggled physically to begin with. Do you think giving young players like Iliman the exposure to men's football early on is the best thing for their development?

'Definitely. Iliman came to us as an under-17 player, but he played under-19 football to begin with. We were heavily loaded with under-19s at the time and so it wasn't just a case of walking into the team and playing. We were probably the best team in the country for EPPP [Elite Player Performance Plan]; thus, he had to deal with struggles and setbacks, especially in playing against bigger and older lads than he was. However, he loved it and embraced the challenge, and learned during that time how to use his body properly. I feel that has stood him in good stead now.'

Was there a moment when you thought, 'We have a Premier League player on our hands?'

'When players are with us, you never know whether they are truly capable of going on to play in the top flight, as it is often such a big gap. Did I know he was special? One hundred per cent. Did I think he would become the player he has today? I believed he could, but wasn't sure. There were moments when you stood back and thought "WOW". We were at St George's Park once in a PGMOL [Professional Game Match Officials] tournament, and he picked the ball up and ran from his own half before slotting it into the bottom corner. I think even the opposition realised he was a bit of a freak and a special talent.'

Sorba Thomas wasn't ripping up any trees for Boreham Wood, but Huddersfield Town took the plunge to sign him. What do you think they saw in him?

'You only have to see Boreham Wood's decline from when he left in the January of that season [not making the play-offs] to understand what a special player he was. Especially, at the age he was at the time. He was playing wing-back at Boreham Wood and so was perhaps not getting the goals that would put him in the limelight, but for me he was the reason why they were doing so well. He is great on and off the pitch. He has Premier League pace with lovely quality on the ball, and he was certainly worth taking a chance on; it certainly paid off for them as he has been terrific for them since.'

Why do you think he was able to adapt so quickly from the National League to the Championship?
'I love Sorba, and I always see him as another son to me. He worked on his ability every single day. Every level he got to, he was hungry to push himself and get to the next level, and so on. I never doubted he would get to that level one day. I had a phone call with him shortly after he joined Huddersfield Town and he was frustrated that he wasn't playing for them at first; that's how much he believed in himself. He expected to go straight from the fifth tier into the second tier and start and play every minute of every game. As soon as he got his chance, I knew he would fly.'

What makes Sorba Thomas such a good player?
'He is quick and strong, direct and can play off either foot. One thing he has done is work so hard to make his game unpredictable; that is a really unique quality to have. As a full-back, he is a nightmare to play against as he can get at you and cause you problems in so many different ways. Like Iliman Ndiaye, he has fantastic quality, but he coupled that with brilliant work-rate and a hunger to win the ball back. He tries to affect games in and out of possession, and that is what managers love.'

4

The Non-League Messiah

WHEN YOU ask anyone about the greats of lower-league football, one name that will – or at least should – be thrown into the mix is John Still. The Non-League Messiah. The man responsible for springboarding Luton Town's eventual rise through the pyramid, there are very few personalities in the game revered as much as Still; he is very much regarded as 'God' at Kenilworth Road in some quarters. If there is anyone who can identify a talented young player from non-league capable of making the move up the levels, Still is the master; been there, done it and got multiple T-shirts. In particular, Still has a track record of unearthing centre-forwards, several of whom have since gone on to have successful careers in the EFL and above.

Wes Thomas

One of Still's earliest success stories was forward Wes Thomas. Thomas, now in his late 30s and retired, went on to make 344 appearances in the Football League and Conference Premier/National League and scored 90 goals; his best individual season coming in 2010/11 for Cheltenham Town with 18. Born in Barking, Thomas was spotted by Queens Park Rangers as a youngster, and he went on to complete a two-year scholarship with the Hoops. He was let go at its conclusion and decided to drop into non-league to balance playing semi-professionally with his studies.

That proved to be a hugely beneficial move for Thomas in his development as a young forward, joining Waltham Forest – now Walthamstow – upon his release by QPR. He had a memorable first season for Waltham, scoring 17 goals in 32 appearances to finish as top scorer and helping them to finish eighth in the 2005/06 Southern League Eastern Division. His form alerted the attention of Conference South side Thurrock and manager Hakan Heyrettin, who had managed Thomas at Waltham Forest. He hit the ground running at Thurrock and went on to finish as the side's top scorer. That – coupled with Thomas falling out of favour with Heyrettin – saw him on the move, with fellow Conference South outfit Fisher Athletic making a £15,000 bid. It was with the now-defunct Bermondsey-based club that Thomas really made his mark, being his team's leading scorer for a third season running – this time with 17 goals – and catching the attention of John Still.

Thomas joined Still's Dagenham & Redbridge, and would go on to spend two years with the club, although he found game time hard to come by and uncharacteristically only scored three times in 27 appearances. Loan spells at Grays Athletic and Rushden & Diamonds were to follow before he was transfer-listed and eventually allowed to join Cheltenham in July 2010. Still may look back and regret his decision to let Thomas go and not persevere with him, as he would go on to forge a successful career in the EFL. The very next season he would excel at Cheltenham with

18 goals in 41 appearances, adding yet another top scorer's medal to his ever-growing collection, despite only netting once from March until the end of the campaign.

His displays for the Robins saw Crawley Town come calling for his services, with highly regarded manager Steve Evans making a move for him. If there was one thing Evans knew like the back of his hand it was top forwards; he had also been responsible for the form of Matt Tubbs, prolific in his two years at Crawley. Evans had found another gem; such was the regard in which Thomas was held, he only played six times for Crawley before the cash was once again being splashed for him. Bournemouth came knocking, agreeing a loan-before-you-buy deal that saw Thomas become a Cherries player for a six-figure fee. Given that Bournemouth had struggled so much with finances over the years, for them to have got the chequebook out for six figures at that time showed that Thomas was a good player. He would maintain a one-in-two record for Bournemouth during his loan, scoring seven times, albeit he would only go on to score four more during his permanent spell.

For the next five years, Thomas would drift around various clubs in League One and the Championship, making 156 appearances in all competitions and scoring 37 times; by no means a prolific 30-goal-a-season striker, but a steady one-in-four type. He would finish his career with spells at Oxford United (57 appearances), Grimsby Town (40 appearances) and Notts County (42 appearances) during which he scored 37 goals; a tad better than the one-in-four ratio. He may not have gone on to have as illustrious a career as some of the other examples in this book, but all the while he provides a fitting and perhaps more traditional epithet for 'unearthing a diamond' from non-league.

Paul Benson, Josh Scott and Jon Nurse

Without a doubt Still's biggest success was underlined by the 2009/10 campaign, with strike partners Paul Benson and Josh Scott – ably assisted by supporting act Jon Nurse – all playing an integral part in firing Dagenham to promotion into League One. Their success provides a fitting microcosm of Still's hugely impressive record of talent identification, with all three having been signed from the non-league circuit. Let's start with perhaps the pick of those in the form of Paul Benson.

Benson was signed by Still five years previous to that play-off final triumph at Wembley. Still was born in West Ham, with the bulk of his professional career in the east London, Essex and Kent area; he both played and managed for Leytonstone and Dagenham, and – at the time of writing – is the director of football at Southend United. That part of the country has been Still's bread and butter; if there's a non-league player with promise in that region, you can bet your bottom dollar Still has at some point been sniffing around them. Indeed, Benson was born in Southend and went on to represent his boyhood club at academy level, before his eventual release ahead of the 2003/04 season.

Benson moved into non-league in an attempt to kick-start his career, and it certainly proved to be an astute decision. After leaving Roots Hall, Benson signed for local semi-professional side White Ensign in the Essex Olympian League. His record for the Great Wakering-based club is one of the most impressive of any striker that features in this book; there are prolific forwards, then there was whatever

Benson was. His numbers were so impressive that his name was almost forced upon Still, with a whopping 107 goals in 65 matches in all competitions; there wasn't a great deal of 'unearthing' that needed to take place.

Unsurprisingly, Still made the move for Benson – likely before anyone else did – however, to begin with Benson would see his Dagenham & Redbridge career blighted by injuries; his first season, 2005/06, was cut short after he suffered a broken leg. However, Still was more than happy to play the waiting game for the striker, and he showed his true colours the following campaign, vindicating Still's decision to sign him. He finished as the club's top scorer with 28 goals to help the Daggers win promotion from the Conference National.

Upon promotion to the Football League, Benson's season would again be blighted by injuries, although in the same way that he had returned after his broken leg, he bounced back with 18 league goals as Dagenham finished eighth in League Two. Still needed to go out and sign a player who would make the difference and get them into the play-offs; step forward Josh Scott.

That summer, Still again delved into non-league to find another gem, this time 'Heading to Yeading' to newly merged Hayes & Yeading United, who had just been promoted to the Conference National after winning the play-offs, with the key driving force for their success being Scott's 25 goals. Scott had scored 27 in 80 appearances across four seasons with Hayes before the merger with Yeading, and he continued his fruitful spell in front of goal. With Benson excelling as a target man, Still saw Scott as the perfect 'nippy' striker to complete his 'little and large' combination. Target acquired.

Before I talk about the successful 2009/10 campaign, we need to turn it back two years to the summer of 2007 to shine a light on the third of the Daggers' tantalising attacking trio in Jon Nurse. Of the three, Nurse was perhaps the least prominent, very much the third choice – with only 30 starts compared to Benson's 45 and Scott's 36 – but was equally as important to their success. The forward was also brought in by Still from non-league, following their promotion from the Conference, signing from Stevenage Borough.

Let's rewind to where it all started. In 1981, Nurse was born in Barbados; he would go on to play six times for his country. When Nurse was just three years of age, he moved with his family to the United Kingdom, settling near Fulham. Nurse was an avid football fan from a young age and got his first taste in his early teens for local side Malden Vale, before going on to play for Wallington Wanderers. It was clear from the outset that Nurse was a talent, a natural athlete with his pace, and it stood out enough for two professional clubs to come calling for the youngster – Crystal Palace and AFC Wimbledon. It wasn't to be for Nurse, but that would not curb his enthusiasm, and like Benson and Scott, it was in non-league where he would pursue an opportunity.

It was Sutton Athletic to whom Nurse turned, a Sunday league team half an hour across London from Nurse's Fulham home. His form in Athletic colours alerted the higher-ranked local outfit Sutton United, and after a short spell with Surrey side Nuwood in which he helped them win the Surrey South Eastern Combination Junior Division One, the Yellows were to make a move for the Barbadian hotshot. Just 22 years of age, Nurse had to be content with a spot in the reserves to begin with, but he built such a reputation with United that it was not long before he made the transition into the first team. He spent just a single season with Sutton after registering an impressive 24 goals in 30 games.

He departed at the end of the 2003/04 season, but not without his fair share of interest from elsewhere. Old adversaries AFC Wimbledon made another move for him, while Colchester United also took him on trial, but it was Conference National side Stevenage Borough – under boss Graham Westley – who secured his services. His debut for Borough would coincidentally come against his future employers Dagenham & Redbridge.

Nurse would go on to make 104 appearances – scoring 22 times, a decent return for someone who struggled with injury – and like his youth days in Sunday league he flitted between playing on the wing due to his pace and up front due to his finishing ability. The highlight of his time with Borough would have most certainly been in 2006/07 when helping his team to lift the FA Trophy at Wembley; he may not have played in the final against Kidderminster Harriers, but to go from Sunday league to the 'home of football' in four years was an achievement in itself.

Bubbling away in the background of that campaign was interest from John Still, who had seen his star striker Craig Mackail-Smith depart Dagenham, and he had made an enquiry for Nurse. Attempt one, in January: fail. Attempt two, in the summer: success. If Still had wanted Nurse to replace Mackail-Smith, he didn't embrace that burden. Mackail-Smith had scored 15 in 28 prior to his exit; in the following two campaigns, Nurse would score only six in total.

So, going into 2009/10, Still had three main strikers at his disposal: Paul Benson, Josh Scott and Jon Nurse. Were they good enough to fire the Daggers to success? You bet they were. They would forge a successful triad, scoring a combined 34 goals – Benson the highest with 17 – as Dagenham finished seventh and secured a play-off place. In particular, Benson and Scott were responsible for one of the standout play-off games in EFL history, with the Daggers demolishing Morecambe 6-0 in the first leg at Victoria Road courtesy of a brace from Benson and a sensational four-goal haul from Scott. If you wanted a game that encapsulated everything Still was about – signing gems from non-league – then the final was exactly that. They beat Rotherham 3-2 with goals from Benson, Nurse and Danny Green; Green had also been signed by Still from non-league, plucked from Bishop's Stortford in the summer of 2009. The team of 2009/10 was the biggest advert for Still's willingness to sign from non-league: strikers Benson, Scott and Nurse; skipper Scott Doe and midfielder Green. It was an A-Z guide of the best players from the lower rungs of the non-league ladder elevated to success under Still.

Dwight Gayle

Perhaps Still's most high-profile signing from non-league and proudest work is unearthing striker Dwight Gayle. Gayle was one of Still's more obscure captures, joining Dagenham & Redbridge from Essex outfit Stansted – by no means one of non-league's more recognised hotbeds of talent. Let's start right at the beginning when Gayle was in his youth days. As a schoolboy, he caught the eye with his nippy, quick playing style, and that attracted the attention of Premier League giants Arsenal. Gayle was on their academy books until the age of 12, but was let go by the Gunners.

After a five-year hiatus, Gayle went back to playing semi-professionally for Essex Olympian League side Ryan at age 17; the same league in which Still spotted Benson playing for White Ensign. After Gayle had impressed for Ryan, Stansted decided to make a move for his signature. It was with the Airportmen that his career took flight – excuse the pun – with an impressive campaign that saw him register an incredible tally of 57 goals; more than enough to alert John Still.

Still realised the talents of the 22-year-old and signed him for Dagenham in July 2011, although he wouldn't actually feature for the Daggers until the following campaign. Upon signing, Gayle was immediately loaned out, with Still citing financial restrictions as the reason for him not being an immediate part of the first-team plans at Victoria Road; this despite Gayle opting to have a wage of £150 a week. At the time, Gayle was a carpenter, but such was his desire to make it as a footballer and follow in the footsteps of father Devon – who himself was a prolific goalscorer in the Essex scene – he signed traince terms with the Daggers for less money. It would prove to be a decision that paid off handsomely.

Gayle would spend the 2011/12 campaign out on loan with Bishop's Stortford in Conference North, and if Still needed (he didn't) a reminder of what he was capable of and the talent he had, a 42-goal season in all competitions for the Blues would do just the trick. It was no surprise that in July 2012 Gayle signed a three-year professional deal with Dagenham, Still eager to tie down the services of a player who he made clear right from the off was destined for big things.

It was a good job that Still got his man, as after only 18 games for the Daggers in League Two – scoring seven goals – the EFL's higher-league vultures would come circling to sign him; Peterborough United would win the race for his signature, with a loan-before-you-buy deal agreed. Gayle went on to score another seven goals in just nine games. Indeed, I saw Gayle score one of those for the Posh at Ashton Gate against Bristol City; I was in the away end as a guest of then-Peterborough goalkeeper Bobby Olejnik. United lost, but Gayle scored; even then you knew he was a super talent. He just had that something about him. His deal was made permanent for around £500,000 upon the opening of the January window.

At this point, Gayle's progression had been meteoric and jet-propelled as he continued to make waves. He would finish the season with 13 goals and 29 appearances; not even the most optimistic of fans would have foreseen what was to follow. It would transpire that his last goal of the season – in a 3-2 win over Watford – would indeed be his last for the Posh, despite having only signed in the January. Such was the interest in Gayle, higher-placed teams would come calling; Crystal Palace would be the destination. The Eagles, fresh from promotion to the Premier League and against whom Gayle had played his final game for United, spent a club record £4.5m on him. In the process, it earned former club Dagenham & Redbridge an initial £1m; for Peterborough, circa £3.5m wasn't half bad for someone who had only played 29 games.

Gayle would go on to enjoy a successful spell with the Eagles, with his first career top-flight goal coming in August 2013 in a victory over Sunderland. His first hat-trick would come over a year later in a 3-0 League Cup win against Walsall. Gayle's time at Selhurst Park would be best remembered – albeit not fondly in Liverpool circles – for the role that he played in the Reds seeing their title prospects falter; Gayle scored a brace in a 3-3 comeback draw live on Sky on Easter Monday in 2014, severely denting the Anfield club's hopes of winning the Premier League under Brendan Rodgers. His efforts were so impressive the following season that he finished the 2014/15 campaign as the Eagles' top scorer in all competitions despite finding minutes hard to come by; you can't stop a natural finisher.

In 2016, Gayle was on the move again as Newcastle United – with lofty ambitions of their own to make an immediate return to the Premier League following relegation – came calling; a lucrative five-year deal came his way. It would prove to be an outstanding first season at St James' Park, finishing as their top scorer with 23 goals in 32 Championship appearances as the Magpies indeed won the league. Gayle's exploits earned him an inclusion in the PFA Team of the Year and the EFL Team of the Season, and he was even voted the PFA Fans' Player of the Year for the Championship; it was certainly a step up from Stansted.

Despite a decent season in the top flight in 2017/18, much of Gayle's time in the north-east would be blighted by injury, interspersed with a standout campaign in 2018/19 as he again hit 23 goals, doing so on loan at Championship outfit West Bromwich Albion. So, did he make the right decision to take a pay cut as a carpenter? You could say so. A Championship title; two 23-goal seasons; 145 appearances and 26 goals in the Premier League. Not bad for a lad from the humble roots of park football in non-league.

Oliver Hawkins and Fejiri Okenabirhie

Over the years, there have been games that stick out in my head. Be it big wins, calamitous defeats or just matches that intrigue me from a nerdy, tactical point of view, there's a long list of standout contenders. One of those was certainly one of the least exciting contests – a drab 1-0 National League win for Torquay United over Dagenham & Redbridge in 2016/17. Yet, in terms of intrigue for me as an observer, that one was fascinating.

At the time, I was already a fan of John Still. From an early age, I had an interest in non-league and being able to find 'gems' from the lower leagues, and Still was very much billed as the 'Grand Master'. That Dagenham side was like a homage to exactly that, and they could certainly play. The game was like an insight into how to build a side full of lower-level talent and turned a light bulb on in my own mind as to the strength of non-league's lower reaches. The two players who stood out that day were Oliver Hawkins and Fejiri Okenabirhie. The two poster boys of that side had both been plucked by Still from clubs lower in the non-league pyramid. They both impressed, plus I have a penchant for a 'little and large combo' and they were the perfect pair.

Hawkins signed for the Daggers from Hemel Hempstead Town, but his time with the Tudors was merely the crest of his non-league wave, having enjoyed seven successful years proving himself in non-league prior to moving to Dagenham.

How Hawkins came to move to Victoria Road came almost by chance, and he could have very well gone elsewhere, but for now let's rewind right back to the start. Born in Ealing, the towering forward would stay local to home in starting out with North Greenford United at the age of just 17. Hawkins may not have been the prolific scorer that some of the others in this book were in their non-league days, but there was still a suitable level of proficiency in front of goal that got teams turning their heads.

Hawkins first rubber-stamped his competency with Hillingdon Borough, scoring ten goals in his sole season there, sufficient to prove himself as a capable finisher. Such is the volatile nature of non-league that Hawkins would be on the move at the conclusion of 2010/11, swapping Hillingdon Borough for Northwood. It was there that his career would indeed start to go 'North' with back-to-back campaigns in which Hawkins would hit double figures. If it wasn't the fact that he amassed a whopping 112 games across the two seasons that got managers interested – the best ability is availability, after all – then hitting 19 in all competitions in each of them certainly did.

There was interest in Hawkins, and Hemel Hempstead Town made a move for him. Initially they took him in on trial during pre-season, but that only reinforced to the Tudors that he was a talented player. A step up, but still in the Southern League. To begin with, Hawkins' time at Vauxhall Road would false-start and it was on loan with their Isthmian League counterparts Harrow Borough that he would receive a jump start.

He would only play 11 games with the Reds, and a return of just two goals was hardly anything startling, but his performances convinced Hemel Hempstead boss Dean Brennan to reintegrate him into their side towards the back end of the campaign; it proved to be an inspired decision. Hemel Hempstead would romp to the league title with 102 points, and Hawkins would go on to be a key part of that, helping Town to score a whopping 128 goals in the league.

The Tudors would have a strong first season in National League South, finishing ninth, and Hawkins' game would come on leaps and bounds, too; another double-figures campaign. For Hawkins, it wasn't just his goalscoring that caught the eye. It was more so the complete package and his unorthodox frame and stature. If you ask managers what is the hardest profile of a player to try and sign, a target man will more than likely be the answer; it's difficult to find target men, let alone good ones like Hawkins.

He was courting a lot of interest by this point; where good strikers in non-league are concerned, a certain John Still will more often than not come calling. This was no different, with the veteran manager scouting Hawkins when he was at Luton Town. However, Hawkins ended up at Dagenham & Redbridge, where his career took a somewhat different yet continually upward turn. While Still may well have scouted the lanky frontman when at Kenilworth Road, he ultimately lost his job with Luton in December 2015. Just two weeks later, Still would take over at Dagenham. One person's loss was another's gain; #WelcomeToLutonTown #WelcomeToDagenhamAndRedbridge, Oliver Hawkins.

Hawkins signed for Dagenham, and while they may have struggled and ultimately got relegated out of the Football League in his first season, the young forward played 18 games. His capture and subsequent integration into the side was perhaps a ray of sunshine in what was otherwise a rather cloudy time for the Daggers. The next season, however, would be a far more positive one for both player and club, but for now I park Hawkins' journey and turn my attention to Fejiri Okenabirhie. They were the perfect combination when under Still, and so it is only right that I explore their successful 2016/17 season together, too. First, however, let's go back to 2005.

There is a running theme throughout of players who perhaps don't make it right from the off on the top stage, released by Premier League or upper-echelon EFL academies, and then forced to turn to the solace of non-league in order to get their career up and running once more; Okenabirhie is another who subscribes to that school of thought. At the age of just nine, he joined the youth ranks at Arsenal. While still at school he dreamed one day of going on to play for the Gunners. Yet those dreams were dashed at the age of 16 as he was not taken on by the London club into their academy, and instead it was back to the drawing board.

That drawing board led Okenabirhie to join Stevenage. At the time, Stevenage were plying their trade in League One, and Okenabirhie felt this was a good avenue in which he could follow his dreams of being a professional. He signed as an apprentice initially, and progressed through to signing full-time forms at the age of just 18 in May of 2014. If Okenabirhie did have ambitions of getting into the first team at Stevenage, they were likewise dashed as he would last just the two seasons with Borough, making only three appearances in the process. The Stevenage manager at the time, Graham Westley, decided against extending his deal with the club, eager to try and make the improvements to build on a sixth-placed finish in League Two.

While Okenabirhie found his breakthrough into the senior side somewhat problematic, he was still able to get first-team football under his belt with a plethora of loans into non-league; his 'schooling', if you will. And despite Okenabirhie having impressed at youth-team level – playing a key part in helping Stevenage get to the fourth round of the FA Youth Cup in which he was the jewel in their crown – it was without a doubt his time in non-league that caught the eye of John Still. Okenabirhie may not have been prolific, but Still certainly liked what he saw. Still is to non-league what Simon Cowell is to a fresh-faced contestant on *The X Factor*; he doesn't need to see an 'all singing, all dancing' global star hitting all the high notes to identify a future platinum-selling artist, simply the odd note. While Okenabirhie only scored eight goals in 45 appearances across the Southern League with Bedford Town, Cambridge City and Royston Town plus a more concrete loan spell at Farnborough in Conference South, there was enough for Still to think, 'Yeah, there's something there.' It was after his first permanent spell away from Broadhall Way that he really showcased his credentials: 34 games for Harrow Borough, ten goals. Still had seen enough.

He would go on to flourish in Daggers colours just like he did in the red of Harrow, hitting eight goals in his first campaign. Indeed, it was in that 2016/17 season that I first saw Okenabirhie live, in a 1-0 win for Torquay United at Plainmoor. That Daggers side was a testament to vintage John Still, with a strike force of Okenabirhie and Oliver Hawkins. Wherever you looked, it was awash with players Still had plucked from lower non-league, be it while in charge of the Daggers or previously in his managerial career elsewhere, or who had also come from humbler non-league roots. He'd plucked Elliott Justham from East Thurrock United while Justham was playing part-time and working on the London Underground. Craig Robson came from East Thurrock United, Scott Doe from Kettering Town. Frankie Raymond arrived from Eastbourne Borough, Corey Whitely from Enfield Town, Cristian Assombalonga from Waltham Abbey; that was just in the squad on that day at Plainmoor. In the wider squad, you had Luke Pennell from Dunstable Town, Liam Gordon from Carshalton Athletic, Curtley Williams from Lowestoft Town, Elliott Romain from Eastbourne Borough and Shomari Barnwell from Bowers & Pitsea; that Daggers team had non-league fingerprints all over it.

Okenabirhie and Hawkins have both gone on to have good careers in the EFL; the former to the tune of three separate spells in League One, and the latter having played for Portsmouth and Ipswich Town in the third tier and winning the EFL Trophy with Pompey in 2018. Their combined appearances total is in excess of 400 games; two of Still's finest finds.

* * *

While visiting Roots Hall to speak to John Still in 2024, I took the opportunity to ask him about some of the best striking talent that he has had over the years, their roots, what made him sign them, and why he feels they have gone on to have successful careers.

You signed Dwight Gayle at Dagenham & Redbridge; what was it about Gayle that you liked and made you want to sign him?

'He scored goals! I saw Dwight playing really low down in the pyramid for Stansted. It was weird because when I saw him I also saw his dad; his dad also used to play for me, and so that tells you how old I am. I brought Gayle into Dagenham & Redbridge and we immediately loaned him out as I didn't feel he was strong enough. However, he went to Bishop's Stortford and scored a lot of goals. We brought him back and he just hit the ground running. He is a natural goalscorer; he just has that knack. He was quick, sharp, for his size he was terrific in the air, and most importantly of all he knew where the goal was. With the greatest respect to players nowadays, if you know where the back of the net is and can score regularly then you are going to make a good career for yourself no matter what.'

When you got promoted at Dagenham, you had Paul Benson, Jon Nurse and Josh Scott. Was that 'Vintage Still' as an advert for what you do in finding talents from the lower leagues and developing them on?
'Probably. Paul was local from round the corner at White Ensign. He was another player with a knack of scoring at the level he was at and was worth a chance. Nursey was a goalscorer and hard-working; a lovely guy. Josh was one we took from Hayes, and he was big, strong and powerful. I always like to take a gamble. It tests me and tests the player. They were three terrific players for the football club.'

I remember you bringing a Dagenham side to Torquay United with Oli and Fejiri Okenabirhie leading the line. What were they both like?
'They were good. Fejiri was quick, and Oli was a typical centre-forward in terms of his attributes. Oli Hawkins

didn't really know the game when I initially signed him, but he soon got to grips with it. Fejiri always had a little bit of unpredictability about him which is good for a forward. They have both gone on and had good careers. They were the perfect partnership in many ways. They were very different, but one playing off the other. They can both look back on their careers and be proud of where they have come from. Two boys from Hemel Hempstead and Harrow; I love it. Finding that gem. I still do it now at Southend United with our team in trying to find players from the lower leagues that can come in and do well. It is a massive part of what I have always done.'

You have managed lots of good forwards, but not all have gone to the top level and made careers for themselves. What do you think allows a forward to go to that next level?

'It is not the goals they score, but the way they score them. With Dwight Gayle, I would put him at the top of the list of strikers you have mentioned. He doesn't smash goals in; he just side-foots them. They are goalscorers' goals. The type of goals that you would still score if you did it in the Premier League as they just caress the finishes into the corner and there is such good technique. It is amazing really having that awareness of where the ball is going to drop, and so many top strikers have that ability to be in the right place at the right time. A second too early is no good. A second too late is no good. It is about having that anticipation to time their runs perfectly.'

5

Posh Persuasion

PERHAPS THE biggest and most openly receptive club that has shown a willingness to take a chance on and invest money in non-league is Peterborough United. Ever since Irishman Darragh MacAnthony became chairman of the Posh in 2006, the Cambridgeshire outfit have forged a reputation within the industry for being ardent supporters of non-league. Such is the reputation that they have built up, there is a degree of acceptance that whenever there is a budding young hotshot in non-league with any ounce of talent, the chances are that they will in time end up at London Road.

In his mission statement upon taking over as chairman, MacAnthony pledged to supporters that he would aim to guide United from League Two to the Championship. He more than lived up to his promise. In 2007/08, his first full season as chairman, the Posh successfully tackled the first hurdle of their mission, with Darren Ferguson securing a second-placed finish and with it automatic promotion to the third tier. In the following season, they made back-to-back promotions with a second successive runners-up spot to clinch a place in the Championship at the first time of asking. Easy as you like.

Four players who had played key roles as central figures across both promotions were Aaron McLean, Craig Mackail-Smith, George Boyd and Chris Whelpdale; they had all been plucked from the non-league circuit.

Aaron McLean and Craig Mackail-Smith

The major success stories were Craig Mackail-Smith and Aaron McLean, who – of the nine forwards the Posh had on their books from 2007 to 2009 – struck up a successful partnership as the leading lights of the promotion push; they were very much 'the' partnership of any in the EFL at that time. Across the two seasons, they scored a combined 78 league goals; McLean landing the Golden Boot in 2007/08 with 29, and Mackail-Smith earning an individual honour of his own in the following campaign with 23 league goals to finish as the team's top scorer. These goals alone accounted for 48 per cent of their entire tally in those two promotion campaigns combined; the pair scored as many league goals during that time as the whole team did in the entire 2008/09 League One season. It is no exaggeration to say they are one of the best strike pairings that the Football League has ever seen. Both were signed by the Posh in the 2007 January window, with McLean turning a loan deal permanent, while Mackail-Smith was transferred in for a fee.

Craig Mackail-Smith was a player equally applicable to the previous chapter, with the English-born former Scottish international yet another to count John Still as their former boss having been snapped up from Arlesey Town in 2004, early in Still's second spell with the Daggers.

Mackail-Smith is one of several players in this book with Hertfordshire roots; St Albans City to be precise.

He started out at the age of just 15 in the academy with the Saints, and such was the prolificacy and promise of the prodigy that he was put into the first team just a year later. Indeed, just 16 days after his 17th birthday he got the perfect belated present: his debut. And yet, for all of his early promise and big billing in Saints colours, his time with St Albans was uneventful to the tune of just two goals in three years; it was hardly 'wow, this lad is going places' form. So much so that Mackail-Smith was sent on loan to Arlesey Town then let go on a free to the Blues. That would ultimately be a decision that would work wonders for Mackail-Smith's future prospects.

A game for Arlesey in the 2003/04 FA Trophy would prove to be career-defining for Mackail-Smith. They had already beaten Fleet Town, Hampton & Richmond, Boreham Wood and Hayes to get into the fourth round against none other than Dagenham & Redbridge. Against a team managed by the very manager with the reputation for signing the best up-and-coming talent, in particular strikers, in non-league, Mackail-Smith – with the greatest of respect to Arlesey – got the chance to put himself in the shop window to potentially prove he was worthy of a higher move; that he did. The Daggers would draw 3-3 with Arlesey in the original fixture, before the Blues would cause an upset by knocking their higher-level opponents out in a 4-2 victory with Mackail-Smith scoring a brace. He had booked Arlesey's place in the fifth round, and with it his own move to Dagenham. John Still would – despite a lot of interest from elsewhere – make a move for Mackail-Smith ahead of the 2004/05 campaign.

Signing who performed against your side can sometimes be a dubious tactic as a coach, yet not on this occasion; it would prove to be an inspired move. Mackail-Smith would spend three seasons with the Daggers and maintain a ratio of slightly better than one goal in every three games: 119 appearances and 42 goals at the time of his departure. He would increase his output season upon season in Daggers colours, scoring 12 and 14 in each of the first two campaigns and playing in excess of 40 games in each, yet he surpassed that with 16 goals in just 31 games in 2006/07. His goalscoring form was, capturing the attention of Peterborough.

The Posh would come calling for his services and almost immediately they would find themselves 'licking their lips' with the view that they'd signed a bit of a special talent. You might think Mackail-Smith could have taken a while to adjust to life at London Road; wrong. He hit the ground running with eight in his first 15. His return would be so impressive that it would help propel the Posh to promotion to League One, and then he'd go and eclipse his own return with an even more impressive tally of 26 in playing such an integral role in United's promotion from League One. In total, Mackail-Smith spent four and a bit campaigns with the Posh, scoring 99 in all competitions – an incredible return from one of non-league's finest ever exports.

Aaron McLean, meanwhile, was no stranger in the Football League when joining Peterborough, having been on the books of Leyton Orient as a youngster and playing 40 games in the Third Division, but it was in non-league where he saw his career take off. Following his release by Orient in 2003, Hammersmith-born McLean was signed by newly promoted Aldershot Town. McLean had spent the last few weeks of the 2002/03 campaign on loan with

Town, scoring six in 11 appearances, and thus decided to turn his move to the Recreation Ground (as it was called at the time) permanent that summer having helped them to win the Isthmian League Premier Division. Despite being only 20 years of age, McLean became a regular for a Shots side that secured consecutive play-off finishes, making a total of 72 league appearances.

At the end of the 2004/05 season, McLean was let go by manager Terry Brown and signed for Essex outfit Grays Athletic on a permanent deal having scored three in six on loan with them during his time at Leyton Orient. The diminutive forward impressed, scoring 25 goals in 52 appearances for the Gravelmen. His form alerted the attention of Peterborough and they initially agreed a deal to take McLean to London Road on loan in October 2006. He certainly impressed Darragh MacAnthony, with four goals in nine appearances, and that persuaded the Irishman to shell out £150,000 to sign him. He finished the season well, maintaining a one-in-two goal ratio with ten goals to his name. The 2007/08 campaign would be a hugely successful one in Posh colours for McLean as he would finish as the top scorer in League One with 29 goals, and an astonishing 33 in all competitions. When you've got two strikers scoring a combined 41 goals between them followed by 40 more in 2008/09, is it any wonder that Peterborough went on to get promotion from League Two to the Championship? Ridiculous figures.

As far as strike partnerships go, Mackail-Smith and McLean go down as arguably the best we have ever seen in the Football League: one shy of 400 games, a total of 182 goals, both players hitting 30 once during their time together. Both former England C internationals.

Mackail-Smith went on to excel for Brighton & Hove Albion, seeing himself capped for Scotland, while McLean played – among other things – a sole game in the Premier League for Hull City.

* * *

Nowadays, Aaron McLean is a pundit-turned-presenter extraordinaire, commentating on all things EFL and National League. In his busy schedule, he was kind enough to sit down and talk about his rise from non-league, to playing for Peterborough and his success beyond that. He also gave me an insight into how important non-league was for his development as an aspiring striker.

What do you think playing non-league gives you as a player in being able to prepare for the step up into the EFL and beyond?
'I think non-league gives you a good standard of football. I have seen the progression from when I first started playing in the leagues to what it is now; it is on par with the Football League. There are some teams in the National League that would comfortably compete with teams in League Two, and we have seen that with so many clubs going on and doing well after being promoted into the EFL; the likes of Wrexham and Stockport County are just two examples. The biggest thing is young players go and learn what football is about; what it is like to play in front of fans, training all week, competing for three points. It is that ability to go and hone your craft with "less eyes" on you than trying to prove yourself at a higher level as a youngster. You can just go and develop your game.'

You made 40 appearances for Leyton Orient, and then dropped into non-league. How beneficial was that move – and decision – for your overall development?

'It was hugely beneficial for me. I spent four years with Leyton Orient; two years as a YTS, and two years as a professional. I had got into the first team at a really young age; even in my first year of being a YTS, I was in and around the first team. I was always viewed as a young, up-and-coming player. I was seen as someone that – if we were winning – I could just come on and run defenders ragged, and – if we were losing – could come on and nick a goal. Yet I was never really looked at as a starter, and so never really understood what football was about and the importance of a Saturday; going into non-league gave me that. I was quite a small player, and so going into non-league, playing men whose livelihoods were on the line every time they played, that toughened me up. Going into non-league was the best thing I could have done.'

If you had to pick one – or more if you wish – is there a striker currently playing in non-league who you think is capable of doing what you did in being able to play in the Premier League and at the top end of the EFL?

'It would be difficult to pick a player that I felt could go on and play in the Premier League. However, in terms of being able to go on and play in the Football League and having a good career, I would pick Zak Brunt [of Barnet]. He isn't a striker, but he has shown already this season that he has goals in him. He is working under a top manager in Dean Brennan who is so demanding of his players, and always asking for the players to go and show more; in Zak's case, Brennan always wants him to go and score more goals. If he can do that, I think he can go and play in the EFL as he is only 22 years of age. For me, I think he just needs to change his mindset to be a little more selfish in and around the box, as that is what top players have. Another one is Kairo Mitchell [of Rochdale]; I really like him. I think that he has all the attributes to be a top striker, and for him it was just about finding a home where he feels loved and can play week in, week out. He is playing in a team that very much plays to his strengths. He has a brilliant manager in Jim McNulty, and he is thriving in the setup. He's scoring a lot of goals this season, and I wouldn't be surprised to see him back in the Football League and scoring goals on a regular basis in the coming seasons.'

Increasingly, more and more players from non-league are getting moves up the pyramid. When you returned to non-league in 2015 at the end of your career, was there a notable improvement in non-league, in terms of the standard, setup, etc?

'I think the biggest change – coming back into non-league – was the professionalism of the players and clubs. I think the Premier League has had a huge say in that, as there are so many foreign players being brought in to raise the profile and the standard of the Premier League, and the quality then filters down the divisions. Players that years ago would be in the Premier League are now in the Championship, and so on; it filters down the pyramid. Also, the facilities and the finances have both gone up. The professionalism of the clubs; the physios, the nutritionists, the quality of the training setups. You look at a lot of the pitches now and they are like Wembley. The standards have gone up massively, and I very much look at the National League now as League Three; so many of the players and clubs could quite easily go into the Football League and hold their own.'

What is the one thing that you think you need as a player to be able to go from being a non-league centre-forward, to one capable of performing in the EFL and beyond?
'I think you need a huge amount of desire and application. Being a striker is a difficult position to play. As much as you get all the glory, you carry a lot of the pressure; you are the one that has to score the goals. I was very fortunate that I played in teams that allowed me to go and play my game, and perform to my strengths. It is key that you are in a team that suits you and the attributes you have, but in order to get to the top you have to want to be ruthless, and work hard more so than all the other players around you. If you can do that, and score goals consistently, you have a chance of making it as clubs always need someone that can score goals.'

What was the one thing that you learned or developed during your time in non-league that helped you have the career you did?
'The biggest thing that I learned during my time in non-league was how to look after myself away from the football pitch, in terms of what I was eating, how I was sleeping, etc. I needed to make sure that I was giving my body what I needed, and that I had enough rest. Early in my non-league career, I probably didn't have the know-how or the right information and guidance on what to do. As I progressed, and I worked with different people, they worked with me to ensure that I implemented all of the

right information. I found that I was better as a result of that, as my concentration was higher, I had more energy, etc.; I was able to go out and perform to a higher level on a more consistent basis.'

You played for Peterborough United, who of course sign so many players from non-league. Are you surprised that teams don't do it more? Also, why do you think Peterborough are so successful in doing so?

'I'm surprised that people don't look into the non-league market more. Over the years, we have seen so many players from non-league go on to have top careers in the Football League. Yet there are so many that slip through the net. I would like to see teams use that avenue more, be it loaning players into the National League, or taking players from non-league teams to go and play in the Football League. In my time at Peterborough United when Darragh MacAnthony came in, I was his first signing from non-league and there were about seven or eight at the time that all came through with United having played in non-league. We went on to get back-to-back promotions. Peterborough United are so successful with it as they take the time to go and see teams, watch players, and invest time in seeing who is doing well in the National League. I am always in discussion with MacAnthony about which players are doing well. I think that clubs that benefit from signing from non-league the most are the ones that invest the most resources and effort into ensuring they have the most knowledge they can about the individual players, and who is best-placed to step up into the EFL. They have reaped the benefits of that over the years, as they bring them in, improve them, and sell them on for millions.'

You've seen so many players get big moves into the EFL in your time as a pundit. What do you think sets apart those real top-level players who can make that step up, to your generic, good non-league players?

'I think that the one thing which sets players apart is the consistency. On their day, any player is capable of going and having a good game. But, being able to keep a level of consistently high quality is what sets them apart. Also, it's important to not get carried away with being a footballer, and always having that drive and that desire to want to do better, and improve as a player; you've got to have that mindset to keep improving and evolving. Never be satisfied with where you are. If you get a chance to play in League One or Two, don't be happy with just staying at that level; try and work your way up the ladder, and be prepared to put the work in to do so. The top players perform at a consistent level, be it training or in a game.'

You came through an academy when you were younger. How did that pathway compare to getting your first minutes in men's football in non-league?

'I came through at Leyton Orient, and I would say that there was no pressure on me when I got into the first team. I never felt there was pressure to do well; I could just go out and play. I think that you need pressure to get the best out of yourself, and so I never felt I was a man; I was a boy playing in a man's game. When I went into non-league, I felt I was a man; I was brought in to score goals, create goals, and I was viewed as a man. I had to make sure I produced. If I didn't, I would find myself criticised by the fans or out of the team; it all helped me to mature.

Playing in the first team and playing academy football is very different. Being in a dressing room as a man at Aldershot Town is definitely one of the highlights of my career, looking round the dressing room and knowing I have 15 or 16 other players willing to fight for three points.'

* * *

George Boyd

While perhaps not the most high-profile of names in this book in terms of what they went on to achieve, a player without doubt synonymous with the Football League is George Boyd. With his luscious, long-flowing locks and a lovely left foot he is someone who graced many a pitch and who I remember fondly.

Boyd was one of Darragh MacAnthony's earlier success stories, joining Peterborough United back in 2007. When I think of 'Vintage Peterborough', Boyd was a key component of the side that won back-to-back promotions in 2008 and 2009. I have talked already about the success of Aaron McLean and Craig Mackail-Smith, but I am sure that if you asked the pair of them about that period then they will reference the impact that Boyd had.

For now, I go right back to the start of Boyd's career. It should not be surprising to read that Boyd started out life on the books of Charlton Athletic as a youngster. That in itself should be a badge of honour; the alumni of past Addicks academy graduates makes for impressive – and all the while exhaustive – reading: Lee Bowyer, Joe Gomez, Scott Parker and Ademola Lookman are examples. If you spend time in the club's youth ranks, there's a good chance you've got something about you.

Boyd got his first taste of football in the academy system at The Valley, but he would not follow in the footsteps of so many others who had played for the young Addicks and was let go at the age of just 15; perhaps a decision they went on to regret. He wouldn't, however, let that deter him; he was intent on making it as a professional, and from a young age he lived and breathed football. So much so, in order to be able to attend training, Boyd had to juggle working in a sweet shop just to raise the money to pay for his transport to training. That commitment would ultimately pay dividends.

Despite his release by Charlton, there was interest in Boyd. Born in Chatham, he would spend a short time playing for Chatham Town, but he would look for a permanent move soon after. He could have signed for Football League side Bristol City, or for non-league club Farnborough Town, but it was Stevenage Borough to whom he turned. Boyd worked at Hitchin railway station and was studying at North Hertfordshire College at the time, so it made geographical sense for him to remain close to home. Joining at just the age of 16, it didn't take long for Borough to realise that Boyd was a considerable talent and they opted to give him his debut just a year later. While still on scholarship forms, Boyd was thrown in for his first game on home soil in a league match against Margate.

It would take two years for Boyd to prove his worth, but he would establish himself as a fixture of a Stevenage side that in 2004/05 finished fifth and qualified for the end-of-season eliminators. He would adapt his role from initially being a winger to playing centrally in the wake of Graham Westley's exit, and it proved to be a move that seemingly benefitted him as he earned a reputation for being a goalscoring midfielder. So impressive was he that not only did Peterborough spend a six-figure sum on him, the £260,000 fee was a record for a Conference player at the time. It was a big outlay, but one that the Posh wouldn't regret. Colloquially termed the 'White Pelé' such was his popularity at London Road, the long-haired Boyd flourished with a reputation as one of the best midfielders in the Football League, going down as one of the club's greatest ever players and one of their best signings from non-league.

Chris Whelpdale

The other player who played a key part in the early success in Darragh MacAnthony's tenure was midfielder Chris Whelpdale. Whelpdale's career suffered a false start of sorts in not making the grade after being at some top academy setups yet failing to transition into the first team. He hit the 'peak of his powers' very early on in his career and has never hit the heights of the Premier League so may well feel a tinge of disappointment that he hasn't gone on to play right at the top level as he is a hugely talented player, but he will nonetheless be proud of what he has achieved in the game.

While he was born and bred in east London, and spent his youth playing at local level in Brentwood, Whelpdale's first real foray into football at any recognised level was with Norwich City. The Canaries recruited him to link up with their academy, but it wouldn't be long before he was on the move again. This time he would sign closer to home as he joined the youth ranks at Arsenal while Arsène Wenger was at Highbury. After spending a brief period with the

Gunners, he would sign for Ipswich Town, Norwich's East Anglian neighbours.

It wasn't to be though for Whelpdale and he was let go by the Tractor Boys before he could make the first team and was back to square one. Yet, as is the way with so many in this book, Whelpdale would not let that setback curb his enthusiasm. Instead it would only spur him on to go and get his big break. The base camp for his Kilimanjaro would be Maldon Town, and when Whelpdale was with the Jammers he was still playing for England Schoolboys as part of the 'Class of 2005'. Some notable players to have featured in the 2004/05 campaign alongside Whelpdale went on to have successful pro careers: Chris Lines, John Mousinho and Russell Martin to name just three.

Whelpdale would receive a lot of interest while playing for Maldon, also representing the Essex county side. He would spend two seasons with Maldon before the higher-ranked Billericay Town came calling. His time with the Blues would prove to be his major break, with just a single season under his belt before the big boys of Peterborough were on his case. The Posh weren't alone in their move for Whelpdale's services, with Southend United also putting in a bid, but he decided that London Road would be the best next step.

Whelpdale's career perhaps didn't hit the heights that his undoubted technical ability was capable of, and didn't go the way of some of the other players in this chapter with non-league roots to have gone on to play for the Posh. Indeed, while his first three years at London Road were upward-facing, his career since then went slowly down through the professional ranks and out of the EFL; at the time of writing he found himself back where he started, in non-league football. Nonetheless, he did forge a successful 20-year career.

Peterborough United and Barnet

I can't possibly do a feature about United's success of dipping into non-league and signing players without covering perhaps the most well-established partnership in English football in terms of a conveyor belt of talent between two teams: that being the Posh's long-standing links with Barnet. Chairman Darragh MacAnthony and director of football Barry Fry have been able to maintain a strategic partnership with the Bees, and that has enabled them to bring in a whole host of talent. It perhaps shouldn't be surprising that they have done so, with Fry having managed Barnet twice between 1978 and 1993, and he has always remained an avid watcher from afar.

Jack Taylor

One of the earliest examples of a Barnet player to have been plucked by the Posh that perhaps started off their obsession with the Bees was midfielder Jack Taylor. Jack's brother Harry is also a footballer, playing for Southend United at the time of writing, and the pair were like many in this book, turning to the opportunity of the lower leagues after being deemed not good enough to make the grade at a Premier League outfit. Born in Hammersmith, Jack joined the academy at one of London's footballing juggernauts – Chelsea – at the age of just seven. He would spend seven years with the Blues, before he was like so many; a by-product of the ruthless nature of the academy system and tossed on to the scrapheap of 'what could have beens' and 'nearly rans'.

What I particularly like about Jack's journey is that he shares a real bond with his brother in terms of their pathway into football; the pair both joined Chelsea in 2005, before their release in 2012 and subsequent moves to Barnet. The spooky thing is that they also then both played for Hampton & Richmond Borough as part of their development – albeit at different times – and so it is certainly a case of 'what could have been'; Harry has gone on to forge a decent career in the game, but perhaps not the heights of that of his younger brother.

When you look at the real top players, often a common denominator is an ability to get a high number of minutes at a young age, and exposure to first-team football as early as possible. That can certainly be said about Jack, who made his senior debut for the Bees as a 15-year-old. Taylor wasn't by any means a regular at this point – understandably – but to throw a youngster in at this age into men's football, even if it was only a local cup competition, certainly extended beyond merely being a 'token gesture'; Barnet realised even at that stage that he had a bit about him.

The Bees wouldn't waste any time in tying Taylor down to a professional deal, understanding the potential that they had on offer. Say what you want about Barnet chairman Tony Kleanthous, but one thing for sure is that he is an intelligent businessman; he knows a future money-making asset when he sees one and has had his fair share of them over the years. Indeed, despite Barnet already having some top midfielders on the books at the time – the likes of Curtis Weston, Sam Togwell and Andy Yiadom before he was converted into a right-back – they knew that they had to keep hold of Taylor, handing him a two-year-deal. The following 2016/17 campaign – the first of his two years – would prove to be a defining one for the youngster, with his first loan out in men's football, at Hampton & Richmond, before making 14 league appearances for the Bees in a chaotic-yet-middling 15th-placed season. Taylor was without doubt the shining star in that campaign, and the seeds were sown for him being an integral part of their side.

He'd go on to establish himself as a regular for Barnet, ending up with a total of 129 appearances by the time of his eventual exit in early 2020. With Barnet, he had gone from being a budding young starlet starting out in the game at 15 to being one of the leading lights of a side that made the play-offs aged 21. He had learned how to play the game, honed his technical ability and developed his physical side; all in the pressure cooker of non-league football. There was nothing like the learning curve that the National League had to offer. The contrast between the fresh-faced prodigy against Hatfield Town to the precocious talent against FC Halifax Town in his final game in Bees colours was night and day. He had – during that spell – built up a reputation for being one of the standout midfielders in the fifth tier; when the January window opened and he'd just completed his seventh straight 90 minutes and scored his fourth goal in seven, he had admirers from the EFL seeking his services.

Peterborough was his destination and after four seasons in Posh colours, including a League One promotion for good measure, he signed for Ipswich Town in the summer of 2023. He had left The Hive in 2020 trying to get promoted out of the top tier of non-league, and yet in the space of five seasons he had got promoted to the top tier of English football, with Ipswich reaching the Premier League in 2024. As far as an advert for non-league goes, Taylor provides hope and inspiration to players let go by top-level academies and especially those who have not had their big break by the age of 21 that non-league can provide solace to them and get their career on the right path. He's now a top-flight player and also a senior international with the Republic of Ireland, qualifying due to his Irish father.

Ronnie Edwards

Peterborough have had several Barnet-based recruits over the years who have gone on to have success. I could have easily put winger Ephron Mason-Clark and midfielder Ryan de Havilland under the microscope. The former graduated through the youth teams at The Hive prior to establishing himself as a fixture of the first team, while the latter turned to Barnet after his release from Fulham aged 20. The pair also spent time out on loan in non-league with Metropolitan Police before making their mark with Barnet. But perhaps United's proudest 'find' is young defender Ronnie Edwards. To be able to identify any young player from the non-league scene capable of making the step up into a side expected to compete at the top end of League One as a minimum is one thing, but the fact that they were able to identify Edwards was all the more impressive considering that he had only played one league game for Barnet's first team at the time of his transfer.

Edwards is another prime example of the benefit of getting exposure to men's football at an early age; he was just 16 when he was thrust into the heat of the battle for Barnet. As far as 'meteoric rise' is concerned, Edwards is the very definition of that. On 17 December 2019, he was making his senior debut for the Bees in a Middlesex

Senior Cup tie and yet within nine months he was lining up for Peterborough in the EFL Trophy; how time flies when you are a generational talent. Edwards' journey is even more unique given that he didn't even go down the route of going out on loan to get game time; he by-passed all of that. He got a bit of an introduction – if you can call it that – in playing for Barnet's first team with a handful of appearances, restricted largely to cup competitions, and before you knew it Peterborough were on the phone. Initially taking him on trial, United certainly liked what they saw. The trial was like taking a top-of-the-range sports car for a test drive; you aren't driving it to see whether it is a good car! Peterborough were clear that they wanted to sign Edwards, and that they did, as they forked out for the youngster confident that they had found another 'gem'; they certainly know their onions. Only their 'onions' are actually elite-level young footballers.

Edwards has more than lived up to his potential; indeed, he has far surpassed what even the Posh may have felt he would go on to achieve. He earned international recognition with England's youth teams less than a year after moving to London Road and he went on to win the European Under-19 Championship with the Three Lions in 2022, earning a big-money move to Southampton. In terms of the best players to have come out of non-league, given what he has already achieved at the age he is then the potential is certainly frightening; he's merely scratched the surface. That is a testament to the environment of non-league academies and the pathway provided by clubs at that level. Edwards progressed all the way through Barnet's academy before being put into the first team and he has not looked back since. He remains the gold standard for former non-league centre-backs and the biggest advert for the grounding that non-league football can give young players.

6

Safe Hands

REPRESENTING YOUR country is the pinnacle of any footballer's career; an honour bestowed upon statistically so few. For those plying their trade in the lower reaches of the pyramid, it is a dream that every player has but so seldom achieves. There seems to be a glass ceiling even now that if you don't play in the top flight, you don't have a chance of representing England at national team level. However, while the challenge may still be just as intense and demanding, there is no doubt that goalkeepers have a greater sense of confidence that they can one day go on to represent their country. Indeed, since 1960, of the 38 goalkeepers who have pulled on an England shirt, ten of those have started out in non-league. A conversion rate of around 26 per cent is a pretty impressive statistic and provides hope for non-league goalkeepers that over a 65-year period, roughly a quarter of the stoppers to have played for England started off in the humble beginnings of non-league.

Alex Stepney

When you think of the true pillars of English football, you think Manchester United: 20 First Division or Premier

League titles, 12 FA Cups, 21 Community Shields, three European Cups or Champions League trophies, and a plethora of other accolades; they are the most successful club domestically in England with 60 trophies. And, in 1967/68, the Red Devils became the first English club to win the European Cup. The goalkeeper that day was Surrey-born Alex Stepney. While Stepney may have tasted success on the European stage with United, it was in non-league that he started his career.

Indeed, there is a poetic look to Stepney's journey, with his 21-year career being book-ended by spells in non-league, both in its inception (with Tooting & Mitcham United) and at its finale (with Altrincham).

Stepney was born in Mitcham, so the logical starting point was to join his local side Tooting & Mitcham; I'll admit, I didn't even know Mitcham was a place, and instead thought that it was the prefix to the Terrors' United surname. It could have been grander pastures for Stepney to start out his career, having the opportunity to join Fulham – or at the very least compete for a deal with the London outfit – as he got a trial. It would turn out to be unsuccessful, and he would instead turn to non-league in joining Tooting & Mitcham.

It wasn't long, however, before Stepney had developed a reputation for being one of the standout goalkeepers in non-league. His form for the Terrors earned him a window into the professional game, signing for Millwall on a 'try before you buy' style deal in which he signed purely amateur forms with the Lions. However, it didn't take long for Stepney to prove that he was worthy of more and he would be rewarded with a professional deal only months into his career at The Den.

Stepney would go on to play at the top level of the game for Chelsea and Manchester United; minimally with the Blues (just the single appearance) but principally for the Red Devils. He would forge out a successful 12-year career primarily under Matt Busby and Tommy Docherty, the latter of whom signed Stepney at the Blues. Criminally, Stepney would only be recognised once at international level by England, but he would still go on to write himself into the record books as one of the best goalkeepers to have ever pulled on the United jersey.

After leaving Old Trafford, Stepney would spend time playing in the United States with a team called Dallas Tornado; the North American Soccer League was popular for players at the back end of their careers at the time. He would call time on his professional career with the Tornado, and would return to England with time at Altrincham in the Alliance Premier League (the equivalent of today's National League). Initially on loan, he'd return permanently and spend a year with the Robins prior to his eventual retirement in 1982. The move to Moss Lane provided the perfect ending to a career that started and finished in non-league football, and was just a matter of a few miles as the crow flies from where Stepney had made himself as a fixture for the most successful club in English domestic history.

Ben Foster

One goalkeeper who has also represented England is Ben Foster. He is perhaps better known more recently for his exploits on YouTube, be it on a golf course or in a recording studio, as well as having a GoPro camera in his goal during matches. Because of that, the general footballing public and indeed the younger viewer forget that Foster was – in the prime of his career – a top performer. Foster's rise through to the national team was nearly as quick as his progress as an up-and-coming YouTuber; only seven years on from establishing himself as a regular at first-team level, Foster was pulling on a jersey for England at Old Trafford in 2007. It was quite the upward trajectory. Indeed, it was even more impressive considering that his first call-up for England was as early as 2006.

While Foster made a name for himself at the top level, it was in the tenth tier of English football with Racing Club Warwick that he cut his cloth. Foster began playing in Warwick's youth team, and got his first taste of success at the end of the 1999/2000 campaign as part of the team that won the Midland Floodlit Youth League. Foster may not have been the first choice, but he was handed an opportunity to be part of the first team for Warwick aged 17, a benefactor of circumstance as regular number one Craig Glover and youth-teamer Richard Morris left for Bedworth United and Leamington respectively. Warwick's Billy Hollywood decided to chuck him in at the deep end; another Hollywood would be important at the end of Foster's career too.

And, like he did behind a vlogging camera, Foster was a natural. He attracted a lot of early interest in his displays and Stoke City were one of those tempted into sniffing around for his services. Potters scout Colin Dobson took the short trip to Townsend Meadow to watch Foster; he certainly didn't disappoint. Foster was one of the key players under Hollywood who saw the Racers secure their safety in the Southern League Western Division. Dobson liked what he saw in the young goalkeeper, and that persuaded Stoke to make a move for him. Initially, Foster was brought in on trial; he impressed. He then had a more thorough assessment of his quality by then City boss Gudjon Thordarsson; again, he impressed. They had seen enough.

City wasted little time in getting a deal over the line. John Rudge was the architect behind the transfer, securing Foster's services for a hefty five-figure fee the likes of which was rare for Racing Club Warwick. To this day, Foster is revered at Townsend Meadow, with a picture of him, his first contract and first team sheet still proudly on display. Foster himself still pops back to see his former side on occasion; he is certainly appreciative of his non-league roots. The Racers, too, are proud of the role they played in his development, and so they should be. It could have been so different for Foster who – while playing for Racing Club Warwick – was training to be a chef. Indeed, he was working at Café Rouge. Yet, it was the rouge and white of the Potters that Foster opted for, agreeing a one-year deal with room for an additional two.

In the 2001/02 campaign, Stoke were promoted from the Second Division via the play-offs, so understandably chances were at a premium; especially with first-team regular Neil Cutler in good form. Coincidentally, Cutler would go on to be West Bromwich Albion's goalkeeping coach, ending up being Foster's coach at The Hawthorns.

Foster had to sit on the sidelines for much of that season. He likewise had to sit and watch during his loan with Bristol City, albeit the spell was a useful one for him. He would eventually manage to get some first-team minutes under his belt by joining Tiverton Town, making

16 appearances. His time in Devon would be very much solely for experience, with Foster still remaining part of the Stoke first-team squad during the duration of his loan, initially under new boss Steve Cotterill and then latterly his replacement Tony Pulis. Such was the success of his loan with Tiverton and the part they played in his early development as an aspiring goalkeeper, Foster left a pair of signed gloves for the Yellows; they were framed and are proudly shown on display at Ladysmead to this day.

The 2003/04 campaign would be a frustrating one for Foster. Again out on loan in the Southern League Premier Division – this time at Stafford Rangers – he made just the single appearance. Yet he bounced back with a hugely defining following season, as he would get his first taste of professional football with loans at Kidderminster Harriers and then Wrexham, making a total of 19 appearances. It was with the Red Dragons that Foster would get his big break, signing for the Welsh club in February 2005. But it nearly wasn't to be, as he was only allowed to sign for Wrexham, who were in administration at the time, with special dispensation.

Foster is like many in this book, who was a fortunate benefactor of circumstance that ultimately saw his career take off. At the back end of the 2004/05 campaign, Wrexham made the Football League Trophy Final against Southend United at the Millennium Stadium in Cardiff. Among the observers that day was none other than Sir Alex Ferguson, whose son Darren was playing for Wrexham at the time, and thus Foster had – as well as 36,251 supporters – the eyes of the country's best manager on him. He didn't disappoint.

At the time, there weren't many better 'carrots' for young players than to be rated by Sir Alex Ferguson, and such was Foster's display in the final that the iconic manager decided to make a move for the 22-year-old. Ferguson had struggled to adequately replace Peter Schmeichel after his exit in 1999 with United going through Mark Bosnich, Raimond van der Gouw, Fabien Barthez, Andy Goram, Paul Rachubka, Massimo Taibi, Nick Culkin, Ray Carroll, Ricardo and Tim Howard; all with limited success. Ferguson saw Foster as a potential contender for that throne.

His time at Old Trafford would go on to be uneventful, featuring sparingly, and instead sent out on loan before being let go in 2010. He would go on to establish himself as a regular across two separate spells in the Midlands, with Birmingham City and West Brom, before a move to Watford. After amassing over 400 league appearances, Foster would sign for Wrexham and help them to achieve their own ambitions of playing at a higher level in winning the National League title in 2023. Foster saved a stoppage-time penalty against Notts County to give the Red Dragons the upper hand in the race for the title late in the season. He would retire shortly after their promotion after playing just a handful of games at the start of the 2023/24 League Two campaign.

He remains one of the best goalkeepers to have been produced in England, winning the League Cup on three occasions, receiving international recognition, and playing just short of 550 games across a 23-year career that saw him end up selected – and playing for – the Three Lions at the 2014 World Cup.

Jordan Pickford

If you ask modern-day fans about the best players to have pulled on the goalkeeping jersey for England, one name that will get a mention is Jordan Pickford. A consistent performer for the Three Lions and remembered fondly for his penalty save against Colombia in the 2018 World Cup last 16, Pickford counts time in non-league as his first real taste of men's first-team football.

Pickford started out on the books of Sunderland as a youngster, joining in 2002 at the age of only eight, and was such a high flyer early on in his youth that he was only 17 when he was moved up into the Black Cats' reserve team. Like many on this list, with first-team chances at a premium, Pickford turned to the loan market to experience senior football. Darlington would be the destination. If Pickford wanted to go out on loan and get the taste of making saves at first-team level, he would certainly get that; he was without doubt kept busy with the Quakers, who were competing in Conference Premier at the time and struggled throughout. At the end of the 2011/12 season the club folded after entering administration.

That spell would certainly be filed under 'character-building'. It was a far cry from an environment of experienced players who had been there and done it. Pickford's debut saw Darlington welcome runaway leaders Fleetwood Town to Blackwell Meadows; it was fair to say that he had to grow up fast, with the struggling team that he joined being awash with players stepping up – some for the first time – out of the academy. Much of the loan spell was a case of picking the ball out of his own net, but it was one that was hugely beneficial for his development.

Pickford would get further experience of non-league with another short-term loan, joining Alfreton Town in Conference Premier in February 2013. He would impress with the Reds, and in his 12 games he kept five clean sheets; a decent 42 per cent record. That would prove to be the extent of Pickford's non-league exposure, but it set him up nicely for further outings in first-team football with a quartet of deals in the EFL: League Two with Burton Albion, League One with Carlisle United and Bradford City, and mid-table in the Championship with Preston North End. Experiencing play-off challenges and relegation struggles was all vital to dip his toe into the water for his eventual integration in the Sunderland first team.

Pickford's perseverance at doing the hard yards out on loan was rewarded in January 2016 when he made his debut for the Black Cats in the FA Cup against Arsenal, following that up with his Premier League bow at home to Tottenham Hotspur. He made one more Premier League appearance before the end of the season, at Watford, but he would go on to establish himself as the bona fide number one in 2016/17, making a total of 29 league appearances. Despite Sunderland going down, Pickford caught the eye. Granted, he was kept busy across both seasons – particularly the latter – but that didn't detract from a hugely impressive campaign as he made it on to the PFA Young Player of the Year shortlist, joined by Dele Alli, Harry Kane, Michael Keane, Romelu Lukaku and Leroy Sané. It was fair to say Pickford was in good company.

Pickford had excelled so much at the Stadium of Light that Everton came calling for his services. The Toffees have spent a fair bit of money in recent years, and they loosened the purse strings sufficiently to sign Pickford in the summer of 2017, making him the most expensive British goalkeeper of all time for around £30m. There were high hopes for Pickford to go right to the top, and he's certainly done that. At the time of writing he remained with Everton, as the undisputed number one at club level and for his country. He has put himself in the conversation as one of the best British goalkeepers of all time. Indeed, for all that he has achieved since signing for the Toffees in 2017, it was his loan spells in non-league – and youth international recognition for England while at Alfreton Town in 2013 – that set his career up and running.

Nick Pope

The pinnacle of Jordan Pickford's career came in the 2018 World Cup with his penalty heroics against Colombia. Looking on from the bench that day was Nick Pope, who has also played in non-league and – also like Pickford – has links to the Tyne–Wear derby.

At the time of writing Pope was on the books of Newcastle United. His journey is indebted to his time in non-league in ultimately providing him with a second chance after being given the axe by Ipswich Town's academy aged 16. For Pope, his dream was to one day play for Ipswich. He was a season ticket holder at Portman Road, raised as an Ipswich fan and used to attend games with his dad as a youngster. At the age of just ten, Pope was handed a deal in the academy at Portman Road and hoped that one day he could follow in the footsteps of Tractor Boys stopper Richard Wright, who started off at Portman Road before going on to represent England. Yet his footballing world came crashing down in his mid-teens as Pope was released and had to go back to square one.

Pope's journey is like so many players in this book: rejected by a top academy in his youth, and turned to non-league to rebuild his career. He turned to the local town of Bury St Edmunds following his release by the Tractor Boys, and signed for the now defunct Team Bury. Team Bury had been formed in 2005, initially as West Suffolk College, and would run until 2018 as a feeder for higher-ranked non-league club Bury Town. In his youth, Pope would attend the sports academy at West Suffolk College; he is without doubt their most successful alumnus.

The pathway into Bury Town would prove to be a hugely beneficial one for Pope's early development, with exposure to first-team football as early as 16. So many of the finest talents have gained men's minutes in their mid-teens and been chucked into the deep end from an early age. Pope had made 27 appearances by the age of 19 and had even played for England at college level; just seven years later he would pull on the jersey for the Three Lions.

Nigel Spink

One lesser-known name that played internationally and also started out in non-league is Nigel Spink. Spink made a single appearance in England colours, and prior to embarking on a successful 19-year spell in the First Division he was given his first taste of men's football in non-league.

It was in the claret of Aston Villa that Spink made his name, making a total of 361 league appearances during his time at Villa Park, having started out with the Clarets of Chelmsford City. As a Chelmsford boy born and bred, it was perhaps not surprising that Spink's first footsteps into first-team football were with his hometown club, spending a single year with City before he got his high-profile move to the Midlands.

That transfer shouldn't have come as too much of a surprise to those who knew Spink, who had been highlighted as a potential star of the future right from before his days with Chelmsford. After a spell with Writtle Minors, Spink would go on to spend time with West Ham United on schoolboy forms before his eventual release. The convenience of joining Chelmsford gave him the ideal chance to showcase his talents and develop into the role, and this ultimately played an integral part in fashioning him the chance to sign for Aston Villa.

There was a poetic ending to Spink's playing career as far as his association with non-league is concerned, as – having represented Aston Villa, West Bromwich Albion and Millwall – he ending up with Forest Green Rovers in a player-coach role; there is something deeply romantic about going full circle and ending up back in non-league. He would eventually call time on his playing career in 2002, having won the European Cup with Villa 20 years previously; winning just one cap for England (and two for England B) was a criminally low number for a goalkeeper so talented. However, Spink's spell in non-league had paved the way for him to go from playing against Margate in the Southern League to beating Bayern Munich in the European Cup Final.

Nigel Martyn

Another player who played for both England and England B and started out in non-league was Nigel Martyn.

Martyn's journey is interesting; even in how he became a goalkeeper, let alone a successful one. Like most other football-mad individuals he worked for a living, had a 'normal job' and played for his local team on the side. Seemingly he was content with doing his nine-to-five working two jobs – in a plastic factory and at a coal merchant – and then supplementing that by playing football in whatever spare time he had left. What makes Martyn's proficiency in goal all the more impressive is that during his youth days playing in his native Cornwall he actually started out as a midfielder, and it was only by chance that he landed on being a goalkeeper. His brother's team were short one day, and Martyn – the ultimate team player as he was – volunteered, or rather was pushed into the job. Better still, Martyn could've quite conceivably pursued a different sport, representing Cornwall at cricket as a wicketkeeper to a relatively high standard; we might have had the next Mark Boucher or Kumar Sangakkarra.

He opted not to pursue cricket to a professional standard, going down the route of football instead, albeit it should perhaps not be all that surprising that he would end up being a goalkeeper given that he was adept with his hands.

It was after playing for Cornish side St Blazey that Martyn's aspirations for being a top-level goalkeeper came to fruition, although his big break came about somewhat by chance as the story goes. He was playing one afternoon for St Blazey. At the same time, a local passer by happened to stumble upon the game and was rather impressed by the young stopper they saw that day. As it happened, she worked at Bristol Rovers as a tea lady and was holidaying in the area. Upon returning to the Gas – proud of her 'latest find' – she said there was a player that they, and more specifically manager Ian Holloway, should look at. Holloway duly obliged and Martyn initially trained with the reserves. When I say initially, I mean that it was no time at all before the Gas realised that the recommendation from their tea lady was not just capable of pulling off the odd save, but was more than useful with his hands, and they signed him without hesitation. Just like that, Martyn had landed himself a professional contract.

It wasn't long after signing for Bristol Rovers that other clubs came knocking for Martyn's services, and in 1989 he created history when he became the first £1m goalkeeper in British football by signing for Crystal Palace, who at the time were managed by the legendary Steve Coppell and had just been promoted to the First Division. He would go on to represent two of the giants of English football in Leeds United and Everton, while playing internationally for his country 23 times. All because of a tea lady. Who'd have thought it?

Joe Hart

There are often players who are underappreciated with praises so seldom sung, and one who I'd say falls into that category is Joe Hart. He played on the biggest of stages domestically and internationally, is one of the best goalkeepers to have ever played in the Premier League, and is without a doubt in the conversation among the best English stoppers in history; not bad for someone who started out in non-league.

Like many of the entries in this list, Hart's journey saw him bide his time before he was handed an opportunity. He'd first make a matchday squad, however, as early as the age of 15, yet it wouldn't be until he turned 17 that Hart would receive his debut.

Hart was always a high performer, be it on the football pitch, on a cricket field or in the classroom. While he forged a successful career in football, it could have quite easily been so different as he was a talented cricketer – a strong bowler who played for Shrewsbury Cricket Club as well as being capped at county level. However, his proficiency with a football would soon take centre stage.

Born in Shrewsbury, Hart was rewarded for his footballing talent by being invited in the summer of 2002/03 to train with Shrewsbury Town on an informal basis. Initially it was nothing serious, just a chance for a talented, young, local player to train with his hometown club. As it would turn out, his perseverance to turn up and prove his worth would eventually open the door for the start of his playing career. At the time, Shrewsbury had two goalkeepers on their books: Scott Howie and Ian Dunbavin. Howie had suffered an injury, meaning that they were down to only one recognised goalkeeper; a club going rogue and not including a replacement on the bench wasn't the 'done thing' as it perhaps is now. As such, the Shrews had to bring in a short-term replacement; where would they turn? A classroom in Meole Brace School.

Hart was only 15 at the time, but so impressed were Town in his ability and so great was their need for a quick resolution to their problems that he would be called out of the classroom and on to a coach down to Exeter City for his first inclusion in a matchday squad. It is somewhat poetic that his first taste of men's football came at one St James Park, and that his first realisation of his supreme, top-level talent came at the other St James' Park – four levels and five years apart. He travelled with the Shrews to Devon and was an unused substitute.

The 2002/03 campaign proved to be an unsuccessful one for Town, with relegation out of the Football League, but the integration of Hart into the first-team setup was one of the few positive takeaways. Hart would have to wait until 2004 to be handed his debut for the Shrews; coincidentally, just a day after his 17th birthday. Not a bad present. The game was against Gravesend and Northfleet, a 1-1 draw under the lights at Gay Meadow. In total, Hart would go on to make just a single further appearance that season. The 2004/05 campaign was again a tough one for the youngster, resigned to simply making up the numbers as part of the bench.

The 2005/06 campaign was when Hart would properly establish himself in the first-team picture with the Shrews finishing tenth, five points off seventh, the young starlet making 46 League Two appearances. While Shrewsbury struggled for consistency, Hart would excel with his performances earning him recognition as the division's standout goalkeeper and a spot in the PFA Team of the Year. If prospective clubs needed it – they didn't – that recognition rubber-stamped his quality and potential, and turned the heads of many top-flight clubs. One of those was Manchester City, who'd held a long-standing interest in Hart and for months had been sending goalkeeping coach Tim Flowers to Gay Meadow to watch him play. For someone who had made just over 500 league appearances, was named in the Premier League Team of the Year twice and indeed won the top division once, Flowers knew a top goalkeeper in the making when he saw one.

Hart would continue to prove himself to Flowers, and the former England man persuaded City to part with a reported sum of £100,000 – a far cry from the riches they have since spent – to land their man. The Citizens would not live to regret the decision as Hart would go on to write himself into recent legend as one of the best goalkeepers to pull on their colours, if not *the* best. The 2006/07 campaign would be an 'adaptation year' for the youngster, before he would go on to make himself a mainstay of the Manchester City side over the next eight years, with a total of 348 appearances in all competitions. However, 2016/17 saw Hart seemingly cast aside under Pep Guardiola in favour of a more 'modern-day' option, eventually confirming his exit from the club in the summer of 2017 having won two Premier Leagues, one FA Cup and two League Cups, as well as the Premier League Golden Glove four times, and two PFA Premier League Team of the Year inclusions. He goes down in history as the first title-winning Manchester City goalkeeper since 1968. Hardly the worst return for a goalkeeper signed for just £100,000.

7

A Trip on the Tube

LONDON IS widely regarded as the epicentre from which the 'beautiful game' we have and love today blossomed. In 1863, modern football was codified in the capital. The Football Association was founded and its first secretary – Ebenezer Cobb Morley – hailed from Barnes, a small district in the London Borough of Richmond upon Thames, after moving to the Big Smoke from Hull ten years prior. The first governing body of the sport had its inaugural meeting in the Freemasons Tavern, located just 12 miles as the crow flies from Wembley, the 'home of football'. Fulham were founded in 1879 and are the oldest club in London to still be playing professionally, while Royal Arsenal were the first club to turn professional in 1891; now Arsenal (becoming so in 1913). The first winners of the prestigious FA Cup, in 1871/72, were Wanderers, founded originally as Forest FC in Leytonstone before adopting their new name five years after their foundation in a nod to their nomadic nature.

Thus, while the London football scene today is regarded as a salmagundi of cash-splashing, superstar-studded teams playing to the gallery of a global audience, it actually has humble beginnings and is the bedrock for the game. Cray Wanderers – founded three years prior to football's codification – are regarded as the oldest extant club in Greater London, founded in St Mary Cray, Bromley, which is located in the modern-day capital. They continue to this day to ply their trade in non-league and have done so for their 167-year existence. Indeed, despite the capital having produced so much talent, so many of the players who have gone on to make a name for themselves at the top level count the London non-league scene as the roots of their career.

With that in mind, I take an explorative trip round London – metaphorically speaking, via the medium of the Tube – to shine a light on the best players to have started off in non-league and gone on to play at the highest level, and unearth where their journeys began.

Stop 1: South Ruislip

I start where so many of my London footballing gallivants have taken me: South Ruislip, a short ride round the corner from Grosvenor Vale, home to National League outfit Wealdstone. One of the so-called 'minnows' of the fifth tier, the Stones are a community-focused semi-professional club; they have been in Ruislip since 2008. Grosvenor Vale sits on the doorstep of Wembley, and has provided me with the 'base camp' for many weekend trips to the national stadium, staying locally at the Barn Hotel. A real unique club with the humblest of non-league roots and some brilliant people at its forefront – and behind the scenes – the Stones can claim to have played a part in the development of some iconic players in English football.

Two of the most notable players to have come through with Wealdstone – and coincidentally two who go down in history as the most attritional and committed that we have ever seen – are Stuart Pearce and Vinnie Jones. Both represented the club during arguably their most successful period, between 1982 and 1985. The pair made a combined 214 appearances and are regarded as two of the best to have played for Wealdstone.

Stuart Pearce

The first to break through into the first team was Stuart Pearce. Pearce – famously nicknamed 'Psycho' – was handed an opportunity by manager Alan Fogarty at just 16 years of age, playing for the sum of just £15 a week alongside training as an electrician. He quickly established himself as a regular as Wealdstone won promotion from the Southern League and had a couple of years in the Alliance Premier League between 1979 and 1981.

After breaking through and gaining initial attention for his displays at left-back, Pearce was the subject of an approach from Hull City of the Fourth Division. Pearce – along with Stones skipper John Watson – trained with the Tigers and played a trial game against a Grimsby Town reserve side. Hull offered Pearce a deal off the back of it, consisting of a playing contract as well as, unusually, a job with the local council as an electrician; not a bad outcome, I suppose. Despite the offer, Pearce turned it down in favour of sticking with Wealdstone.

In 1981/82, Pearce played an integral part in one of the most successful Stones sides in recent history, only their third post-war title-winning campaign. In the same season, the Stones made it a quadruple with triumphs in the Southern League Cup, Southern League Championship Shield and Southern League Championship Cup, as well as winning the Southern League itself. Pearce was only 19 at the time, impressing with his 'hard-tackling nature' as part of a backline that conceded only 32 goals and kept 33 clean sheets in all competitions.

At this point Pearce was one of the best defenders outside of the Football League, and interest continued to circle around him. In 1982/83 Psycho would indeed get his big move, becoming one of the first to go from non-league to the First Division in a single move. Coventry City boss Bobby Gould went to watch Pearce play at Yeovil, and off the back of that he was convinced sufficiently in his qualities to spend £30,000 on the Shepherd's Bush boy. Pearce naturally jumped at the chance to sign for the Sky Blues, even accepting a wage of £30 a week less than what he was on at Wealdstone; the price of making it in the big time.

And make it in the big time he did. To this day he is regarded as one of the best left-backs of a generation, and certainly one of the best that the country has ever produced; up there with the Ashley Coles of this world. Pearce would spend just the two seasons as a Sky Blue before being plucked by City's loftier Midlands neighbours Nottingham Forest – led by the infamous Brian Clough – and would go on to break 500 appearances with the Reds with four cup winners' medals across 12 years. He forged a reputation in his career for being a bit of a 'hard nut', playing to the gallery of being a 'hardened ex-non-league defender', and yet in three of his 12 years at the City Ground he hit double figures for goals and scored a combined total of 88; a nod to the attacking escapades of his time in a high-flying Stones side that ultimately earned him the higher-level interest for his break.

Vinnie Jones

Notoriously – and wrongly, may I add – non-league is perceived by many as being a 'rough and tumble' environment. Tough-tackling footballers on poor pitches; the school of hard knocks, if you will. Now, if I was to say to you to suggest one player from history who you feel would fall into that description, you give back Billy Bremner, Roy Keane, Ron 'Chopper' Harris, or Kevin Muscat. Eventually, someone you would no doubt mention is one of the members of the infamous 'Crazy Gang': Vinnie Jones. And, Jones – before hitting the heights of the FA Cup Final in 1988 – had started out his career in non-league with Wealdstone.

I have talked in this book about the importance of non-league and the role that it has in the development of certain players, and in the case of Jones, one thing that he can certainly credit to his early career is giving him the experience of knowing how to win. Some players can try their whole career to get to Wembley, and yet Jones made it within a year, helping the Stones on their way to winning the FA Trophy Final in 1985. In his first two seasons of football, he would end up with three winners' medals to his name – league titles with Wealdstone and during a loan spell with Swedish side IFK Holmsund, along with the FA Trophy.

What I find hugely poetic about Jones's journey is the fact that the crowning glory of his career – beating Liverpool in the 1988 FA Cup Final – came only a couple of miles from the very place that he started out; I have done the trip from Wealdstone to Wembley many times, and it is literally a stone's (excuse the pun) throw. One thing that playing for Wealdstone certainly gave him was the experience of appearing alongside older, more experienced players and having to grow up quickly; that's perhaps why he had such a tough football persona. He was one of few younger players in an otherwise experienced team, so he had to learn the physical and mental sides of the game quickly. It was sink or swim.

Not only would Jones 'swim' in Stones colours, he would go on to do likewise at the top level after his big break in 1986. His form for Wealdstone would see him signed by Wimbledon; up until that point he was also working in construction. Less than two years later he was an FA Cup winner. While Jones's bread and butter had been in the construction of buildings, between his move to Plough Lane and lifting the FA Cup he was working on a construction of his own; building a reputation for being one of the top midfielders in the country. He'd spend the remainder of his career largely in the top flight, interupted by a single season in the Second Division in helping Leeds United to win the title, then ending his playing days in the second tier with Queens Park Rangers. Internationally, he won nine caps for Wales – qualifying through his Welsh grandfather – and appeared alongside the likes of fellow non-league alumnus Neville Southall.

Jermaine Beckford

If I asked most football fans for their standout memory of Jermaine Beckford, I'd imagine the majority would mention his infamous goal for Leeds United at Old Trafford in the FA Cup to knock the Red Devils out in January 2010. I'd have an even bigger wager that few would single out his time in Wealdstone colours and yet for someone who has won at Wembley, it was five miles around the corner where the forward started out.

The halcyon days of Beckford's career came at Leeds and later Preston North End, in between times playing 34 times in the Premier League for Everton, having earlier cut his cloth in the men's game in the Isthmian League Premier Division. He spent three years in non-league, predominantly with the Stones and a brief loan spell at Uxbridge. While Beckford would – four years after playing for Wealdstone – go on to play regularly in the top flight, it was the opportunity to play for the Stones that helped him to realise his ambitions of hitting the big time having previously had a potential route to the top level with Chelsea in his youth days after the turn of the millennium.

Delving back through the archives, Beckford's pathway is like so many: playing part-time in non-league alongside working full-time, after rejection from a top-level academy earlier in their career. Beckford was let go by the Blues at the end of his scholarship but it wouldn't halt his ambitions, with the rejection only inspiring him even more to become a professional. Instead, he would have to juggle playing football while earning his 'moolah' working nine to five as a window fitter, then quarter to eight to half past nine as a goalscorer.

From there, Beckford's career went the way of so many: a prolific goalscorer at non-league level and plucked by a Football League club. Nowadays, Wealdstone are well known for the 'Wealdstone Raider' – supporter Gordon Hill, whose matchday rant on the terrace at a 2013 fixture went viral online – but back in 2006 Beckford was the main attraction; the Panjandrum of Ruislip. He could have ended up as the Panjandrum of the Palace as Crystal

Palace had been circling for his signature in 2006, offering him a trial, yet Leeds landed him in March that year. Owner Ken Bates had openly vowed to find the best non-league talent; as the ball flew past Tomasz Kuszczak at Old Trafford in January 2010, their decision to sign Beckford was certainly vindicated.

Looking back on his career, for me Beckford may feel he was capable of achieving more, but two promotions, over 400 domestic appearances, almost 170 goals, three League One Player of the Year awards, three League One Player of the Month prizes and playing international football – he won six caps for Jamaica, eligible because of his Jamaican father. He goes down rightly as one of Wealdstone's proudest products and one of the most feared marksmen to have ever played in the EFL.

While the Stones may play at Grosvenor Vale at the time of writing, they are set to be on the move in the next few years. In 2023 they announced plans for a new stadium at Freezeland Way, close to Hillingdon Underground station, which is fittingly the location of our next stop.

Stop 2: Hillingdon

Yannick Bolasie

Yannick Bolasie only spent a brief period in non-league yet his roots are well publicised. A winger well renowned for his mercurial skills and trickery with the ball, Bolasie has since gone on to play in the top divisions in England, Turkey, Italy, Belgium and Portugal, amass a total of 119 Premier League appearances, represent DR Congo at the African Cup of Nations win promotion at Wembley and play in an FA Cup Final for good measure; not the worst résumé in the world.

Bolasie was on the books of Maltese side Floriana at the time of earning a transfer to Plymouth Argyle, having spent a single season there after a similarly short stint in non-league at Hillingdon Borough. At the time, he was only 17 years of age and so his spell with the Hillmen was more to allow him to 'dip his toe' into men's football; that was indeed his first chance in the men's game. Bolasie had started out in the academy at Rushden & Diamonds, and prior to making his debut for Plymouth under Paul Sturrock he went back to the Diamonds where he would continue his development in the 2008/09 Conference Premier campaign. That loan would be short-lived, however, and with that loan plus his earlier time at Hillingdon, he only made 15 appearances. And yet it was non-league that very much had a big influence on his early career and that gave him the platform to go on and make it as a professional. It may not have been an exhaustive spell outside of the Football League, but it did give him a useful window into the physicality and challenges that non-league has to offer.

Paul Canoville

One player who perhaps didn't go on to have as extensive a top-level career as some of the others in this book, but is similarly symbolic of a non-league alumnus who went on to reach the old First Division, is Paul Canoville. The former Chelsea man takes on even greater importance, given that he was – in many ways – a trailblazer when stepping up from non-league to sign for the Blues. When he joined in December 1981, Canoville wrote his name down in history at Stamford Bridge as being the club's first black player. As such, his career and rise to the top is even more so worthy of recognition; the knock-on effect that Canoville's move had in terms of providing a gateway for black players at the highest level of the game is not to be underestimated.

In general, Canoville's route into professional football is one of the more complex of any in this book; he had to go through a fair few challenges to get where he did that others wouldn't even dream of, or indeed wish to. It was the solace of professional football that provided Canoville an 'escape' at an important part of his upbringing. Landing the move to Chelsea at the age of 19 played an integral part in ensuring he stayed on the straight and narrow. Even better still, the six years combined that he spent on the books of Chelsea and Reading were very much halcyon days of what has been a somewhat difficult life, a ray of glorious sunshine on a chapter in the life of a person who had an undeniable talent but who had to give it up professionally early into a career that could – and should – have delivered so much more.

Born in 1962, Canoville had a childhood with the odd hurdle to clear along the way. Canoville was raised in a fatherless household, and not helped by not having a fixed residence and reportedly having to rough sleep at various locations during his adolescence. The fact that he was able to pursue a career within professional football is all the more remarkable and epithetic of his unwaveringly strong character and mindset. The sport was the perfect distraction for him, and he started out playing for Hillingdon Borough at the age of just 17. In many ways, the challenges that Canoville had to overcome make him one of the most inspiring examples of players to have gone from non-league to experience a career at the top; this is someone who got his break while having to sleep in an abandoned car on the streets. Not taxied around by their parents and pampered with academy football; Canoville had to work even harder for the chances that he got.

His efforts would be rewarded as in 1981 he would get a dream move to Chelsea. When I say 'dream', the chance to be a professional gave him a purpose. His time at Chelsea would on the one hand provide him with the opportunity that so many budding youngsters dream of in being able to play for a professional club, and yet as if his route in wasn't hard enough, he had to overcome being subjected to racial abuse from his own supporters for much of his time at Stamford Bridge. With racism still rife, Canoville was seen – in many people's eyes – as a bit of a 'one-off'; up until that point, there had not been a black player to have represented the Blues. So, with his slice of history, Canoville would also have to stomach unwanted abuse; only further rubber-stamping the pride in his achievements.

He would end up winning the Second Division with Chelsea in 1983/84, the pinnacle of a career in west London that was unfortunately awash with racism, injuries and controversy; the defender-turned-winger didn't even achieve half of what he could have been capable of. That same mantra could be extended to his whole career. Canoville showed more than a glimpse of a winger who had such strong potential to go right to the top. His spell with Reading would ultimately persuade him to call time on his professional career, as injury woes really started to mount and take their toll; cruciate ligaments and knee problems were the fixture of his fight to stay fit. The Royals had shelled out £60,000 for Canoville, who had already proven his talent, but unfortunately supporters would only get the benefit of seeing him showcase his abilities 21 times across two seasons. The proverbial last straw came in 1988 when Canoville was left in the unthinkable position at just 24 with having to walk away from the professional game with a total of eight children to provide for while having to battle his own problems with injury; it is a crying shame that such a talented player had to give up his dreams at such an early age.

Canoville would, however, still play; in fact, for another seven years. This would – unfortunately – only be at semi-professional level as he drifted around various clubs in and around London. It coincided with a really difficult period of Canoville's life, as he battled a much-publicised drug addiction; if you haven't read his autobiography, entitled *Black and Blue*, then I highly recommend that you do, as he so eloquently describes the battles that he had to go through. If his drug addiction didn't present him with enough problems, he was diagnosed with non-Hodgkin lymphoma in 1996, which forced him to abandon any plans he had of continuing playing; he had last played two years previous to that with Egham Town.

His career was not given the limelight that others have had in stepping up from non-league, or at least a focus not maintained on the weight of his footballing abilities above publicising the demons that he had to face; thankfully, he is now clear of any such drug or illness problems and is on the straight and narrow. Only now do we illuminate just how talented a footballer he was; while his career was before I was even born the reports and tributes that you hear from those of a Chelsea persuasion – my dad, especially, who grew up as a Chelsea fan just a stone's throw from Stamford Bridge – paint the picture very much as a 'what if' of a career that could have been. Regardless, Paul Canoville was a tremendous talent out of non-league.

Stop 3: North Greenwich

Ian Wright

Ian Wright, Wright, Wright. The man so often on our TV screens spreading laughter and joy, a regular on *Match of the Day*, and seemingly a fashion mogul, Wright is one of the best strikers this country has ever produced. It was with non-league side Greenwich Borough – merely 15 minutes along the banks of the River Thames from North Greenwich station – where Wright's football career was born. He had a tough upbringing, which is perhaps one of the reasons why he has become such a positive role model in his own right to so many. Amid the trials and tribulations of his youth, Wright would use football as a welcome escape. While a teenager, his first introduction to the sport would come with a local Sunday league team, Ten-em-Bee, which gave him the chance to get out on the grass and forget about everything else.

Back in 2018, Wright did an interview with the Players' Tribune website where he detailed his upbringing and route into football, and spoke fondly of the role that two guys – Tony Davis and Errol Palmer – had in making him the man he became. Wright was a football-mad kid in his youth, yet was not afforded the luxury – at home, at least – of doing so, so he would spend a lot of time honing his skills; just the ability to do what he loved was oxygen for him. Davis and Palmer were in charge of Ten-em-Bee. It is perhaps this pair to whom we should be thankful for the footballer Wright ended up being. They would pick him up from home, look after him and take him to training. For the hours he would spend with the team kicking a football around with his mates, it was his paradise.

It was clear that even at Ten-em-Bee's level – perhaps even more so – Wright was a talent. He had the chance to sign for Southend United and Brighton & Hove Albion, with the pair both bringing him in on trial, yet Wright could not bag himself a contract and his dream of becoming a professional was fading away. He would, of course, go on to make it, but not without his fair share of hurdles to overcome along the way. What makes Wright's story all the more impressive is that at the age of 19 – when most young players make it into the game – he was on his way out of it. That proved to be a hugely difficult spell as he turned his back on football following his rejection by the Seagulls and a spell in prison. Wright quit the game completely, and instead focused on a 'proper' career, training to be a labourer. By 21 he had still not had his break in the game; a late bloomer.

And yet, even though he was working as a labourer, Wright couldn't keep himself away from the game he loved. It was no surprise when he indeed returned, signing for non-league Greenwich Borough to fulfil his football passion. For Wright – who was supporting his partner, and stepson Shaun Wright-Phillips, the future England winger – the extra money playing semi-professionally was invaluable. He earned £30 a week with the Cannons, but at the same time was being paid in the greatest commodity: the chance to do something he loved. What I find particularly poetic is the fact that Wright's playing career started with the Cannons, and he made a name for himself at the peak of his powers for a club with a cannon on its emblem. I like things like that. Anyway, back to his journey.

So, where were we? Greenwich. Wright would take to the semi-professional game like a duck to water; he was a natural. He may have had a tough upbringing, and a late entry into playing, but you can't beat talent. And boy did Wright have it, to the degree that Crystal Palace came calling. What I find amazing is that – at first – Wright turned the Eagles down. In the end, however, the temptation was too much and he took Palace up on their offer, not signing outright to begin with, but instead spending a three-month trial working with one of the great managers in the form of Steve Coppell.

Coppell is one of the very best British managers we have seen in this country. Back in the 1980s he was just embarking on an initial nine-year successful spell with the Eagles. As a top player in his own right who appeared alongside some of the most talented players in Manchester United's history – the likes of Lou Macari, Ray Wilkins, Norman Whiteside and Bryan Robson – it was safe to say that Coppell knew a star when he saw one. Having seen Ian Wright, he liked what he saw, enough to want to take a chance on the Greenwich goalscorer in August 1985. Now, this bit I have to smile at. The fee? Well, it's funny you should ask: £10,000, £50,000? Nope. A set of weightlifting equipment. Brilliant.

The Eagles quite quickly realised that they had pulled off a blinder in working the deal, with Wright excelling straight from the off in a Palace shirt. The seeds were sown for the eventual success that he would have with back-to-back campaigns in which he hit nine league goals both times. In 1987/88 Wright would lay down a marker that he was a top player in the making, thriving alongside new frontman Mark Bright.

Wright would average a goal every other game in 1987/88, netting 23 times in all competitions as a precursor to 1988/89, when he almost single-handedly fired Palace to promotion from the Second Division with an impressive tally of 24 in 42 games, hitting 33 in all competitions. His form would earn him recognition at international level with a call-up to the England B squad. An England B team hasn't played since 2007; it had originally been brought in to act as an ancillary squad for the main side to bring in players with promise to soften the step up to international football. Players to have pulled on the B team jersey include the likes of Gary Pallister, Paul Merson and Viv Anderson.

Wright made a handful of appearances in the First Division before his call-up, yet his return would perhaps bring the most iconic Ian Wright moment of all time: his famous equaliser in the 1990 FA Cup Final against Manchester United. He went on to score again in extra time, putting Palace ahead only for United to come back and draw 3-3, then win the replay 1-0. Wright's feat announced him on the big stage as not just a former non-league player with a bit of talent, but a bona fide top-flight star in the making.

That was merely scratching the surface for Wright, as the following season he took his game up another level and rubber-stamped his reputation as one of the country's finest strikers. He would swap B team for full team, earning senior recognition on the international front just six years after he had been plying his trade for Greenwich Borough. He also wrote himself into Crystal Palace history books having scored his 100th goal for the club, joining esteemed company behind some leading lights of yesteryear in Peter Simpson and Edwin Smith. And along came his first bit of silverware, winning the Full Members' Cup, at the time sponsored by Zenith Data Systems. Wright scored two decisive goals to help Palace beat Everton 4-1 in the final at Wembley.

His exploits would attract the attention of Arsenal; I'll let you fill in the blanks from here. His spell with the Gunners is well documented: a successful seven seasons and 185 goals in 288 games was not a bad return. He hit double figures for league goals in every single season at Highbury, going beyond 15 six times; he certainly knew where the back of the net was. To think that one of the best English forwards to have ever graced the game hailed from the humble roots of non-league just goes to show what can be achieved by players lower down the levels. Not everyone is going to end up being a 324-goal FA Cup and Premier League winner, but you get my drift. Wrighty will no doubt doff his rather suave cap to non-league; it has been unimaginably transformative for his career in setting him on his way.

Mo Eisa

A name that perhaps goes under the radar to the footballing public as a non-league alumnus, more than likely due to the fact that he's not hit the headlines of the Premier League and likely even less so now that he is plying his trade in the Persian Gulf League, is forward Mo Eisa. He was given his break by a manager in Gary Johnson who – to his credit – has a strong track record of unearthing talent from non-league. Paul Terry (Dagenham & Redbridge), Adam Stansfield (Elmore), John Akinde (Ebbsfleet United),

Sam Foley (Newport County), Kieffer Moore (Dorchester Town) and Jamie Grimes (Dover Athletic) are his finest examples, along with – of course – Eisa.

Eisa's story is actually rather textbook in many ways; a prolific lower-league striker that a league side took a chance on. There's a book on players of that ilk alone. As of the time of writing he finds himself playing outside the EFL and indeed outside of the UK; Iran to be precise. He's proven to be a capable goalscorer (primarily with Cheltenham Town, with 25 in 50 across all competitions in 2017/18). Eisa certainly isn't one of the higher-profile names to feature in this book, but I think that the Sudanese international provides a good advert for the many local footballing academies that have played such a key part in the development of so many players in this book. He started out in his youth days with Pro Touch Soccer Academy, and they also played a role helping his brother Abo to get his career up and running.

Stop 4: Tooting Broadway
Michail Antonio

One player on whom the spotlight is often shone when it comes to providing examples who started out in non-league and have gone on to forge a career in the Premier League is Michail Antonio.

In terms of 'meteoric rises' from non-league, Antonio has to take the top prize having got his big move after just four league games in men's football; any advance on that? He was one of those non-league players you looked at and got the 'future top-level player' vibes; his physicality, speed and athleticism set him apart. Especially in the modern-day game, it's that pace and power that stands out like a sore thumb; I got the same 'Michail Antonio Energy' when seeing Sinclair Armstrong on loan at Torquay United from QPR in the 2021/22 season.

Despite Antonio getting such a significant transfer, the fact he got a move into the Football League perhaps shouldn't have come as a surprise as even before making his first-team debut with Tooting & Mitcham United he was highlighted as being a 'player of promise' to the tune of a trial with Tottenham Hotspur. They say that everything in life happens for a reason, and while it's difficult to say he wouldn't have gone on to have the career he has done if that opportunity hadn't worked out the way it did, the rejection and having to return to non-league certainly helped. The fact that his mother rejected the trial on his behalf was a blessing in disguise for Antonio as he has since gone and proven himself, and been able to forge out a good career in the Premier League.

Antonio would get further chances to kick-start his career with trials at Brentford and Queens Park Rangers, yet he was unsuccessful once more. He would eventually swap the stripes of Tooting for the blue and white hoops of Championship side Reading in 2008, although he returned to the Terrors on a short-term loan deal to get more first-team minutes under his belt at an important stage of his career, before going on various loan spells in the Football League. It wasn't until 2012/13 that he would tie down regular first-team opportunities after signing for Sheffield Wednesday. His career since then is widely publicised and he's spent the best part of a decade at West Ham United, making in excess of 300 appearances and winning the UEFA Conference League in 2023. I find it somewhat poetic that for all of the opportunities he got in the early years of his career in the London footballing scene to join up with top-level academies, the prime years have come roughly 15 miles from where it all started for him in non-league with Tooting & Mitcham.

Stop 5: Harrow-on-the-Hill

John Barnes

When you ask fans of a certain generation – we are talking the 1980s and 1990s – to write down the best players who spring to mind, one who will most certainly crop up is John Barnes. He broke through during the 1980s, joining Liverpool towards the latter years of a decade in which they were the dominant force in English football, winning six league titles and finishing below second just once, and went on to weave himself into the fabric of one of English football's biggest institutions. In 2023, I went to Anfield for the Football Content Awards and was able to see a special plinth erected outside the grounds of Liverpool's stadium to mark his ten years of service with the Reds.

While his best football came with Liverpool, Barnes spent six years at Watford prior to his move to Anfield, playing alongside legendary striker Luther Blissett and under one of the greatest managers that this country has ever produced in Graham Taylor. However, his start in football did not come with the Hornets, but in fact was in non-league with a side called Sudbury Court, based in Middlesex.

From Sudbury Court, Barnes got his big break when signing for Watford in 1981 after a successful trial appearance for the Hornets' reserves. Taylor made the decision to hand the Jamaican-born winger a permanent deal, the nature of which certainly plays to the gallery of the hyperbolic, often misguided, fabricated construct of 'non-league': spotted on a local park pitch, and a move completed to the tune of a set of kits as opposed to a transfer fee. It did little for the image of non-league, but was transformative for Barnes's career.

It is no surprise that Barnes's time in football turned out the way it did from there, spending his formative years learning under Taylor and his prime years with Kenny Dalglish. And yet all of that wouldn't have been possible if Barnes, new to the country at the time, hadn't had the opportunity of playing for Sudbury Court and showcasing his talents and that chance spotting by Graham Taylor; who knows what he would have gone on to achieve if Taylor hadn't seen him? It just underlines the importance of going out and playing in non-league; get your name out there, play games and you just never know.

Albert Adomah

The final player on this leg of our journey is Albert Adomah. At his best, Adomah has been one of the most dynamic and simply unplayable footballers in England with his trickery, quick feet and pace on the ball; he's been a joy to watch over the years in the Football League. At the time of writing he was on the books of League Two outfit Walsall on the 'homeward stretch' of what has been an 18-year career that has seen him play in the Premier League, win promotion at Wembley, play at the African Cup of Nations and appear in a World Cup. Looking back on that, he may well feel that from the humble beginnings of non-league he has gone on to forge out a successful time in football that many aspiring players would snap your hand off for.

Born in Lambeth, the Ghanaian international got his first taste of the game as a junior playing for a team called Old Meadonians. Adomah was like every other football-mad youth, spending much of his time playing with his mates in the local cages and on the street; it should – perhaps – come as no surprise given his unwavering devotion to endlessly kicking a 'bag of wind' around with his friends in these humblest of beginnings that the lovingly named 'Uncle Albert' has developed such a reputation for being a tantalisingly tricky and technical, quick-footed wide player with skills that wouldn't look out of place in the great Brazilian teams of yesteryear. To this day, his social media is adorned with a showcase of his artistic talents: it's the 'artistry' which gives such a subtle nod to his roots.

While Adomah remains one of the big success stories out of non-league, he is also one of the poster boys and 'Mount Rushmore figures' for the Championship; he still holds the record for the most appearances in the second tier since the renaming in 2004, with 526 games under his belt. It was after back-to-back 49-appearance seasons for Barnet that Adomah got his move into the Championship, moving to Bristol City in the summer of 2010. His record is hugely impressive; in the 14 seasons he spent in the second tier he made 33 appearances and above in all but one – his last. He even got his shot – albeit sparingly – to play in the top flight, making two Premier League appearances for Middlesbrough in 2016/17. The 2024/25 campaign saw him smash through the 800-game mark in a career that has spanned 18 years and counting at the time of writing, and saw him gain international honours with Ghana. For all of his appearances, it was the 80-odd in non-league that undoubtedly gave him the grounding that he needed to go and achieve what he has.

* * *

Shortly after Albert Adomah represented Ghana during the international break in late 2024, I had the privilege of speaking to him about his humble roots in non-league, the journey he has been on to create the career he has, and how he is now helping several non-league alumni at Walsall to get their careers up and running.

You started out at Old Meadonians as a teenager. What was that like for your development as a footballer?

'It was massive for me; all the way from amateur to youth level. They have got nine different teams, and I started out in the lowest team and went on to play for the first team. In the end, I was playing with men at the age of 16. I was playing men's football on a Saturday, and it was a better standard than the alternative of playing on a Sunday. It was more competitive. Playing at amateur level was more a professional setup than Sunday league, as others my age were doing, and so it was a hugely important stage of my career.'

The 2006/07 season was when it really clicked for you as a player, with 52 appearances and 11 goals. What was key to that form and success?

'Simply, I was scoring goals. Throughout the age groups, I scored 30 goals in nine, then 15 in 18, and then 11 goals at first-team level. You train to score, and then you have to perform on the pitch. You have got to learn to be proactive and be in the right place at the right time. At amateur level,

I was watching Queens Park Rangers and Manchester United at the time and I tried to imitate the likes of Andy Cole and Dwight Yorke who I looked up to.'

While you played for Harrow Borough, you were studying. Did the fact you were studying alongside playing football take the pressure off your football and allow you to play with freedom?

'Yes. I knew my direction at that time; I knew that I was going to be a footballer, or at least wanted to, and so there was in many ways little pressure on me. Sometimes, I had to ask for time off and to be allowed to leave work early so that I could catch a train and go to training, and so I was wholly committed to making it as a professional footballer. The fact that I was studying alongside playing football gave me a Plan B to fall back on if my footballing ambitions didn't work out the way that I hoped.'

As someone who has come out of non-league and had a successful career at the top level, what would be the biggest bit of advice you'd give to young players thinking about dropping into non-league?

'My advice is to be yourself. It is never too late to get your big break in football, and so don't rush things. Stay motivated to be successful and you will get your break at some point. I would also say to express yourself, and most importantly enjoy football. When you do get a chance to play at a higher level, make sure that you take it; stay true to yourself, work hard and grasp it with both hands.'

You went on to play for a Barnet side with a good recent tradition of giving a platform to players to go on and

achieve bigger things. How useful was your time at Barnet in shaping your career?

'My time at Barnet was amazing. The highlight of my career was signing for Barnet. I will never forget the manager Paul Fairclough; all the work he did for me and the belief he had. Fairclough was a special manager. He had that personality that you respected. His one-on-one management and communication skills were superb, and he had a skill at being able to put so much belief into players. He has had so many successful stories in management of being able to produce players, and it is no coincidence. I am still very close to [chairman] Tony Kleanthous, and I will always hold Barnet dearly to me.

The legendary John Motson sponsored you during your time at Barnet; he must have realised your talent. How proud of a feeling was that?

'It was amazing. For you and others, you all know his voice; it is so recognisable. For him to support his local side was nice, and for him to back me and support me – given all of the players that he has commentated on – was an extra special feeling. It is nice for him to want to give back to and invest in Barnet; it is nice to see. I didn't expect him to choose me, but the fact he did gave me extra motivation to want to do well.'

How did you find the transition from non-league to playing in the EFL?

'The major difference was the technical aspect; my technical ability certainly improved drastically during my transition to the Football League. At Old Meadonians, I only trained once a week. At Harrow Borough, I trained twice a week. However, when I made the move to being a professional footballer, I trained nearly every day and had an improved standard of coaching. If I was part of an academy, I would perhaps have been better technically from the outset. The rawness was always there in my game, and it was about being able to refine that and develop my craft that was key and it was having played against men in the lower leagues and the extra coaching I got when making the step up that allowed me to handle the transition easily.'

Did the physicality and demands of being in non-league help you develop and sharpen up the technical side of your game, for which you are now so well renowned?
'Absolutely. My pathway allowed me to be ready for and handle the physicality of playing in the Football League. The fact that I played in non-league allowed me to develop the physical side of my game, as I played against men. I had to adapt the way that I trained within a professional environment. The talent has always been there, and it was just about getting the right coaching to get the best out of me.'

Do you feel the fact you went through non-league and not the perceived 'robotics' of academy football help give you the playing style that you have now?
'It is difficult to say, as I didn't play in academy football in the formal sense; just simply in the youth teams at Old Meadonians, and then made my way through the age groups and into the first team. I started playing street football, and so that helped with developing my skills. I

was never taught the skills or tricks; I had to learn myself while playing in the park with my mates, playing cage football, and on the streets. I had to express myself, and be a bit selfish; that comes across in the way that I play. When I was playing street football, I was trying to beat everyone, but when I made the transition into the EFL I only had to work on beating one player and so found it easy.'

You're on the books of a Walsall side that have signed players out of non-league in recent campaigns. Does the fact they stepped up so well into League Two show how strong non-league is and how successful it is in producing and developing players?
'Definitely. Walsall have some great talent, and that is something which extends to non-league. All you need is your chance and to be scouted. The likes of Jamie [Jellis] and Harry [Williams] have come into our team at Walsall and not just been key parts of our side, but been among the standout players in League Two; you wouldn't know that they came through non-league. They needed to adapt to begin with, and it wasn't easy, but they are now flourishing and have been able to show what they are about.'

You've been able to sponsor some youth teams at Harrow Borough. How nice and rewarding has it been to give back to the club that played such a big part in your career?
'It is an honour and a privilege. I was actually able to sponsor youth teams at both Harrow Borough and Old Meadonians, and it is just nice to be able to give back to two clubs that have helped me so much in my journey and give back to the local community.'

Stop 6: Hayes and Harlington
Cyrille Regis

One of the earliest examples of players who have started out in non-league and gone on to have success in the Football League and beyond is a legend within the Midlands footballing scene: Cyrille Regis. In terms of reaching the heights in the game, I would say winning an MBE for services to football and having a statue erected of you outside of The Hawthorns ticks the box. At the end of the day, when you have Johan Cruyff trying to sign you as a replacement for Marco van Basten, you've got a bit about you. When we talk about the best players to have ever stepped on a pitch in the Midlands, Regis is right up there in the conversation.

From an early age, Cyrille was always into sports. His first real true love was cricket, the man himself saying that he was always a better cricketer than he was a footballer; crikey, we could have done with him for the England cricket team then. His cousin – namesake John – was also into sports, you could say; he was a Commonwealth, Olympic Games, World Championship and European medallist as a runner. Thus, Cyrille certainly had a lot of early exposure to sport, but he would – in the end – turn to football rather than opt for a bat and ball and cricket whites.

When Regis was 17, he signed for Molesey. He would only spend a single season with the Moles, but he would certainly make an impact; 25 times in front of goal, in fact. For someone who – by his own admission – played football as 'a sport he did with no passion' then he wasn't half talented at putting the ball in the onion bag.

Regis would resist approaches from elsewhere to join Hayes in 1976, and very much like his time with Molesey it would be for a single season. His time with the Missioners was short-lived as he soon jumped up the ladder to join West Bromwich Albion. If Regis ever needed a boost for his ego, the nature of that move would underline his quality. The Baggies' board would initially not support the idea of shelling out for the youngster, but chief scout Ronnie Allen – who would go on to manage Regis at The Hawthorns – was adamant that the young player had what it takes, so much so that he actually paid for Regis out of his own pocket; a first in this book. That would prove an inspired decision, with a goals ratio of one in three, ranking tenth in the club's all-time scorers' list, almost 740 career appearances in all competitions for the Baggies, Coventry City, Aston Villa, Wolverhampton Wanderers, Wycombe Wanderers and Chester City, five England caps, an FA Cup winners' medal and inducted into both Coventry's and England's Hall of Fame; you could say that Allen's opinion was vindicated.

Les Ferdinand

When you think of the great strikers to have graced the top flight, one player who always enters the conversation is Les Ferdinand. He perhaps didn't get the plaudits that his talents deserved as he wasn't playing for a Manchester United or a Liverpool, but he was the type who would – in today's game – be worth a lot of money: big, strong, capable of leading the line, good in the air, a top finisher and a proper handful. His best performances came pre-millennium – when I was merely a twinkle in my parents' eyes – but I remember watching footage of some top Newcastle United games in the Premier League years and he was always someone who stood out.

Indeed, Hayes and Harlington station is just a stone's throw from where Ferdinand started out his journey, at nearby club Viking Sports. Viking Sports – or Viking Greenford as they were renamed in 1991 – were from 1945 to 2003 in Greenford, originally set up by former non-league player Roy Bartlett. They ended up dissolving in 2003 due to a reported lack of funding, but they can count themselves as having played an integral part in the development of one of this country's finest ever strikers.

Viking Sports would provide Ferdinand with a pathway into football, yet it was at Southall where he would get his first chance in the senior game. The Ealing outfit have played a part in the development of several top players to play at a higher level. Ferdinand's time at Southall gave him an insight into playing on the big stage as he helped the club to the 1986 FA Vase Final at Wembley in his final year, before moving to Hayes. His transfer to the Missioners would put him firmly on the map as he struck 20 goals in the space of 42 appearances to develop a growing reputation as one of the best strikers at non-league level, all while working full-time as a painter and decorator. He may well have been a dab hand with the paintbrush, but he was even more skilled with the football and his exploits with Hayes caught the attention of Queens Park Rangers. At the time, Rangers had several good strikers at their disposal – Gary Bannister, John Byrne, Leroy Rosenior and Clive Walker – yet so convinced was boss Jim Smith that Ferdinand was the answer that he persuaded the board to part with £50,000; a lot of money in those days.

Looking back on it, I think he made the right decision. Particularly fruitful spells with Newcastle and Tottenham Hotspur were to follow for Ferdinand, along with 17 caps for England. While he goes down as one of the best strikers to have ever played in the top flight, it was the lessons in working hard, rolling his sleeves up and having to earn an opportunity, as he had to with Southall and Hayes, that stood him in good stead throughout his career, battling through being a bit-part player in the early years post-Hayes to excel on domestic and international fronts. That work ethic and determination to be a success got him to where he did, and non-league had a lot to do with that.

Alan Devonshire

While on the subject of Les Ferdinand, one thing he shares in common with the next name on this list – former West Ham United player Alan Devonshire – is that he played for Southall. While Devonshire may well be more recognised to the present-day audience for his exploits with the long coat and flat cap in the managerial dugout in non-league, the older generation will certainly remember what a top player he was in his own right. In sides that boasted such rich talent as the likes of Billy Bonds, Trevor Brooking, Frank Lampard Sr and Alvin Martin, Devonshire remains one of the best to have pulled on the Hammers' colours with just shy of 450 appearances.

Devonshire is a player whose journey was very much one of triumphs over adversity: not one, but two setbacks. He was born in what is now west London in Park Royal, only 12 miles as the crow flies from Crystal Palace. As a junior, Devonshire joined the Eagles as part of their academy setup but would quickly be turned away at the age of just 14 after he was adjudged to have been too small. Fast forward to the prime years of Devonshire's career, and while he may have been small, he could most certainly pack a punch in the tackle. Despite being let go, there was undeniably a talent there as Palace would return for the youngster years later and bring him back into the fold for some games with the academy on an ad hoc basis, but it would be a 'difficult second album' for the young midfielder. It was Southall to whom Devonshire turned upon his release by Crystal Palace to keep alive his dream of being a footballer.

Devonshire juggled working in a Hoover factory with playing part-time for Southall, and it wasn't long before he was hoovering up interest (I'm disappointed in myself for that pun, I'm going to be honest) as sides higher in the pyramid came knocking. However, it was by way of a fortunate act of kindness from two individuals – Eddie Baily and Charlie Faulkner – that his career took its next turn. At the time of Devonshire's spell with Southall, Baily was six years out of his playing career. He was working as an assistant for Spurs, but also operated as a scout. Baily liked what he saw in the youngster and recommended him to West Ham. I'm a tad surprised that Baily didn't tell Tottenham Hotspur about the young prospect, yet nevertheless Devonshire had been found.

Ron Greenwood was the manager of West Ham at the time, and spent 13 years with the Hammers in that capacity. If there was a top player out of West Ham, there was a good chance Greenwood would have managed them at some point. Off the back of Baily and Faulkner's recommendations, Greenwood decided to make a move for Devonshire, who went on to make a name for himself as one of the best players to have ever appeared for the Hammers. In the 2003 book *The Official West Ham Dream Team*, the authors asked 500 West Ham fans to put together their all-time 11. Such was the impact that Devonshire made during his 14-year career at Upton Park that the supporters included him in the team.

For all of the successes that Devonshire had at West Ham, there is still – looking back on his career – a tinge of 'what if?' and disappointment that he didn't achieve more. He suffered with injuries for parts of his career, particularly towards the back end of his time with United. An ultimately damaging Achilles injury would see Devonshire have to sit on the sidelines for over a year, and the impact of his absence was felt immensely. Indeed, from the glitz and glam of the 'vintage' West Ham sides of old, the Hammers were relegated out of the top division in 1988/89 as Devonshire could only manage 14 games.

But Devonshire did have some fond memories in a Hammers shirt. Perhaps one of his highlights was helping the club to win the FA Cup in 1979/80 despite only being a Second Division side. Devonshire scored a key goal in the semi-final against Everton in that run. Further highlights include the following season as Devonshire helped United to win the Second Division and only miss out on making it a brace of silverware that year with defeat to Bob Paisley's Liverpool in the League Cup Final.

Devonshire would leave West Ham at the conclusion of the 1989/90 season, signing for Watford at the age of 34. In truth, his spell with the Hornets never really got going by way of both his age and the injuries that had plagued his final years, and Devonshire officially hung up his boots as a professional in 1992. The destination? Non-league. A seldom-documented spell with Chippenham Sports was to follow as he played the final knockings of his entire career, while he laid the foundations for a hugely successful managerial life that was to follow in juggling playing with a coaching role, too. His first official foray into management would see Devonshire leave men's football entirely, taking over with Brentford Women. It wasn't long, however, until Devonshire was back in the men's game as he took charge of Osterley, in Isleworth, west London. Little would he know that his next job would see the start of a career off the field that was arguably as successful as his one on it. He took over at Maidenhead United in 1996, spending seven years there before an eight-year stint at Hampton & Richmond Borough, then four years at Braintree Town, followed by a return to Maidenhead in 2015. He was still at York Road at the time of writing, continuing to battle against the odds in keeping the Magpies in the National League.

DJ Campbell

Over the years, there have been players out of non-league who have been mavericks, whose undeniable talent has taken them onward to a successful career despite perhaps not adjusting to the pressures and permutations of the professional game; I certainly feel that much is true of DJ Campbell. While away from the pitch Campbell had one or two distractions, on it there was no getting away from the fact he was a hugely talented player; indeed, despite playing in the Premier League and making in excess of 400 career appearances with more than 170 goals, he will no doubt look back on his career and feel that he only achieved a fragment of what his future in football had – at one stage – promised. He may have played for England C during his youth days, yet there was expectation at one point that he would go on to get his full-blown Three Lions colours; he was that good.

Campbell could, however, have got an earlier break than he did actually receive. He started out on the books of Aston Villa as a youngster up until his release at the age of 19 and maintained ambitions of playing for the Villans until his eventual release at the turn of the millennium. He'd have to turn to non-league after being let go, joining Chesham United. That would set his career up and running, with a successful spell returning 16 goals in the space of 29 games, yet it wasn't until 2003 in joining Yeading that Campbell would earn his reputation as a bona fide goalscorer. He would forge out a fruitful stint in front of goal to help Yeading to the Isthmian League Premier Division title in 2004 after back-to-back campaigns with more than 30 league goals each time and a total of 68 in all competitions across the two. His stock would infinitely rise in January 2005 as he got the chance to showcase his talent when Yeading played Graeme Souness's Newcastle United in the third round of the FA Cup live on the BBC; he may not have scored, but he certainly impressed. That would put him in the shop window, and luckily for him it was Brentford who would peek inside, signing Campbell and giving him his golden ticket to the big time.

The big time he most certainly got to, albeit perhaps not as 'big' as his talent was capable of, yet it was still a career to the tune of promotions from the Championship with Birmingham City and Blackpool, more than 50 appearances in the Premier League as well as his consistent appearances and goals records. His career would finish up going full circle, calling time on his career while playing for Maidenhead United. The Magpies' boss at that time was

Johnson 'Drax' Hippolyte, who had managed Campbell during his time at Yeading. Hippolyte played a key role in enabling Campbell to achieve what he did – in getting him his move, getting him playing, getting him his England C cap – and the player remained indebted to him.

Jason Roberts

The final player on our trip is quite aptly connected to our penultimate name, in the form of Jason Roberts. I grouped these two together under Hayes and Harlington purely due to where they started out playing, and yet it is quite poetic in that with the many striking partnerships we've seen in history these two share the limelight at the end of this chapter as Jason Roberts is Cyrille Regis's nephew.

Like Cyrille, sport was pushed upon Jason at an early age. As well as Cyrille, and popular athlete John Regis, Jason had two further uncles who were also both footballers. Dave Regis played at the height of his career with Stoke City and Notts County, as well as drifting around the non-league circuit with various teams, while Otis Roberts only forged out a short career in the game that wasn't nearly as successful as that of his nephew. Sport was a big part of Jason's life so it would have been no surprise that he chose to go down that route and pursue a career in the game.

Quite quickly it was clear he was talented. Having started playing as early as six years old, Roberts would regularly have scouts from top-level clubs in attendance at his youth games playing for Parkfield Youth, and he got the chance to train with the likes of Tottenham Hotspur and Chelsea. And yet it seems almost unthinkable to learn that Roberts – for a player clearly with so much ability –

would actually contemplate giving up his dream to be a footballer; after seeing a trial with Wycombe Wanderers go unrewarded, he stopped playing. But, luckily for Roberts, he had two things in his favour: ability, and an uncle who realised his ability. So sure was Cyrille Regis that Jason had talent, he put in a word for him at his former club Hayes and the Missioners would heed such advice and hand him a trial. Unlike his audition with Wycombe, this trial with Hayes would be a successful one and Roberts would earn a deal, never looking back. His career from there certainly took a rather rapid rise: in his first season he won promotion from the Isthmian League Premier Division to the Conference, and within seven games of his third campaign he got a big-money move to Wolves for £250,000, albeit without making an appearance for the Molineux club. It was a lot of money for a player at that level at the time – even now – and that just underlined his talent.

After loans with Torquay United and Bristol City, Roberts would move to Bristol Rovers then follow in Cyrille's footsteps by signing for West Bromwich Albion then moving to Wigan Athletic in 2004. His prime years were in the Premier League with Blackburn Rovers from 2007 to 2012.

Roberts' career highlights the value of an opportunity and how transformative non-league can be. A player had seemingly seen his pathway into the game blocked, a chance trial in non-league, a life-saver of a contract; his reward? A career that spanned in excess of 560 games including eight seasons in the top flight.

8

EFL Striking Greats

FOR NON-LEAGUE players, the EFL is very much regarded as the 'promised land'. Once you have played at that level, there is a sense of completion. Just the very words 'promised land' bring back memories of the most memorable piece of commentary in my time as a Torquay United fan in the play-off final against Cambridge United at Wembley: the euphoria and elation of Setanta commentator Steve Bower after Tim Sills's famous 'Zorro' goal. Despite the EFL just being 'another league' in practical terms, there is still something hugely appealing and all the while captivating about the divisions sandwiched between the glitz and glam of the top flight and the perceived grit and guile of non league.

The EFL is single-handedly responsible for giving us not just moments that live long in the memory, but those that are synonymous with English football. If you were to ask supporters to create a top ten of standout moments, one that would most certainly be on that list is Troy Deeney's last-ditch goal for Watford in the play-off semi-final against Leicester City. Aside from Sergio Agüero's title winner for Manchester City, Deeney's strike will go down in history as one of the most iconic moments we have ever witnessed.

Deeney is one of a long list of iconic strikers to have graced the EFL having started out in non-league. Understandably, EFL clubs have in the past demonstrated a willingness to take a 'gamble' on non-league striking hotshots; after all, goalscorers don't grow on trees. The chances are that any striker finding the back of the net regularly will at some point be plucked by a side in the EFL. I have gone back through the archives and picked out some of the best goalscorers that we have seen grace the EFL (or its predecessor equivalent). To start, let's go to Birmingham.

Troy Deeney

Birmingham, West Midlands. Home of the Peaky Blinders but more famously home to the scorer of one of the EFL's greatest ever goals: Troy Deeney. In 1988, the now Watford legend was born, but it was in nearby Chelmsley Wood – in the Metropolitan Borough of Solihull – that Deeney grew up and where his football career started. As a youngster, Deeney was raised as a Birmingham City fan, providing the ideal distraction amid the chaos of a difficult neighbourhood upbringing. He was by no means the most committed of players, but it was clear that he had ability. Such ability saw Deeney offered the chance to impress the Blues' biggest rivals, Aston Villa. Aged just 15, the youngster was given a four-day trial by Villa but was ultimately not offered a deal, with Deeney himself claiming he was more focused on 'chasing girls at the park' rather than playing football on it.

However, that rejection did in no way curb his involvement. At 16, Deeney left school with no qualifications and turned to bricklaying on just £120 a week. While he may not have been the most committed student in the classroom, he was a 'student of the game' and juggled bricklaying by laying the foundations for what he hoped would be a successful football career. He signed for local side Chelmsley Town and was handed an opportunity to make his debut for the Coleshill-based outfit in October 2004, included only as Town were low on numbers as a result of their game being moved to an early kick-off to avoid a clash with a World Cup qualifier for England. Deeney certainly didn't pass up his chance, graduating from the reserves after just a handful of appearances to become a fully fledged member of the first team at 16.

He went on to establish himself as a regular for Chelmsley but, by his own admission, Deeney was contemptuous of the Midlands outfit, purely as 'all the cool kids local to Chelmsley Wood' did it. What he lacked in enthusiasm and commitment, he made up for in talent. During his time at Chelmsley he scored 23 times in 59 appearances; not bad for someone who would often work 13-hour shifts as a bricklayer before playing football on a Tuesday evening, all without the drive to be a professional beyond it being simply a 'hobby' to keep him occupied and out of trouble.

As is a feature of several of the stories in the book, Deeney was a beneficiary of circumstance and a huge slice of luck for his break; in a similar fashion to that which had earned him his debut two years prior. Deeney was spotted by local EFL club Walsall, albeit not by way of a qualified scout sent on professional business but by an ad hoc passer-by. The scout in question was the Saddlers' head of youth, Mick Halsall. Halsall's son was also a player at Chelmsley Town's level, and one Saturday Halsall made an opportune visit to watch him merely because another match he had been tasked to watch had been called off. It is fair to say that Halsall would count his lucky stars that day. He would go home slightly disappointed, with his son's side losing 11-4. And yet, in his role overseeing youth development, Halsall would go home largely happy with the display of one young player he had seen that day: Troy Deeney. If he needed a microcosm of what he was capable of, Deeney turned up 'steaming' from the night before at only 18, and yet walked away with not just a match ball but also seven goals to his name. Halsall was straight on the blower to his club.

Off the back of that game, Deeney was unsurprisingly offered a trial by Walsall. Now, you'd be forgiven for thinking that a spotty-faced Deeney from a council estate in the West Midlands would jump at the chance to earn himself a contract with the League Two club. Nope, not Troy. Such was his lack of interest, he wasn't even planning on turning up. Chelmsley Town realised that Deeney was a super talent and the enormity of the chance at stake; even if he wasn't bothered, the club weren't going to allow such an opportunity to pass. Deeney's manager at the club called round to Chelmsley Wood, got the teenager out of bed, and sent him on his way to Walsall with a taxi fare in his pocket. Looking back, Deeney will be pleased that he did.

Deeney would impress enough for Walsall to offer him a deal in December 2006. The club would immediately send him out on loan to Halesowen Town for the remainder of that season, and if the Saddlers needed a reminder of the talent they had signed then eight goals in ten Southern League Premier Division appearances would more than do that. He returned to Walsall that summer with expectations high but the first year and a half, in truth, would be a little underwhelming with only three goals. However, Deeney would alleviate any such concerns as a change of manager at the Bescot would result in a return of nine in 12 in the spring of 2009; that was the Deeney that Walsall had signed, and his form was very much the catalyst for his success.

He would spend four years with the Saddlers before moving on to Watford, where he would spend the peak years of his career. His time with the Hornets would initially be stop-start due to the odd off-field issue, but he enjoyed a particularly successful three consecutive campaigns in which he passed 20 goals in all competitions each as he helped Watford win promotion to the Premier League in 2015, then stabilise themselves at the top level. In the first of those three seasons, he was responsible for one of the most famous moments in English footballing history as he scored against Leicester in injury time to send Watford to the play-off final, just seconds after Leicester had seen a penalty saved which would have secured their own spot at Wembley. In total, Deeney scored 140 goals in 419 games for the Hornets; a ratio of one in three that was all the more impressive given quite a few of his campaigns with Watford were amid relegation scraps in the top flight.

He would never get a chance to play right at the top of the game with England as was mooted a couple of times, but that should not take away from what was a hugely successful playing career. Deeney is a great example of what can be achieved with hard work, dedication, and more importantly having to bounce back from heartbreak and setback. He spent time in prison, suffered violence at home, expulsion from school, and yet he still didn't let that deter him in forging out 706 appearances in the game, a total of 217 goals, two promotions, an FA Cup Final, and he captained both Watford and Birmingham City. Well done, Troy.

Charlie Austin

During the height of Deeney's success at Watford, there was constant dialogue speculating that he might get a call-up for England. He had even turned down a chance to play for Jamaica in the hope of representing the Three Lions; unfortunately, the call never came. One player who did get selected for a squad – albeit without winning a cap – was Charlie Austin.

Originally from Hungerford in Berkshire, Austin's first real involvement in the game came as a teenager, playing for nearby Reading in their academy. Yet his ambitions of one day making it at the Madejski were dashed at just 15 years of age, and Austin was forced to drop into non-league. At 17, Austin signed for nearby Kintbury Rangers, just an 11-minute bus commute from Hungerford. After joining Kintbury, Austin made himself a regular and hit the ground running. In 27 appearances he bagged 20 goals, which alerted the attention of Hungerford Town, who at the time were playing in the Hellenic Premier League. The Crusaders signed Austin in 2007 and he went on to play a total of 30 games as part of a Town side that finished third in the league and scored a whopping 118 goals; they have scored more in a single season only once in their entire history, 130 in 1970/71.

Hungerford made the decision to let Austin go at the end of the 2007/08 season as part of squad reshaping ahead of mounting an ultimately successful push for promotion in 2008/09. He signed for Thatcham Town, but left the Kingfishers without making a single appearance as – aged 19 – Austin moved with his family to Bournemouth, forcing him to find a new team. He would end up grateful for this as his career as a prolific goalscorer would lift off.

Austin signed for Poole Town, juggling playing semi-professionally for the Dolphins under legendary local manager Tom Killick with working as a bricklayer. It was his spell at the Tatnam Ground that laid the groundwork for what was to follow. Indeed, in 2014, Austin recalled a game back in 2008 for Poole against Brading Town where after finishing work on the building site as a bricklayer for his dad's company, he had to make his way to Lymington ferry port to make a trip to the Isle of Wight for a 7.45pm kick-off under the lights. Such hardship did not deter him, and he returned home at 1am the next day with the match ball under his arm after bagging a hat-trick in a 4-1 victory.

Austin quite quickly developed a reputation for being one of the sharpest shooters and the pick of the Wessex League forwards. The 2008/09 campaign was one of particular success in front of goal as he netted 34 times in 34 league appearances for the Dolphins; that really got teams interested.

Having moved to Bournemouth with his family, it would be no surprise that the Cherries came calling. With a player scoring as frequently as Austin sitting on their proverbial doorstep, Bournemouth had the catchment area for attracting the best local talent. Manager Eddie Howe liked what he saw so, prior to the start of 2009/10, he approached the young forward to see what he was all about. Austin went on to trial with the Cherries during pre-season and impressed at Dean Court. Howe was a talented young manager who was developing a reputation for assembling successful sides, and he was also a huge fan of Austin.

However, it was sod's law for Austin; the opportunity had presented itself, he had made his mark and looked poised to take it, but the deal would fall through. The Cherries had suffered with financial problems – entering administration in February 2008, and had failed to navigate a CVA – and had seen a transfer embargo placed upon them. As a result, Howe was unable to wrap up the signing and had to let Austin return to his parent club.

However, Austin was not back at Poole for long as Swindon Town would make a move for him, with Robins scout Ken Ryder opting for 'stealth tactics' in order to land him. Ryder decided to pay for his own entry into a game in which Austin played, rejecting any notion of free entry in his role as a scout, as to not give anyone the heads up that a professional was in attendance. That proved to be a smart move from Ryder, as he got to see Austin doing what he did best; scoring goals. Four of them, to be exact. He went away from that game glowing with praise for Austin before returning the following week. Would Austin perform? He certainly did; another hat-trick ball ended up under his arm.

By this stage Ryder had all but made up his mind that Austin was the real deal and wanted to approach Poole. But, like all good scouts, he wanted to do his due diligence first and get an alternative perspective; of course, that was always going to be positive. So positive, in fact, that the next scout sent on orders to watch Austin rang Ryder at half-time purring; he had already scored three goals. Thus, in the space of two and a half games, Austin had got three hat-trick balls. Swindon didn't need telling four times; they'd seen enough to be convinced that he was a special player.

Austin went on trial with the Robins, having impressed in his mock exams; the final exam wasn't too bad either. He was put into the reserves for a game against Swansea City. The result? Another hat-trick. Swindon couldn't get Austin signed up quickly enough, only giving the 20-year-old a deal until the end of the season to begin with, but the main thing was they had their man.

Any fears over whether or not Austin would hit the ground running were to be quashed in emphatic fashion. He went on to score 19 goals in 33 appearances in the 2009/10 League Two season; not bad for someone making his debut in the professional game. Swindon handed him a new extended deal at the end of the campaign amid interest from elsewhere. The next season would see Austin suffer somewhat with injury but he was rarely off the scoresheet: 17 goals in 27 games in all competitions despite a dislocated shoulder showed that he was a natural born finisher. Despite suffering from injury in September, his season and a half with the Robins would see bigger clubs come calling.

Swindon received bids for the forward, but safe in the knowledge he was under a new deal, they batted away that interest. Austin, however, was on a mission to make it to the top and decided to hand in a transfer request. The Robins reluctantly agreed, and entertained – and indeed accepted – a bid from Ipswich Town. The two clubs may have agreed, but Austin had other ideas and turned the deal down in favour of an alternative deal from someone else, a certain Eddie Howe.

Howe may not have been able to land Austin while he was at Bournemouth, but such was his admiration for the forward that in his new job at Burnley, he made sure that he got his man. The Clarets went all out to land him, sealing his signature on a three-and-a-half-year deal. Howe would only last in charge from January 2011 to October 2012, yet Austin would spend the best part of three seasons with the Clarets with his last particularly impressive as he hit 25 in 37 Championship appearances. And it was his move to QPR directly after this that would rubber-stamp his reputation as being a goalscorer. You only need to look at his record to know that – 48 in 89 over two and a half seasons in all competitions, including 18 in the Premier League in 2014/15.

In terms of goalscorers, Austin has to, for me, go down as one of the greatest to have come out of non-league, if not *the* greatest. On reflection, I think that he should have achieved more for his talent; what he did produce wasn't shabby, mind you. His time in non-league was exemplary, followed by 31 league goals in 54 for Swindon. 41 in 82 for Burnley and 45 in 82 for Queens Park Rangers, continuing to score freely into his mid-30s. To maintain such a high goals-to-game ratio in the EFL and at the top level despite not always being a guaranteed starter tells you all you need to know about Austin. A classy operator, and one of the best non-league alumni to have played the game.

Glenn Murray

One of the true striking greats who I often associate with the vintage years of the Football League is Glenn Murray. Murray called time on his professional career in 2021 while on the books of Nottingham Forest having maintained a scoring record of over one in three, with 217 goals in 624 career appearances in all competitions. To have amassed that many games in his career, playing at the top level and finishing with such an impressive record underlines Murray's ability; he lived and breathed goals.

Murray would end up signing for Carlisle United in 2004, but it was years previous to this that he had got his first taste of football with the Cumbrians as a youngster. His dad was a footballer in his youth, and so Glenn was eager to follow in his footsteps. In many ways, Glenn went down the traditional route into the game with spells playing for his local youth teams on a Sunday before graduating through into academy football with Carlisle. Back in 2020, Murray did an interview with *The Athletic* and talked about how his dad was eager for him to become a pro given that he himself had failed to make the grade, and ferried him around in hope that he could become a successful player.

It wasn't to be for Murray with Carlisle – the first time around at least – and he would be at a crossroads as to what he did with his talent. By his own admission, he found it tough and wasn't wholly committed to whether he wanted to take football seriously and was contemplating packing it in, but like the proud parent he was, his dad wouldn't accept failure for his son. Instead, he made sure that in whatever capacity he could, Glenn would keep playing. That wouldn't take him far – in terms of distance, certainly – as he signed for local non-league side Netherhall. Yet, in terms of where it would take him metaphorically, those humble beginnings would see him go places.

If you were to ask Murray who the main influences were in his football career, two names that would most certainly be in the conversation are Jimmy Irving and Billy Gilmour. They had been players in their own right on the local scene and were running Netherhall at the time, putting their trust in Murray from the outset. They often say it is 'who you know, not what you know' and Murray was a happy beneficiary of the fact that Irving's brother David was a top player. And, when I say 'top player', David played with George Best and Gordon Banks over in the US when the country was the *crème de la crème* of world football. It's still a sought-after destination now – I wouldn't mind playing football in the sun – but when David was still playing it was like an oasis of top-tier talent.

Having impressed with Netherhall, Murray was given a golden opportunity that would ultimately put him on the big stage to ignite his career. David Irving had moved on to manage Wilmington Hammerheads in North Carolina. David had been a striker, and having got word from Jimmy that he had a young hotshot coming through at Netherhall, he offered Murray the chance to go out to the US and play semi-professional football.

By this point, Murray had got a bit of his love for football back, and he was eager to consume as much of the game as he could. He signed for the Hammers, but their season only lasted from March through to September. It spoke volumes of Murray's attitude as in the downtime of the season, he would return home to England and play on the side for Workington Reds. If I had been free for sux months of the year out in North Carolina, I'd have been sunning myself and living the life of luxury, not rushing back to kick a bag of wind around in the cold and wet world of Workington Reds. But fair play to Murray, that's the dedication it takes to make it at the top level.

Aaron McLean and Craig Mackail-Smith scored a combined 182 goals in all competitions for Peterborough United.

Tyrone Mings received his first cap for the Three Lions in a 6-0 win against Bulgaria in 2019.

Kieffer Moore has scored 13 goals for Wales, including against Switzerland at Euro 2020 in Baku, Azerbaijan.

Dwight Gayle scored 23 goals for Newcastle United in 2016/17, as the Magpies won promotion to the top flight.

Ashley Williams scored for Wales in the Euro 2016 quarter-final against Belgium, a game in which he captained his country.

Jamie Vardy scored for Fleetwood Town against Blackpool in the FA Cup in January 2012, in a game that the Cod Army lost 5-1.

Dan Burn scored for Newcastle United in the 2024/25 Carabao Cup Final, days before making his England debut.

Iliman Ndiaye represented Senegal at FIFA World Cup 22.

Jermaine Beckford scored the winner for Leeds United at Old Trafford, as they beat Manchester United 1-0 in January 2010.

Max Kilman sealed a move to West Ham United for a reported £40 million in July 2024, joining from Wolverhampton Wanderers after six seasons.

Jarrod Bowen scored the winning goal for West Ham United in the Conference League Final against Fiorentina in 2024, helping the Hammers win 2-1.

Pelly Ruddock Mpanzu started in the 2022/23 Championship play-off final for Luton Town, as they beat Coventry City on penalties.

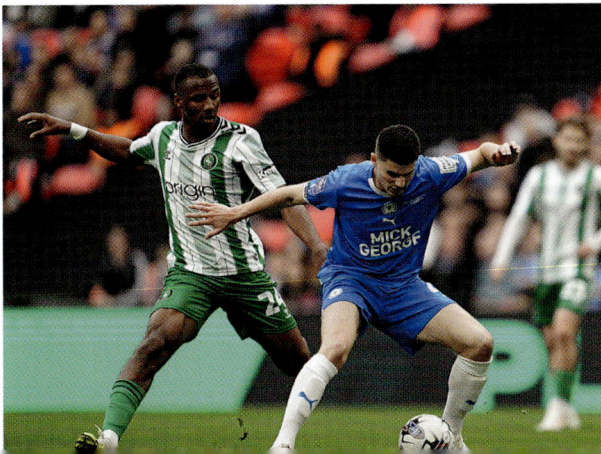

Non-league alumni Ronnie Edwards and Richard Kone went head-to-head in the 2023/24 EFL Trophy Final at Wembley.

Ollie Watkins scored the
winner for England
in the Euro 2024
semi-final against
the Netherlands after
coming off the bench for
the Three Lions.

Josh Stokes sealed a move to Bristol City in January 2024, in a season where he scored 13 league goals for The Shots, including in the FA Cup against Stockport County.

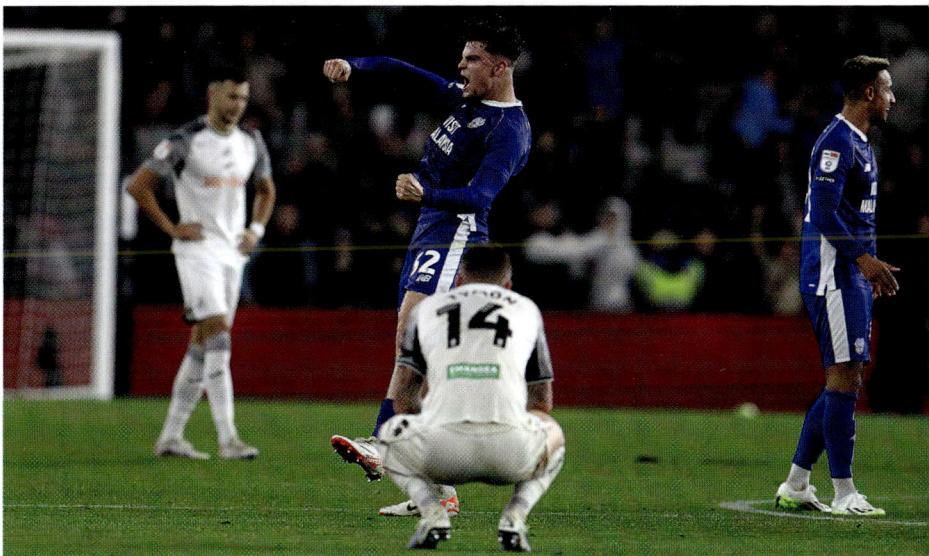

Ollie Tanner scored his first professional goal in 2023, for Cardiff City in a 2-0 Derby Day win against Swansea City.

Jamal Lowe represents Jamaica at international level, but has also played for England C.

Danny Hylton graduated from the Aldershot Town academy in 2006, going on to score 53 times for the Shots.

Tony Book spent eight seasons with Manchester City, winning the FA Cup in 1969.

DJ Campbell played in the Premier League for Blackpool, Birmingham City and QPR, scoring a total of 14 goals in the process.

And make it at the top level he did. He remains one of the best strikers to have ever played in the Football League; a seasoned goalscorer. Despite being a reliable performer, however, he'd never get an England cap. Yet that didn't diminish his career, which included five promotions. It is somewhat ironic that his best years came at Brighton & Hove Albion and Crystal Palace, two big rivals: 111 goals over three spells with the Seagulls being the highlight. Murray is an advert for what it takes – in terms of application, work rate and dedication to the cause – to make it at the top level out of non-league.

Andre Gray

One of the later stops on Andre Gray's career came out in Saudi Arabia earning shedloads; a far cry from the hard graft of playing semi-professionally in England's sixth tier. Gray's light bulb moment when he got his big break and a move higher up the pyramid came while at Luton Town, and that had been a long time coming for the centre-forward having failed to 'hit the back of the net' when he was with Wolverhampton Wanderers.

Born and raised in Wolverhampton, it made sense for Gray to try and pursue a route into the game at Molineux, and that is indeed where he started out. It was with his childhood club that he got that opportunity, joining up with Wanderers as a youngster in their academy while still a primary school student. Wolves have had some top strikers over the years, including their legendary all-time leading scorer Steve Bull, and Gray's dreams of following in his footsteps were dashed as at the age of 13 he was let go. He was forced to look elsewhere, and would turn to Shrewsbury Town.

That spell wouldn't last long before he was shipped out on loan, initially to AFC Telford United and then Hinckley United. He'd opt to join Hinckley permanently and while it was perceived by some to be a backwards step, it proved to be an inspired decision. His initial return would be fairly low-key, but he would find his shooting boots as a permanent Knitter with 37 across two seasons. That would attract interest from Gary Brabin and Luton and after a loan that saw him score seven times in 12 at the back end of the 2011/12 season, Gray would make his move to Kenilworth Road permanent under Paul Buckle. He spent the best part of two and a bit years as a Hatter, and with much of it on the scoresheet too: 57 in 111, with 30 of those goals under transformative striker-loving coach John Still as Luton won promotion out of the Conference Premier. He waved goodbye to non-league and with it said hello to the Championship, jumping two further levels in the summer of 2014 when joining Brentford, before reaching the Premier League with Burnley. He has also enjoyed brief spells in Greece and Saudi Arabia. Gray is one of the highest-profile successes that non-league has to offer.

* * *

I was fortunate enough to speak to former Luton boss Paul Buckle about his time managing Andre Gray and why he felt he went on to have such a successful career.

What attracted you to sign Andre Gray?
'It would definitely be his pace and power. He had the ability to turn 40-60 situations into 60-40 situations; he would be a defender's worst nightmare. He can score all

types of goals. His commitment to scoring goals is scary. You read most stories about players who have gone on to have success at the highest level and they are the ones who dedicate the most time to their profession, in being the first ones on the training pitch and last off; this was Andre in a nutshell. He is also a great team player, and so he has everything.'

Did you always think Andre Gray would go on to have a successful career at the top level?

'Without a doubt; 100 per cent. I was always confident that Andre could go on to play in the Premier League. I wasn't at the club when Gray signed on loan initially for Luton Town, but was there when he turned his loan deal into a permanent one. When I arrived, you could see that he had it all: pace, power and everything you need to be a top striker. He had a strong desire to learn; that is one thing that can sometimes hold players back, and yet with Andre he was the opposite. He was receptive to learning and taking in information; he was a manager's dream. I have worked with a lot of different strikers before, and Gray is different to the rest in that he has every different type of finish. Most strikers often just go for power, but Gray had the placement and the power. He could do it all. And, like Jamie Mackie – who I managed at Exeter City – his success was all on him.

'I have a funny story with Andre during my time at Luton Town. I was in the gym one day with the younger players and Andre was out on the grass hitting balls. I pointed out of the window and spoke to the players saying, "He will play in the Premier League one day." They all laughed at me when I left the room, but I knew that he was going to be successful. It was only ever going to be injury that held him back from being a success.'

In terms of strikers you have managed, where does Andre Gray rank?

'Without a doubt, Andre is right up there as one of the best. He has scored in the Premier League against Liverpool and sealed a big £18m move to Watford. Most things he would have wanted to achieve when he left Luton Town, he has managed to do. The other player that I always have to go back to in terms of the best that I have worked with is Jamie Mackie. Mackie was at Exeter City when I was the assistant manager. He had everything, and I was not surprised that he went on to do as well as he has done. I also offer up into the conversation Ashley Barnes; I managed him briefly during my time at Torquay United, and I knew that he was a player going right to the top and it was purely down to not having the finances to be able to do so that I didn't sign him on a permanent basis from Plymouth Argyle.'

When you have a special talent like Andre Gray, do you have to manage them differently?

'One hundred per cent. You absolutely have to manage them differently. Strikers need confidence. Scoring goals is – in my opinion – the hardest thing to do in football, and so in order to allow strikers to score they have to be given the freedom in the final third. Look at Tim Sills when he was at Torquay United. Before he came into the club, he couldn't score. I believed in him and gave him the freedom to go and do what he does best, and he went on to score 20 goals in 22 games. When Andre Gray missed a chance at

Luton Town, I encouraged him to do it again. Every time he missed, I put the belief in him that he could keep trying his utmost to score. You shouldn't be afraid to go and miss chances. You have to keep encouraging strikers to do extra, and they will get the rewards for that.'

You have managed a lot of top strikers; what do you think is needed to go right to the top?

'The most obvious thing that they need is to be able to score goals! You can have all the attributes you want, but if you don't put the ball into the back of the net then you are not going to make it. Better still, making them! Andre Gray was capable of doing both; he could score goals, and make goals, and he could even go that step further in stopping goals. The work he goes through in tracking back for the team makes him the complete package. You also need to dedicate your life to being a top centre-forward; you need to be obsessed with scoring goals. To begin with, Andre wasn't getting the immediate rewards, but he worked hard and eventually got the big reward in helping the Hatters beat Wrexham in the semi-finals of the play-offs and scoring in the final. His tally that season wasn't big enough for him to get the move, but it provided an early insight into his abilities. When John Still came in, he was an experienced manager, and he knew how to get the best out of him. He got the goals to his name and got a move off the back of it.'

With players like Gray, is there always a responsibility and pressure on you as a manager to ensure you don't hold them back?

'That is a really good question. As a manager, you need the ability to develop players. It is your duty as a management to improve players, and that is something that I have always done in my managerial career. You look at the players that I developed during my time at Torquay United with the likes of Billy Kee and Elliott Benyon, and then at Exeter City with Jamie Mackie during my time as an assistant with the Grecians. So, I would agree; there definitely was a responsibility during my time at Luton Town to help Andre Gray and help him realise his potential. It is my mission as a manager to always act in the best interests of the player; I want to take on that mission personally. It gives you a great feeling when you see players go on to realise their potential.'

You have recruited a lot of players out of non-league's lower tiers; who would you say is the best?
'That is a tough question; there have been a lot! I would have to go with Mustapha Carayol, who I first managed at Torquay United; he was a huge success. Nobody wanted him at the time when I signed him; he had exhausted all avenues. He had taken so many hits, and had received a lot of nos in his career. Nobody would touch him, and every club he had ever been at had got rid of him. I took a chance on him, and it certainly paid off. Have you seen a more exciting player? He was capable of double and triple stepovers; he had it all. After he left Torquay United, I managed to re-sign him while at Bristol Rovers. I was able to sign him for £10,000 for Lincoln City and was able to sell him on for around £750,000. A fabulous player, and one of my proudest achievements in management. If you asked him, he'd tell you what a huge part I played in his development. I was hard on him, but it certainly paid off in the end.'

* * *

Lee Hughes

One player synonymous with early years supporting Torquay United from an opposition perspective is Lee Hughes – someone you'd hate playing against you, but absolutely love in their pomp playing for you. He was a proper pest, never gave defences a moment's rest and was often the pantomime villain of many a Football League stadium up and down and country, more often than not because he was wheeling away celebrating having just slotted one past your team. In that regard, he goes down in the same group as the James Constables, Alex Revells and Matt Tubbses of this world: players who always caused Torquay problems and were never far from a scoresheet.

It was in the Football League where I saw Hughes strut his stuff, but it was in non-league that he started. Hughes would go on to establish himself as one of the great goalscorers in Hawthorns history in West Bromwich Albion colours, but his journey to play for the Baggies was certainly less than straightforward. When Hughes was in education, he regularly turned out for West Brom at schoolboy level in hope of one day progressing into the youth team and then beyond that, establishing himself in the first team. He would do the latter, albeit only after having gone away and forged an opportunity for himself elsewhere first.

Despite being a proficient finisher, Hughes was let go when still a schoolboy at 15, and was back to square one. There was interest in him – as there would be for anyone capable of putting the ball in the back of the net with the consummate ease that Hughes did – but nothing would materialise. Instead, he would have to stick to semi-professional football as the starting point of what he hoped would be a successful career in the game. While playing, he would work as a roofer, and so while he was putting roofs over people's heads, unbeknownst to him his natural ability to score goals would in time put a roof over his own.

He signed for Kidderminster Harriers, who were playing in non-league at the time, although that mattered little to Hughes: he just wanted a route into the game. After spending three years in the academy setup, Hughes would progress into the first team in the 1994/95 campaign. As skilled as he was on a roof, he was even more capable when it came to putting the ball in the back of the net. He quickly established a reputation as a consistent goalscorer and netted 70 times for Kidderminster, with what would prove to be his career-best 34 league goals in a single season, 1996/97.

His exploits for Harriers earned him recognition for what is today known as the England C side, with a call-up and playing just the single game in 1996 for the Non-League Lions; it rubber-stamped his reputation as being one of the best forwards in non-league. Unsurprisingly, clubs higher up the pyramid came calling for him and after his 34-goal haul, Harriers received a bid in August 1997 from a certain West Bromwich Albion. Having let Hughes go at the age of 15, the Baggies were so impressed by what they then saw from him that they felt obliged to sign him; that was £380,000 that they could have done without spending in hindsight. But fork out a hefty fee they would.

He'd served his 'apprenticeship' – so to speak – with Harriers, and it was now time for his shot with the Baggies.

I could continue to describe Hughes' career club-by-club, but it would quite easily last the duration of this book alone. Needless to say, the second opportunity at The Hawthorns would pave the way for a successful 28-year career, the last eight of which were back in non-league, finally finishing in 2022. The prime years of his career would be at West Brom, as well as a four-year spell at Notts County after signing in 2009. It was with the Magpies that I saw him at Plainmoor, in a team that also included a young Kasper Schmeichel; he scored 33 in all competitions that season as Notts won League Two. Largely down to controversies away from the pitch, Hughes perhaps did not reach the height of his potential. And yet he remains one of the best I have ever seen at Plainmoor and is one of the finest players produced in non-league.

Will Grigg

Will Grigg's on fire, your defence is terrified; oops, sorry – a force of habit. I jest, of course, but without a doubt a player who has to be recognised in this section – someone who is perhaps the most widely known among the footballing public alone for the song that is so often sung about him – is Chesterfield's Will Grigg. The man who rose to fame – if you can call it that – by virtue of his form for Milton Keynes Dons certainly knows where the back of the net is, and he certainly knows where the roots of his football career are: in the West Midlands with a spell in non-league.

At least, that was where his first-team footballing journey started. Like so many, Grigg turned to non-league after failing to make it through the academy route in the pro game, formerly with Birmingham City. Grigg's journey is quite unique in that his first real rejection – in being released by Birmingham – came down to suffering from a broken leg at just 15. That was enough for the Blues to opt against persisting with him beyond merely the youth team, and at 16 he was let go having spent a total of nine years with the club. That wouldn't, however, deter Grigg and instead just made him hungrier for success.

Born in Solihull, Grigg attended Solihull College of Technology and so it wasn't a complete surprise that he joined his local club to try and get himself back on the ladder. His time with Solihull Moors was by no means lengthy or eventful, not progressing beyond the youth team, but it was successful in getting him back into football as after less than a year at Damson Park he was signed by Stratford Town. The Bards played in the Midland Alliance – quite the comedown from Birmingham City – and Grigg spent a short period with the club.

Grigg's time with Stratford was successful, courting interest from higher-league teams as a result. He was destined to remain in the West Midlands; West Bromwich Albion were interested but in the end Walsall managed to land him on scholarship forms at the age of 17. While Grigg was merely brought in to continue his development alongside an educational programme, he displayed a maturity and confidence befitting of strikers many years his senior.

He was not the prolific force with Walsall we have come to know today, nor was he at his next club, Brentford. But a loan move to MK Dons in 2014/15 would be the making of Grigg and the origins for the 'Will Grigg's on fire' chant as he would quickly earn a reputation for being a bona fide goalscorer, later playing for Wigan Athletic,

Sunderland, Rotherham United and two more spells with the Dons, as well as winning caps for Northern Ireland (he has an Irish grandparent), before joining Chesterfield in 2023. For a player who suffered such a setback in rejection and a broken leg at an age when so many are just learning to find their feet in the game and hone their craft, it is credit to Grigg that he has been able to have the career he has.

Ché Adams

Another striker who has trodden a similar path as so many in this book is Ché Adams. In terms of using non-league as the environment in which to hone his skills, aid his development and get his career up and running, Adams' journey and involvement with the lower leagues is perhaps one of the more impactful. Adams went from playing in the Northern Premier League Premier Division with Ilkeston to playing in League One with Sheffield United; a five-tier jump straight in one. The timing of this chapter is ironic, as I wrote it while watching Southampton clinch promotion to the Premier League by beating Leeds United at Wembley in the 2024 Championship play-off final, with Adams leading the line. Ten years prior to that he had been playing in the ninth tier; a stark reminder of his rise through the leagues.

Adams hails from Leicester and was, like most football-mad youngsters, playing for his local junior club: Highfield Rangers in this case. It wasn't long though before he was being recognised for his talents, plucked by EFL side Coventry City at the age of just seven. The Sky Blues' academy has shown over the years to be one of the strongest around, with a conveyor belt of talent having come through the doors: Cyrus Christie, Callum Wilson and James Maddison the standouts. While having been signed by the City academy was a strong sign of his ability, their sheer depth of quality did make progress tough; at the age of 14 he was let go by City, his hopes of an EFL career seemingly over before they had even started. Little did Adams know that would prove to be the best thing to happen to him, however.

After leaving Coventry, Adams linked up with nearby St Andrews as part of their youth programme. He would go on to spend just a year with the Poachers, being accelerated into the first team at the age of just 15. That is certainly the earliest I have seen a promising young player be integrated into the senior side; it is perhaps not a surprise therefore that his development and subsequent rise was accelerated. He would play north of 40 times in the first team for Oadby Town in the United Counties League and finished with eight goals to his name; a record of one in five for a 17-year-old making his debut in men's football wasn't half bad, I'd say.

Adams would eventually join Ilkeston aged 17. Manager Kevin Wilson had just started up an academy at the time, and had identified the youngster as a potential signing. However, Adams wasn't brought in for the youth team primarily; he was too talented. Wilson knew – even that early in his development – that he was a player of real potential and quickly made him a regular in the first team. Adams would, however, still turn out for the youth team, in helping them to reach the second round proper of the FA Youth Cup in 2014 – a 1-0 defeat to Accrington Stanley, but further than they had done before. In the main, Adams was very much viewed as a first-team asset as even as a teenager he was special. Even Adams couldn't believe just how quickly he became a mainstay of the side under Wilson; that early exposure to men's football was invaluable in setting him on his way.

His impact on the first team would be almost immediate: his two assists early in 2014/15 against Stourbridge would very much set the tone for the campaign. The New Manor Ground would quickly become something of an oasis for top-level scouts, all clamouring to get a look at the youngster making waves in the Northern Premier League. So good was his form that as early as October he already had 20 goal contributions; he wasn't going to be at the club for long. And he wasn't. Fast forward just a month and Sheffield United would come calling in advance of the January window to secure his services for a six-figure sum. From there, Adams' career certainly saw a meteoric rise and within a campaign and a half he'd swap Sheffield for Birmingham. It was a snowball effect from there, going on to excel at St Andrew's, and he would eventually swap blue for red once more in moving south while his career was going north, joining Southampton for a hefty £15m. Such a move has paved the way to earning international recognition with Scotland, qualifying via his Scottish grandmother. It's been a rapid rise, and one that at the time of writing saw its latest chapter out in sunny Italy with Torino; quite the step up from Oadby Town.

Ollie Watkins

While his time in non-league was perhaps the briefest of any striker on this list, one player who still counts experience outside of the professional ranks is Ollie Watkins. He is one of two players in this book to have started out with Torquay United, with Kieffer Moore –

who features later on – also counting the Gulls among his earliest memories in football with time in their academy. What a forward line that could have been. Yet, like Moore, Watkins had to turn elsewhere in order to get his big break in the game; he joined Exeter City's academy at under-11 level after leaving Torquay. As it turned out, that would prove a wise move for the sake of his career.

Exeter have developed a reputation for having one of the best academy setups in England. As a fan-owned club, they operate by way of a develop-and-sell philosophy, and so the success of the Grecians has centred around having a thriving academy. In that regard, Ollie Watkins represents the most famous alumnus to have come through at St James Park; the roll of honour also includes the likes of defenders Dean Moxey and George Friend and midfielders Matt Grimes and Ethan Ampadu. Of those, Watkins is the only one to have gone out on loan in non-league during his early years; perhaps his career has been the best out of the five, too.

Having joined Exeter as an under-11, Watkins would excel and work his way through the age groups so City felt that he was worthy of a scholarship, signing forms to remain with the Grecians up to and including the under-18 squad. It was in this age group where he would make a name for himself and cause City to realise that they perhaps had a talented player in their ranks; during the 2013/14 campaign, Watkins was a regular in the team that won the Football League Youth Alliance South West Conference. The Grecians played 16 games and scored 40 goals; impressively, Watkins scored 30 of those by himself. Not a bad return.

It was off the back of that form that City signed him up on professional terms in April of 2014. It wasn't long before Watkins would get a taste of the first team either: on the final day of 2013/14, Exeter made the long trip to Hartlepool United and Watkins was called into the squad by boss Paul Tisdale. It proved to be a particularly special day, making his debut in the 77th minute. Just 22 minutes earlier he had also seen fellow youngster and academy graduate Matt Jay – with whom he had forged quite the partnership in the under-18 side – thrown into the fold. Only 18 years of age, Watkins was given his taste of first-team football, a long trip on the team coach and minutes in the Football League; he had made it.

One of the strengths of City's academy has been the club's ability to manage prospects and know the right time to give them exposure to the first team. Conversely, the Grecians also make good use of local connections to give their young players experience of men's football, and in this regard Watkins was no different.

Despite being in and around the first team, the early part of 2015 saw Watkins shipped out on loan to Somerset outfit Weston-super-Mare. Looking back on his career, it would be one hugely important for his development and the success that would follow.

Watkins would not head to Weston-super-Mare alone; he joined the Seagulls alongside best friend Matt Jay. That loan spell proved to be the making of Watkins, remaining with the club until the end of the campaign and scoring ten goals in 25 appearances. He returned to Exeter as a better player, albeit he then had to remain patient upon the start of the following season, restricted to sitting in the stands in a watching capacity. However, when the opportunity presented itself, Watkins certainly made the most of it.

He couldn't have wished for any bigger occasion in which to make his first professional league start in City colours: none other than a derby against local rivals Plymouth Argyle. By the time Watkins faced the Pilgrims in the return match seven months later, he had rubber-stamped his role in the team as a starter. March was when he particularly announced himself on the senior stage by bagging the Football League Young Player of the Month and PFA Fans' Player of the Month awards after scoring four times to help City consolidate their spot in mid-table. As with any emerging young player, while higher teams may sit up and take note of them with a perceived purple patch, it is only when they back that up over the course of a more sustained period that they tend to make their move. Luckily for Watkins, 2016/17 would see him show that his form in the previous campaign was not simply a flash in the pan and he would score 16 goals in 52 appearances in all competitions – including a hat-trick against Newport County. He was then named as the EFL Young Player of the Year.

There aren't many bigger accolades than winning the EFL Young Player of the Year award. Every side is always looking for a top player to invest in for the long term, and the seasons that had gone before had provided a good indication of what was to come. Previous winners Lewis Cook and Dele Alli had both sealed moves directly off the back of taking the same prize, and City were half-resigned to losing Watkins.

That they did, to Brentford. Firmly committed to investing in 'Benham Ball' by this stage, they'd shelled out on Rico Henry from Walsall the previous summer and the Bees decided that Watkins would be the latest investment, brought in for an initial £1.8m. That was the same figure that Brentford paid out for fellow forward Neal Maupay, yet Watkins was very much the main attraction. Indeed, he was certainly the biggest success story and would go on to earn a move to Aston Villa in 2020 off the back of 49 goals across three campaigns, including a standout 2019/20 in which he scored 26 in 50.

Since then, Watkins has proven himself as one of the best forwards in the top flight and in the process earned international recognition. For his former sides back home in Devon – Buckland Athletic, Newton Town and Weston-super-Mare – the moment he got his first England cap was a special occasion, his first goal even more so. A moment when the likes of Sam Matterface can eulogise about where Watkins comes from, his Devonshire roots and who he used to play for in the embryonic years of his career; their moment in the sunshine to steal the spotlight. All while in some local club supporter bar back in Homers Heath there are hundreds of jubilant fans all jumping for joy when seeing one of their own hit the headlines on the big stage. They got their moment of glory when Watkins scored arguably the most prestigious goal in his career to date in helping England to win the Euro 2024 semi-final against the Netherlands. One of the best moments in recent English footballing history was indebted to one of non-league's finest former players; I like that.

Alfie May

The final player in this chapter is Alfie May. In terms of prolific goalscorers, there aren't many in the EFL who have been as consistently proficient; there are very few Saturdays where you look at the vidiprinter and don't see the diminutive dynamo's name on there. While he is now one of the EFL's finest, Gravesend-born May started out with Kent-based outfit Corinthian. He kicked off his senior career with the Hoops after being released from Millwall's academy as a youngster, and it is fair to say that his career has taken an upward trajectory ever since making the decision to drop into the non-league scene.

May's story is like so many of the players in this book; starting out on the books of an EFL academy, released at an early age, and turning to the solace of non-league to 'get back off the canvas'. And, in many ways, his journey from non-league into the EFL is not an unfamiliar one; I could write a whole book on budding hotshots in non-league who have got a move off the back of scoring freely. However, that doesn't in any way diminish May's achievements to get to the point he has. If anything, the speed at which he went from playing in the ninth tier to being promoted to League One, a matter of months, makes his rise all the more remarkable.

May started out at Millwall aged just nine, joining an academy that has produced the likes of Eberechi Eze, Lyle Taylor, Fred Onyedinma and Marvin Elliott. During his time with the Lions, he showed himself to be a more than capable centre-forward and yet he was released at the age of 14. Like so many young players at that age, a decision was made – rightly or wrongly – on whether to give him a contract based solely on whether or not they were physically developed enough. Unfortunately for May, he was certainly not blessed with height. Mind you, Lionel Messi hasn't done badly for himself, has he? May was deemed not tall enough, although his cousin was also in the academy at the same time, reportedly 6ft 6in and one of the biggest for his age group. He was kept on, yet has anyone ever heard of him since?

Following that rejection, May initially found it tough to come to terms with the news; indeed, he gave up football to begin with. Millwall did give him the opportunity to continue training with them for a period of time – a 'loose second chance' if you will – but overwhelmed with the fact he had seemingly had his hopes of being a professional footballer dashed, he stopped playing and pursued other interests for a year. In this respect, the fact that he had such a false start and a break from football at a time when most players are normally just getting into their stride makes his story all the more impressive. It certainly speaks volumes to his character. In life they say to make the most of a second chance, and boy did May do that. He would eventually return to the game after his year-long hiatus, signing for a local Saturday team that was run by a friend of his brother. It was certainly not the glitz and glam of playing for Millwall, but what it did do was give him the opportunity to play regular football and hone his craft. It was clear quite quickly that he most certainly had the talent and ability that needed crafting.

Dropping into non-league at that stage allowed May to enjoy football again. After seeing his dreams dashed by Millwall, it would have been easy to completely fall out of love with the game; there are so many young players who face rejection at that stage, and very few go on to have successful careers or even pursue playing football. He got his smile back while playing for his brother's friend's side; the real Alfie May was back. It was fair to say that the start of his senior career was a little slow in getting going, with several less productive spells, with Corinthian initially before failing to register when on the books of Billericay Town. However, after a spell of 23 goals in 36 for Chatham Town, it was with Kent-based outfit Erith & Belvedere that May well and truly proved what he was capable of; a tally of 41 goals in a single season was enough for him to win the Southern Counties East League's Golden Boot.

That spell with the Deres certainly put May on the map. His next club, Hythe Town, is where he credits as being the real 'runway' for his career to take off, and where he worked with someone who still to this day he credits as being an influential figure for him: Hythe's manager at the time, Clive Cook. May was, upon signing for Hythe, billed as a bit of a 'superstar in the making' having come off the back of an unsuccessful trial with Crewe Alexandra and also spending a brief period of time on the books of Bromley in non-league's premier tier. The trial at Crewe particularly lit a spark in May, giving him a new hunger and desire to want to be a professional.

He signed for Hythe and hit it off from the start in a team third from bottom in their division; from those struggles, May's exploits in front of goal helped the Cannons to get into the play-offs. While Town ultimately weren't promoted that season, May's form reinforced that he was a capable forward and not just content to be playing in non-league, but with the ability and more importantly self-belief to want to be playing higher. One of the key driving forces in that was Clive Cook; as relentless as May's scoring ability was the efforts of Cook to keep motivating him and reassuring him that he would one day make it in the EFL, constantly letting him know how highly he thought of him. He made May feel ten feet tall. Well, maybe six feet at a push. Anyway, Cook realised that May was more than good enough to play professionally and so that proved.

Another opportunity presented itself to him in the form of a trial with Stevenage, again instigated through the efforts of Cook, albeit May had to wait until November 2016 for concrete interest to materialise. Doncaster Rovers were keen, initially taking him on trial to see what he was about; quite quickly they realised he was quite handy, and manager Darren Ferguson offered him a deal. It was a tough decision regardless of May's ambitions of being an EFL player: he was juggling working full-time on a building site with his brother alongside playing semi-professionally in non-league. It was a big move but one he had to take, and on 1 January 2017 Doncaster announced his signing. He had done it. All the hard yards of playing in non-league. All the constant phone calls and messages of support from Clive Cook. All of the rejections he had suffered up until that point; it was all worth it as he was finally an EFL player. No more building sites; the only foundations he was building was that of a successful professional career.

That he most certainly has. Since arriving at Doncaster, May has gone on to prove himself as one of the deadliest finishers that the lower leagues have to offer, although it wasn't until 2021/22 that he really showed the same level of proficiency in front of goal as he had done under Cook at Hythe Town, and during his time with Erith & Belvedere. During the six seasons between signing for Rovers in League Two and his return to League One with Cheltenham Town in 2020/21, May failed to hit double figures in terms of league goals. I think it is fair to say, however, that he has more than made up for it since. From 2021/22 onwards May scored more than 20 League One goals each year, totalling 66, during two relegation firefighting campaigns with Cheltenham and his subsequent move to Charlton Athletic in 2023/24. At the time of writing he was with Birmingham City, joining them in the summer of 2024. May is without a doubt one of the best strikers to have come out of non-league and excelled in the EFL.

9

Top Table

AS A budding young footballer, there are often a handful of accolades that feature on a bucket list by which their career is often marked as a success. For many, the pinnacle is to captain their country at an international tournament, or even better still to taste success on the international stage. Closely following that would most certainly be to win the Champions League or to do well in a European competition. Just to have the chance to play in the Premier League would be enough to instil a sense of immense pride and completion; to go one better and get a taste of the upper echelons of football would be beyond a player's wildest dreams, especially those who start out in the humble beginnings of non-league. Yet there have been several who have plied their trade in non-league and then gone on to follow in the footsteps of football royalty on the greatest of stages.

Garry Birtles

One of the top players in the late 70s and early 80s, Garry Birtles went on to make just over 500 club appearances as well as having the honour of representing his country on three occasions, the first of which came in 1980 against Argentina at Wembley. For now, however, we go right back to Birtles' roots in non-league and discover where the prolific forward started out. While it proved to be Nottingham Forest where Birtles made a name for himself, it was with one of the other greats of English football that he had his first major realisation that he could potentially go on to be a footballer. Aston Villa came calling when Birtles was only 12 years of age, having developed a reputation as being a talented young player with Attenborough Colts.

Even at that age, Birtles was eager to try and make it in the game, and he later made the ultimate sacrifice of foregoing his GCEs in order to attend a trial with the Villans. However, Villa opted against keeping Birtles on and that meant the youngster would have to go back to the drawing board. He later swapped drawing boards for skirting boards and became a carpet fitter while pursuing his love of football on the side, turning out for local side Clifton All Whites, situated on Green Lane, Nottingham – coincidentally, just five miles away from where Birtles would go on to forge a career as one of the best English forwards of his time.

Birtles played for Clifton until the age of 19 when, as a beneficiary of circumstance, he was signed by Long Eaton United. Clifton chairman John Raynor left to take up a similar role with Long Eaton, and took Birtles with him. During his time at Clifton, Birtles was regularly deployed on the wing, but Raynor opted to move him more centrally as a forward and his form would flourish, his career picking up pace as a result.

Birtles' displays were so good for Long Eaton that he attracted the attention of Nottingham Forest boss Brian

Clough, who went to see him play in an FA Cup qualifying game against Enderby Town. Birtles went away hoping that he had impressed Clough enough to earn a deal. In his time as a manager, Clough had several famous sayings. On his talent as a manager he once said, 'I wouldn't say I was the best manager in the business, but I was in the top one.' Following Forest's relegation from the Premier League in 1993, he stated, 'If the BBC had a Crap Decision of the Month award on *Match of the Day*, I'd walk it.' And after Stuart Pearce got concussed in a game, Clough instructed his physio, 'Tell Pearce he's Pelé and that he's playing up front.' And his takeaway from watching Birtles for the first time was 'Classic Cloughie', admitting, 'The half-time Bovril was better than watching him.' As breaks in football go, all signs pointed towards Birtles as having fallen short once again. Yet sometimes in football you need to have a bit of luck; so many of the players in this book have had an opportune moment that has defined their career. Despite Birtles seemingly being deemed inferior to a hot meat drink, Clough – a manager who had a track record for identifying top players – clearly saw something in him and decided to offer him a trial.

Birtles spent a month with Forest, and did well enough for Clough to make an official approach to Long Eaton. The forward moved to the City Ground for a fee in the region of £2,000. Birtles was offered a contract of £60 a week, the same as he was being paid in his day job; in the space of a month he went from laying carpets to laying the foundations of a successful footballing career.

If Birtles thought that his career would be plain sailing from there on in, he was going to get a rude awakening as his ascent to the top was to hit choppy waters. Birtles would have to wait until March 1977 before Clough would take the plunge and put him into the firing line, a run-out in midfield. But the manager wasn't impressed, telling Birtles, 'If I ever play you in midfield again, give me a shotgun and I'll shoot myself.' There have been better debuts. It couldn't have gone any worse for Birtles; the moment that he had been waiting for since turning out as a wee lad had gone terribly. It had been so bad that Clough decided to toss Birtles in the wasteland of reserve-team football for the next 18 months. Despite having got his big move to Nottingham Forest, he found himself back where he started; playing Sunday league. Was his career over? Far from it.

He'd had a break before landing a trial despite having an absolute shocker, and it was another opportune slice of luck that brought about another chance for Birtles to prove himself. Clough had sold striker Peter Withe to Newcastle United, and had put his faith in young forward Steve Elliott. Elliott struggled to find his shooting boots and Clough had no other option than to bring Birtles in from the cold. Shotgun firmly locked away, and played solely in a striking berth, Birtles didn't look back.

Birtles would go on to be one of Clough's proudest – and most successful – finds. Over two spells either side of a stint at Manchester United he would score just shy of 100 goals in a Forest shirt, helping them to win the European Cup in consecutive seasons as well as the European Super Cup in 1979. Such was his form for Forest he was awarded the prestigious Bravo Award, given to the outstanding young European footballer annually from 1978 to 2015. To think that Clough managed to find a player of that ability lurking in non-league was not only testament to his eye for talent, but also an ode to the quality to be found outside of the professional ranks.

Tony Book

Tony Book was a prominent figure in the 60s and early 70s, with his time in the limelight coming as he represented Manchester City in the First Division from 1966 to 1974. His story is perhaps even more unique given that the bulk of his career was played in non-league, rather than simply a brief spell at the start. While his time at Bath City was hugely successful from 1956 to 1964, it was his exploits towards the end of his career that saw him inducted into the Manchester City Hall of Fame; to this day he is still very much regarded in Citizens circles as 'Mr Manchester City'.

But it is in Somerset where I start reliving Book's rise to the top, beginning in Bath. Book was born in the backdrop of Roman baths in the heart of the West Country. While these would provide the roots for his career to take off, Book's story was to take a twist as early as the age of four when he moved to India with his family – certainly not a footballing hotbed. His father was in the Somerset Light Infantry, and so as was the norm for families of the war, the Book family was fairly nomadic at that time. Tony was forced to up sticks and settle temporarily in British India while his father served in Burma during the Second World War. This was where Tony first honed his talents as a budding footballer. In much the same way legends of the game have started out playing on the streets of South America like Brazilian legend Pelé, Tony first learned to kick a football as a barefoot youth on the streets of India amid a backdrop of war. He was part of a family of boys, and so he spent much of his days playing football with them and sharpening his skills.

Shortly after Book's 11th birthday – and indeed, shortly after the end of the war – his father saw his posting in Burma come to an end, and the family returned promptly to their Bristolian roots. He attended the local secondary school in the city, and got the chance to build on his early love for football by playing for his school side, as well as being scouted to play at both city and county level, impressing on both counts. Having left secondary school aged 16, he would eventually end up having to do his fair share of national service, following in the footsteps of his father in serving his county.

Prior to his call-up in 1952 aged 18, Book spent two years as a bricklayer. While he was physically laying the foundations as a footballer, working full-time as a bricklayer for this period would allow him to metaphorically lay the foundations for an eventual successful career in gaining experience at amateur level. He joined up with local side Peasedown Miners Welfare, based in a village called Peasedown St John. Book would go on to establish himself as quite the competent full-back by trade, yet it was at the other end of the pitch that he would get his first taste of men's football, as a centre-forward.

Book would go away to join the army as part of his national service in 1952, but that would not curb his enthusiasm. Posted as part of the Medical Corps, he played for the Royal Army Medical Corps for three years. This almost worked Book an opening into the top level as alongside him in the team was Frank Blunstone, who was on the books of Chelsea. Blunstone would go on to play for the Blues alongside Jimmy Greaves. Blunstone twisted the arm of Chelsea boss Ted Drake to give Book a trial, despite him being stationed. Ultimately it wasn't to be for Book, as Drake closed the metaphorical book on any potential exciting new chapter in his journey.

That would not deter the youngster, who decided to pursue a 'proper' route into the game. Book would get an opportunity to do so for Southern League outfit Frome Town, for whom he signed in 1955. Book would prove himself to be a capable forward, with his exploits helping the Robins to the last four of the Somerset Cup in 1956. If you needed a microcosm as to his quality, in Book's absence the subsequent downfall of Frome would do just that. After the turn of the year, Book would move on for pastures new and indeed go closer to home in signing for Bath City. While Frome would go on to struggle, Book's career would be set for a 'best seller'.

While he would go on to be a true great for Manchester City, he would do likewise at Bath. He went on to make 387 appearances for the Romans, which ranks him ninth on the list of all-time appearances for the club. Book's move to Bath almost came about as a happy accident and by chance, benefitting from circumstance in City's hour of need amid financial woes. Little did they know that Book would go on to be a legend for the club during his nine years at Twerton Park. It would be his time at City that would give him a golden ticket to playing at the top level of the game. Malcolm Allison would manage at Bath for a year in the early 1960s, and would take Book along with him on his managerial travels to Toronto City and then latterly to Manchester City, via a couple of seasons at Plymouth Argyle, Book becoming a Football League player for the first time aged 30. He spent the later years of his career with City, making himself a fixture of one of the club's most successful teams, winning a First Division title, an FA Cup, one League Cup, two Charity Shields and a European Cup Winners' Cup. In the space of five years he'd ticked off the bucket list of domestic football, but it wouldn't have been possible if he hadn't played in non-league.

Ashley Williams

After the trials and tribulations of some players' rises to the top, the next name will appear all the more run of the mill in comparison, but equally as impressive. To have the honour of representing your country is something that only a select few get to experience. To then be picked to captain your country is an even greater achievement, like the 'crème de la crème de la crème'. To then lead your country's national team to its most successful tournament in history scribes your name down in legend. Such an honour was bestowed upon Ashley Williams who, in 2016, led Wales to an unprecedented semi-final of the Euros.

Williams was born in Wolverhampton and from an early age, it was clear that he at the very least wanted to be a footballer. His first real taste of the 'football bug' came when his family moved to nearby Tamworth. Like many of the players in this book, Sunday league was where Williams honed his trade initially, playing for local youth side Belgrave Bullets. For Williams, football consumed him. On Sundays he would run out for the Bullets, and on Saturdays he would watch his dad Errol play. Errol was a player in his own right, as well as latterly a manager, and so football was very much a part of Williams' upbringing.

It was clear quite quickly that Williams was a capable player, and represented Staffordshire at county level; to think that the future captain of Wales would start out with the Lambs has a certain sense of irony to it. Williams was eager to follow in the footsteps of his idol John Barnes; he revered the Liverpool winger as a youngster, so much so that he recalled writing to Subbuteo in disgust at there being no black players depicted in the game; off the back of this Williams got to meet his hero. His desire to make it could not have been stronger.

Williams would get his first real taste of higher-level football at West Bromwich Albion, having been scouted to be a part of their youth setup. However, his dream would seemingly come to a halt at the age of 16 as he was let go by Albion and he was back to playing local football instead, with Staffordshire club Hednesford Town. Errol Williams was the manager of the Pitmen at the time, and Ashley was given the chance of playing for the club. Quite quickly they realised that Ashley was not just 'another player' – he 'had a bit'.

Williams was never able to establish himself at Hednesford, but played regularly enough that soon there was Football League interest in him. Oldham Athletic took him on trial before submitting a transfer bid which was rejected. But that decision would not hamper his progression up the pyramid as Hednesford eventually allowed Williams to leave Keys Park for Stockport County, oddly on a free, and having signed for the Hatters on New Year's Eve, he would enter 2004 as a bona fide Football League player.

It would be three months before Williams was given a run out by the Hatters, making his debut against

Hartlepool United. He would go on to make a total of ten appearances before the end of the season. He impressed so much during this spell that his cameo earned him recognition as the club's young player of the year; that was merely a sign of things to come. The 2004/05 season would see County continue to struggle on the field, finishing 24th in League One and being relegated to the basement tier, yet Williams established himself as a fixture when making 49 appearances in all competitions.

He really started to make a name for himself the following season with the arrival of a new manager in January – the wily Jim Gannon – getting the best out of the young defender. Williams would establish himself as one of the most sought-after young players in the league under Gannon, so much so that Championship club Luton Town launched an unsuccessful bid of around £500,000. He remained at Edgeley Park, but was turning heads of sides higher in the Football League, earning another feather in his cap by landing the 2006/07 player of the year award at County after a strong finish to the campaign.

By 2007/08, Williams was absolutely flying. Now club captain at Stockport and a regular under Gannon, the world was his oyster, and on 26 March 2008 his career really lifted off with his debut for Wales. While born in Wolverhampton himself, his mother Lyn was of Welsh descent and it was due to that of his grandfather that Williams opted against potential English or Jamaican call-ups to take up a spot in John Toshack's team at the age of 24.

Williams made his debut as Wales won 2-0 away to Luxembourg in a friendly, Toshack throwing him in from the off as he played the entire 90. It was nearly a nightmare first game in Welsh colours, with a poor backpass almost gift-wrapping a goal for *Les Lions Rouges*, but in true Welsh fashion he came roaring back. If you had told Williams that would have been the first of 86 international caps, he may not have believed you.

It got better for Williams as just two days after making his debut, he was the subject of a move to League One high flyers Swansea City, featuring three times as they romped to the League One title. City turned his initial loan permanent at the end of the season for £400,000. As the Swans made their bow in the Championship, Williams wasn't just a part of the first team; he was a pillar, playing in all 46 league games. In his first full season, Williams would walk home with another couple of awards for his ever-growing collection, including the prestigious FAW Welsh Footballer of the Year trophy. He was excelling so much that he would go on to make it a hat-trick of consecutive seasons in which he made 46 appearances, with 2009/10 and 2010/11 also seeing him named in the Championship Team of the Year, by this point established as Swansea's captain.

As far as Williams' domestic career was concerned, success with the Swans would be the highlight including reaching the Premier League and winning the League Cup in 2013, yet it would be on the international stage with Wales that he'd have a defining moment. They reached the last four of the 2016 European Championship, and Williams became the first captain in Welsh international history to lead the Dragons into a major tournament semi-final. A humble lad who had his schooling in the lower reaches then achieved such accolade, acts as inspiration for players in non-league aiming to play at the top of the game.

Steve Finnan

For many, the pinnacle of club football is the Champions League. The elite competition, nothing beats the grandeur of those Champions League nights under the lights and that famous theme tune; it is what every footballer dreams of. To go one step further and win it, however, is reserved for only the very elite; at the time of writing, only 23 teams have won the competition since its debut in 1955 as the European Cup. Our next player remains the only person in history to have played in – and won – the Champions League, UEFA Cup and Intertoto Cup, as well as playing in every league of English league football, plus the Conference, where his career began. I'd be surprised if he wasn't the last. Regardless, it's some claim to fame. Step forward, Steve Finnan.

Indeed, going back through the archives to list what he has won, nearly won and played in, you'd have to make a genuine argument for Finnan perhaps being one of the most successful non-league graduates. For now, let's go right back to where it all started: Chelmsford, the Essex town where Finnan grew up. The defender had been born in Limerick – the Janesboro area, to be precise – but when Finnan was still young, he moved with his family across from Ireland and settled in Essex. He got his first taste of football with the now-defunct Wimbledon, given a chance in the Wombles' youth setup. At the time Wimbledon were playing in the First Division, and as a result of playing in their academy Finnan grew up – until the age of 16 – as a devout Dons fan.

That devotion to Wimbledon came to an abrupt halt in 1993 when Finnan was given the news that they would be letting him go. Yet another player given the boot by an academy at 16; that is becoming quite the norm in this book. He wouldn't have to wait long to get back on the bike, so to speak; along came Welling United in that same year with a contract for the Limerick lad. Out with the Wombles, and in with the Wings.

For Welling, Finnan featured prominently in a team that recorded successive bottom-half finishes in the Conference. He caught the eye however and Birmingham City came calling during the summer following the 1994/95 campaign. Barry Fry has since gone on to make quite a name for himself in identifying non-league talent in his role as director of football with Peterborough United, and Fry was in charge of the Blues when Finnan made the move north; as such, he was one of Fry's first. Fry was so sure of Finnan's potential that he persuaded the Blues to fork out a hefty £100,000 fee. To think that Finnan had been let go by Wimbledon for nothing and then two years later would be signed by a First Division side – and one of the biggest footballing institutions in the country – just goes to show how quickly someone's career can change.

Despite having jumped three divisions to sign for Birmingham, Finnan wouldn't just be content with making up the numbers to begin with. The 1995/96 campaign did see Finnan go out on loan away from St Andrew's, ending the season with Second Division outfit Notts County, but he still managed to make a total of 19 appearances for the Blues in what turned out to be his only full season as a City player. Finnan helped Notts County to qualify for the Second Division play-offs, before returning to St

Andrew's in the summer. That re-integration would be short-lived as County opted to sign Finnan on a permanent basis off the back of his successful cameo; a healthy bit of profit for the Blues, as they agreed a £200,000 deal. Fast forward eight months and the Magpies found themselves relegated to the Third Division as they finished bottom of the league. Finnan must have been wondering if County had kept the receipt.

The defender would impress and it was in 1997/98 that he would well and truly make a name for himself, helping County romp to the league title and only missing out on being centurions by way of a single point. Finnan was an undroppable force at right-back, making a total of 51 appearances and controversially missing out on inclusion in the divisional team of the year. Regardless, he was fast becoming a household name, and his form turned the head of none other than Kevin Keegan. A player who won everything in his playing days, Keegan also proved himself to be quite the capable manager – winning three domestic titles. As Notts County made their way to the Second Division, Fulham stepped in to take Finnan to Craven Cottage. The west London club were equally in the Second Division, but such was their desire to win the league they had money to spend and Keegan sent £300,000 of it the way of the Magpies in November 1998. A healthy £100,000 profit for Notts, and Finnan was on the move again.

Fulham would take to the First Division like a duck to the Thames, with Finnan proving himself to be a stalwart of their side – making 45 appearances – as he added another piece of silverware to his cabinet in winning the second tier in 2001. He would brace himself for a debut campaign in the Premier League. So, how would Finnan fare? Playing for the newly promoted minnows of the top flight, might he struggle? In his first season there he earned a place in the Premier League PFA Team of the Year, as well as being named Fulham's player of the year, all the while qualifying for and winning a European competition. In 2003 he moved to Liverpool, where he won the Champions League in his second season and then reached another final in 2007, finishing his playing days in the Portsmouth team defeated by Chelsea in the 2010 FA Cup Final. From the Conference to the very peak of the club game, more than 600 appearances and half a century of international caps; what a career he had.

Vivian Woodward

Perhaps the finest example of coming from non-league to the very top is the legendary figure Vivian Woodward. By far and away the earliest player in this book – having played the bulk of his career in the early 1900s – Woodward is a name synonymous with the London scene and to this day remains a player rightly revered by Tottenham Hotspur, and is regarded as one of the true greats of English football. Of all the players I have read up on and whose careers I have researched, Woodward stands alone with a rather unique journey – not just his exploits as a footballer at club level but also his achievements on the international and global stage, as well as his efforts away from the pitch. I'd go as far as to say that Woodward's career is the most interesting that I have had the privilege of learning about. It is no exaggeration to say that Woodward would not look out of place in a discussion about the best English players in history; right up there with Stanley Matthews,

Bobby Charlton, Bobby Moore and the like. You only need to detail a list of Woodward's achievements to know that we are talking about a special footballer and one simultaneously talented in other disciplines.

Privately educated at Ascham College, Woodward was talented at sports, representing the college in cricket and football. The Kennington-born youngster could well have chosen to commit to donning cricket whites for much of his adult life, yet it was another sport that took centre stage. He was identified early on as being hugely blessed as a footballer, so much so that he was tipped by college staff to go on to represent England and forge a successful career for himself in the game; they weren't wrong. Unfortunately Sky Bet wasn't open for business in 1893, otherwise they may have earned a penny or two as a result of Woodward's powers on the pitch.

What made Woodward's successes all the more impressive was that he was nonplussed when it came to football. He had no real burning desire to achieve in the game; it was more his sheer level of ability that helped him have the career he did. Such was his little interest, Woodward would regularly miss games in favour of playing cricket; he'd happily pass up playing football on Saturday, but not the Spencer Cricket & Lawn Tennis Club. He was perhaps more focused on pursuing other sports. There was hope he would become an early example of a Fred Perry or a Tin Henman. He was not just good – he was one of the best tennis players in the country. The fact he became the successful footballer he was is perhaps not 'luck', but at the very least a happy accident. You couldn't keep down a player of his talent with the ball of a bigger variety.

After impressing at junior level with Ascham College, Woodward would get his first taste of senior football at Clacton Town. Even with the Seasiders, his focus was not solely on football and he would miss games for tennis tournaments or to represent his local cricket team. And yet it wasn't as if his game on the grass suffered; if anything it went from strength to strength. He'd spend five years with Clacton before going on to play for Harwich & Parkeston for a brief period at the turn of the 20th century. During his time with Clacton he averaged a ratio of better than a goal a game; that was a clear warning sign of what he was capable of. Regardless of the level you're playing at, a good ratio is sure to turn heads; indeed it did. He'd go on to sign for the pre-City suffixed Chelmsford and helped them to win the Essex Senior Cup. Such form would earn him recognition by way of a move to Tottenham Hotspur, who coincidentally themselves were in non-league at the time. Woodward still did not take football seriously in his first few years at Spurs, again regularly taking time off to prioritise alternative sporting ventures. It just underlined the talent he had; he was able to do this and still ended his career with a ratio of well above a goal a game.

Woodward's route to the big time was unlike any others in this book, and somewhat fortunate, for he got his break into the top leagues by way of a vote to promote Spurs from the old Southern League into what was then the Second Division in 1908. Eventually, Woodward would prioritise his footballing career – in agreement with most that he was a special talent – and went from architecture to planning teams' downfalls in swapping a pencil for an even more skilled tool: his right foot. Skilled it most certainly was; he would earn England recognition off the back of that by winning his first cap for the Three Lions in 1903 while still in the Southern League. No other players in this book can count getting a full England cap while playing in non-league. That spoke volumes of Woodward; he was one of a kind.

It's fair to say that of the players in this book to have played in non-league, Woodward's career – on paper, at least – is one of the most decorated; his list of achievements during his 25-year career puts him among the best to have ever graduated. There aren't many players who can say they've gone from playing in non-league to winning Olympic gold – Woodward was part of the victorious Great Britain team at the London Games of 1908, retaining the gold four years later in Stockholm – in a matter of months; that merely scratches the surface with Woodward's list of exploits. He rightly goes down among the greats and one of the finest players that the country has ever produced. For a player who spent much of his career either otherwise engaged, injured or working, and for a large part of it outside of the upper echelons of the football pyramid, to still go on to achieve what he did makes you wonder what he could have achieved if he'd have taken it seriously. The *crème de la crème* of non-league alumni.

Chris Smalling

The final player on this list, and someone who – until recently – was playing for one for the big names of European football, is Chris Smalling. When profiling the greatest sides in history on the continent, Italian giants Roma often feature. In the Italian peninsula and only a stone's throw – excuse the pun – from the River Tiber, the city of Rome is known for its famous Colosseum. There is a certain sense of poetic irony to think that from the humble beginnings of playing for the Stones, Smalling eventually found himself plying his trade in a city that is home to one of the most famous stone structures in history.

While Smalling was born in Greenwich, it was in Kent where he would start out his footballing career, moving to the area in the wake of losing his dad aged five. Right from the outset, Smalling was an avid football fan, both in a supporting capacity – growing up an Arsenal follower – and in a playing capacity for local youth sides Walderslade Boys and Chatham-based Lordswood. It was clear that he was immensely talented, not just at football but everything he tried. His former PE teacher Andy Anderson recalled to the *Daily Mail* how Smalling was 'a very good rugby player, talented at basketball, judo, and he even excelled in paintballing'. Indeed, he was a national champion in judo. Yet he opted to dedicate his time to football.

Smalling's ability saw him scouted at the age of 12, signing for Millwall. But his dream of becoming a professional saw its fair share of stumbling blocks, none more so than being unable to make it to training. Smalling's mum couldn't afford a car – she was having to raise Chris and his brother Jason as a single mother. Despite Smalling being a bright young grammar school lad, his mother wouldn't allow him to travel alone into London, so at 14 years of age he had to come to terms with the difficult decision that he would have to walk away from Millwall and make do with playing for his school – and county – instead.

That decision to turn down the Lions wasn't the end for Smalling; instead, it was just the start, a blessing in disguise, as he would opt to join Maidstone United, local to where he lived in Kent.

The architect of that decision was an individual called Peter Nott. A coach at the time, he was in the reserves with the Stones and liked what he saw in Smalling so was an advocate more for immediate progression into the first-team fold for the youngster. Nott signed him initially for the reserves, although he was fully aware of the fact he wasn't going to be there for long, and after he twisted the arm of the first-team manager to give Smalling an opportunity, the defender would indeed get one – and he grasped it with both hands. The picture of a fresh-faced Smalling in a Stones shirt has been widely publicised across social media and it was in his teens that he would be thrown in at the deep end with Maidstone. He made his senior debut in April 2007 in a Kent Senior Cup tie, and his league debut the following December. He wouldn't make himself as much of a fixture in the first team as he may have liked – enforced largely due to international duty with England Schoolboys representation, as well as suffering with injuries during that campaign – but he would still make his mark.

Smalling's break in the game could have gone so differently; he could have quite easily ended up back in non-league with Maidstone having not achieved anything. He initially signed for Middlesbrough in April 2008 off the back of his breakthrough for the Stones, and yet in double quick time he left due to being homesick and returned to his Kent roots. That could have derailed his bid to become a top player; not Chris. There are always buyers for top defenders in the game and Smalling was already looking like one of those. While one door closed in departing Middlesbrough, another one opened as he joined Fulham two months later.

Smalling's rise from there is well-documented, spending just a season and a bit with the Cottagers before joining Manchester United. It was a real badge of honour for Smalling. For all of the Red Devils' success over the years, signing players with non-league roots has not been their bread and butter. Instead, they have favoured promoting from within and signing from abroad. Given it wasn't a regular occurrence, Sir Alex Ferguson being happy to shell out on the youngster off the back of such little evidence was a testament to his potential. Smalling had made just 35 appearances, including those made for Maidstone, and only 13 in the Premier League with Fulham.

Smalling rewarded Ferguson with 323 United appearances in all competitions, winning two Premier Leagues, an FA Cup, a League Cup and a UEFA Europa League, along with 31 England caps. He then moved to Roma for five seasons, adding the UEFA Europa Conference League in 2021/22.

10

Non-League Lions

IN TERMS of the best players out of non-league, often the biggest accolade that can be bestowed upon them as a mark of their ability is to receive a call-up to the England C squad. The team has been running since 1979 and recognises the 'very best of non-league'. Largely made up of players from the National League and its equivalents, there has been a long list over the years of those to have pulled on the famous Non-League Lions jersey; some of the players already discussed earlier in the book have played for England C. I haven't even mentioned the likes of Sam Clucas, formerly of Nettleham; Ricky Holmes of Southend Manor, White Ensign and Chelmsford City; Charlie Goode of Hadley, AFC Hayes and Hendon; Aden Flint of Pinxton and Alfreton Town; James Constable of Cirencester Town and Chippenham Town. That is just five.

I could have written a whole book of players who have played for England C and gone on to forge successful careers in the game. Instead, I've opted to take a closer look at some of the more shining examples to represent the side.

Kieffer Moore

One of the top picks of those to have played for England C under long-term manager Paul Fairclough is Kieffer Moore. Given that Moore was born in Torquay, I feel somewhat deprived that he didn't make his name propelling his hometown club through the leagues. He started out in the youth academy at Torquay United and remained there until the age of 12. Representing the Gulls was very much a dream of his and he had earlier been a ballboy at Plainmoor, but his dream came crashing down in 2004 when United's academy system folded and he left to join local outfit Paignton Saints. He would turn out for the Saints until the age of 20; to think that he was still playing park football until then makes his journey all the more impressive. By 20, most footballers have already had their big break, but not Kieffer.

Moore had already shown plenty of promise at Torquay, then displayed that – and much more – for Paignton. From the outset, it was clear that he was an accomplished goalscorer. His exploits across two campaigns at the back end of his teen years particularly caught the eye of local sides, scoring 47 goals in 43 matches. That form saw Truro City take him on trial at Bolitho Park. At the time, the White Tigers had just lost towering former Plymouth and Torquay striker Martin Gritton, who had retired and decided to focus on post-football work as a result of moving to London. City needed a replacement for Gritton and turned to another ex-Gulls man in Moore to take up the mantle. Moore trialled against Falmouth Town and impressed City boss Lee Hodges, who was a player for Torquay when Moore was playing for Paignton Saints, and so had already seen his talents first hand. Truro's hope that Moore would act as a replacement for Gritton would certainly go to plan with the striker scoring 13 in 22, albeit they would, by Hodges' own admission, lose him out of the blue when he signed for divisional rivals Dorchester Town. In terms of location, Moore would – in the months to come – be happy that he did.

Moore would continue to score freely while with the Magpies, averaging almost a goal every other game in black and white to finish with 20 goals in 2012/13, while also working two other jobs: as a lifeguard and also as a personal trainer. At this point Moore had cemented his reputation as being one of the best local strikers, and his big break was just around the corner.

In 2013, Yeovil Town won promotion from League One, winning 2-1 against Brentford in the play-off final, and they began preparations for their first campaign in the second tier. Manager Gary Johnson – a man with a proven track record for signing from non-league – needed some extra firepower ahead of their Championship season. Moore was playing in Conference South, five levels below the Championship, so it was a huge gamble but it was one that Johnson was willing to take as he signed Moore on a two-year deal; a big vote of confidence in him.

Moore's time with the Glovers was hampered somewhat due to injury, and he was released by Paul Sturrock – who had earlier unearthed Craig Noone from Southport when taking him to Plymouth Argyle – in 2015. After a brief spell out in Norway with Viking, Moore would end up back in non-league after signing for Forest Green Rovers, where he was playing when he won his England C cap. In the 2015/16 campaign, he would feature sparingly as Mark Cooper's side reached the National League play-off final. The following year would also see Moore used only occasionally, and yet while he failed to make himself a fixture at Forest Green it would be that season – out on loan at Torquay United – when he would really make a name for himself. It was only a brief loan, but five goals in four games, including a hat-trick against Solihull Moors, and some impressive performances meant that despite Torquay being cash-strapped, boss Kevin Nicholson agreed a deal for the forward. The eagle-eyed among you will recognise that he didn't go on to sign for United; instead Mick McCarthy dashed the Gulls' hopes by coming in with an 11th-hour bid to prise him away to the Championship's Ipswich Town in January 2017. Progression with the Tractor Boys would stutter, and it would only be upon joining Rotherham United on loan and joining Barnsley permanently that Moore would finally excel in the EFL. A subsequent spell with Wigan Athletic would see him really showcase his talents and with it receive his first call-up for Wales, qualifying through his Welsh grandfather. He's not looked back since, eventually signing for Bournemouth in 2022 then winning promotion to the Premier League and going on to score in the top flight. To think that a fruitful spell at the bottom end of the National League for a struggling Torquay United side has paved the way for the successful career at both domestic and international level; a testament to the value of getting out and playing minutes.

Jamal Lowe

Another name highly synonymous with the England C side is Jamal Lowe. Anyone you ask about England C is often quick to point out the rise of Lowe and the success that he has had after playing for the Non-League Lions. In

2017 he was playing in non-league, yet fast forward just six years and he was in the Premier League; there's not many bigger adverts than that. As far as doing the hard yards is concerned, Lowe has one of the most extensive experiences of playing in non-league of any player in this book; from the point he first became a senior player in 2011, he'd go on to spend six years in non-league. He had eight clubs during that period and yet in the time since he has only had six.

Lowe's career has gone full circle; he started off with Queens Park Rangers aged 14, and fast forward 15 years he played for the Hoops in the Championship. He didn't make the grade with Rangers initially, moving to Farnborough for a brief period before signing for Barnet; it was with the Bees that he'd find his way into senior football. Lowe would progress into the first team and got his chance to prove himself in 2010/11 in the Herts Senior in what was a chaotic season for the club, with four managers and finishing 22nd in League Two, but a useful one for Lowe himself. He would continue to play predominantly in the youth team, but in 2012 got an opportunity to show what he was about on a more consistent basis under new manager Edgar Davids. However, the Bees were relegated to the Conference Premier that year and it would ultimately see Lowe's first-team opportunities limited; he would embark on a tour of non-league instead.

Lowe would hardly rip up any trees in loans at Hayes & Yeading, Boreham Wood, Hitchin Town, St Albans City, Farnborough and Hemel Hempstead Town. Even in deciding to sign permanently for two of those there was seemingly little to show for his efforts; a total of 91 games and only 17 goals. It was hardly 'future Premier League player' material. Yet his defining years were to be just round the corner as he signed for Alan Dowson's Hampton & Richmond Borough in 2015; a decision that would ultimately be the making of his professional career. With the Beavers, Lowe firmly found his best form over back-to-back seasons in which he'd hit double figures; all the more impressive given that he only joined after 11 games in one season and stayed until the January of the following campaign, yet he still hit 37 goals. His exploits for Hampton & Richmond would ultimately be enough to earn him England C recognition with an appearance against Estonia in Tallinn, indeed scoring in the game. That day, Kieffer Moore, Blair Turgott, Cheye Alexander, Ethan Pinnock, Alex Woodyard and Elliott Whitehouse all played; all went on to play in the EFL.

It wouldn't be long before Lowe would get his big break, with Portsmouth calling for his services. Fellow forward and fellow Beaver Nicke Kabamba followed Lowe to Fratton Park, and the pair won promotion to League One in 2016/17. Since then, Lowe has gone on to have a successful career; winning promotion to – and playing in – the Premier League with Bournemouth, as well as representing Jamaica at international level. Kabamba, meanwhile, remains a non-league player as of the time of writing, with Barnet, and has followed in the footsteps of his former strike partner in winning England C recognition. Lowe has had a stellar career and more than realised the ambitions he had as a 16-year-old with Queens Park Rangers to be a professional footballer.

Ethan Pinnock

Another of the best players to have pulled on the Non-League Lions jersey is Ethan Pinnock. Pinnock's journey is arguably more impressive than many in this book, given the speed of his rise to the top; at the time of writing the defender is playing regularly in the Premier League for Brentford, yet only four years before reaching the top flight he had been playing in the National League. He is certainly what can be described as a late bloomer – at 19 he was only just starting out in men's football and at 23 he was leaving Isthmian League Premier Division side Dulwich Hamlet to join Forest Green Rovers. To think that at 24 he had only just moved to the EFL and then at 31 he had already made over 100 appearances in the top flight, his achievements are all the more unique.

Pinnock's youth upbringing was sporadic to say the least; he played for as many different clubs in five years as a youngster as he has in the 14 years as a first-team player since. It was Glebe where Pinnock's football upbringing started, playing in the academy at Foxbury Avenue. The rise that was to come should perhaps not have come as a surprise, with Glebe having played a key role in the development of a handful of players who have since gone on to bigger and better things – Emile Smith-Rowe started out there, and Lyle Taylor and Manny Monthe also count Glebe as the roots of their careers.

While Pinnock's rise to the top may have suffered something of a late start, his youth career certainly took flight early on, as by the age of nine he was spotted by Millwall's academy. He spent six years with the Lions before he was let go, with the London club having fears that he wasn't of the physical build to go far. Unbeknownst to Millwall, Pinnock would – in the wake of his release – go and stand in a metaphorical pot of soil; I think they call it a growth spurt!

Pinnock would not let that rejection get to him as he was eager to one day make it in the professional game. He was part of a footballing family, and so was around that environment all the time. Ethan's brother Sol was a player himself in non-league, while his cousin is Nyron Nosworthy, who had played for Sunderland in the Premier League and Sheffield United in the Championship. There was likely a bit of pressure to follow in their footsteps and forge his own career.

After his release from Millwall, Pinnock would find it difficult to settle at just one club, with brief spells with Fisher Athletic and AFC Wimbledon, who were local to where he grew up in south London. It was thanks to Sol that Ethan would finally settle down. At the time, Sol was on the books of Dulwich Hamlet, and after Ethan had departed AFC Wimbledon he managed to get his brother a spot in the Dulwich youth setup.

What made Pinnock's rise all the more impressive was that he started out as a winger, and it was only off the back of a loan spell with Kent-based Holmesdale that he would hold down a position as a defender. He ended up being used as a utility player while with the Dalers, and on his return to Dulwich he underwent the transformation into the player that he is today: a far cry from the lad that Millwall had released. Dulwich Hamlet manager Gavin Rose decided to play Pinnock as a centre-back because of his now large frame, allowing him to follow in the footsteps of Nyron Nosworthy, who himself had been a decent centre-back at a higher level.

Dulwich Hamlet had seen top players come out of their academy before. Perhaps their proudest graduate was George Elokobi, who played in the same team as Rose, giving the future manager an early insight into what a promising centre-back looked like. Pinnock had to bide his time to make a mark in the first team, making only 15 appearances in 2010/11 as well as spending time with Holmesdale. Coincidentally, Pinnock's first game for Holmesdale was against former club Fisher Athletic. Upon joining Holmesdale, Pinnock was billed as a left-back, but his spell was characterised as being one of adaptation in which he showcased his versatility; he played in what was then a more natural left-wing role and even spent time playing as a forward. It is no wonder, therefore, that Pinnock is such an intelligent defender; he knows how to play as a striker, and understands their game.

Pinnock's first few campaigns in Hamlet colours were hallmarked by competing for promotion. In 2010/11 they finished in the Isthmian League Division One South play-offs while the following season saw them go one step further and win the title; Pinnock made 28 appearances during the latter. The 2014/15 campaign was where he really began to make a name for himself; by this stage he had pinned down the role as a centre-back. Not only had he developed physically but also technically, and he played in every league game as Hamlet finished fourth.

Pinnock had marked himself out as one of the best young defenders in non-league by this point, and in particular caught the eye with his physical stature and technical ability with the ball at his feet; so seldom were both present in the same player, showing his unique value. He marked the 2014/15 campaign with individual awards. The Hamlets conceded 51 goals on their way to a play-off finish – with only Maidstone United conceding fewer – and Pinnock was rewarded for that by being named as the supporters', players' and manager's player of the year. He was by far and away the standout player for Hamlet, having also established himself as the captain. After missing out in the play-offs in 2015, Pinnock again led Hamlet into the post-season event, only to again fall short. However, while Hamlet may have missed out on their aim of getting promoted and climbing the leagues, there would be no such shortcomings for Pinnock, as he would make the step up, to the National League. It was abundantly clear that he was operating at least a level above the one he had been playing at with Dulwich Hamlet, and he would get the chance to do so.

In 2015/16 Forest Green Rovers finished in the National League play-off places; they eventually lost out 3-1 in the final at Wembley to Grimsby Town. Under Mark Cooper, they were eager to go one better the following season, so needed to add one or two extra players to their squad to bridge the gap so Cooper moved Pinnock. The manager had also delved lower into the non-league market the previous season when landing Kieffer Moore, and Pinnock was the latest on the production line into the Nailsworth outfit. Cooper was sufficiently encouraged by his displays for Dulwich Hamlet that he convinced Forest Green Rovers to pay out for Pinnock; on reflection, while Rovers had not progressed from non-league at that stage, the relatively hefty fee would end up being one worth paying.

Pinnock's move to the New Lawn would represent a key landmark in his still fledgling career. One of the major milestones in the journey of any aspiring young player in non-league is the transition from part-time to full-time football, and joining Forest Green was very much the realisation that this was now his job; he had to make it work. In many ways, it was also his chance of becoming a man. He'd enjoyed his apprenticeship floating around non-league academies and first-team setups; this was his chance to really kick on and realise his potential. A London boy, it would see him move away from home, too. It was make or break and luckily, it would be the former. Non-league is awash with good players; to make it at the top level you need something different. Right from the outset, Cooper made it clear that Pinnock was someone he felt could go far in the game. He is more than qualified to make that judgement; his dad Terry was a top player for Leeds United and England in his heyday, so Mark had been in and around top players even before he got into football.

Pinnock was indeed a special player, and what made him so was the combination of qualities that he had; certainly a unique skillset the likes of which is so seldom seen, especially in non-league. To begin with, he had the obvious height and physicality that was a necessity for top-level defenders. But he was also quick, comfortable on the ball and most of all left-footed; that combination was very rare, and the same combination that saw Tyrone Mings's accelerated ascent up the pyramid. Pinnock's arrival saw Cooper opt for the use of a back three, citing his abilities as the perfect fit.

Quite quickly Cooper realised that his trust in Pinnock was well-placed. Pinnock would make a total of 45 appearances in all competitions for Rovers as Cooper led Forest Green to the play-offs once more in 2016/17. Building up to the play-offs, Pinnock had suffered with injury; such was his importance to the side he was brought back into the fold for the end-of-season eliminators – starting the final – and that decision proved key. Pinnock was superb against Tranmere Rovers at Wembley, with his height and aerial ability allowing Forest Green to cope with the bombardment into their box, and they emerged 3-1 victors. In the space of a year, Pinnock had gone from playing at Champion Hill to being a champion at the home of English football; it was certainly a poetic rise.

While Pinnock was a key cog of the Rovers backline, even Cooper would have perhaps been a little frustrated to see him spend just the one season at the New Lawn. His displays were so good that Championship outfit Barnsley came calling for his services having finished 14th in the previous campaign, and in the summer of 2017 they made a concerted effort to invest in their squad, particularly in the defensive department. In 2016/17 Barnsley had conceded 67 goals in the league; only three teams had let in more. They also failed to adequately replace Alfie Mawson, who had joined Swansea City for around £500,000 the previous summer.

In came Jason McCarthy (Southampton), Matty Pearson (Accrington Stanley) and Liam Lindsay (Partick Thistle), with Pinnock following suit as very much the jewel in the crown. However, it would be a frustrating first season at Oakwell for Pinnock following his £1m move as he would only play 11 times due to injury struggles, while Barnsley were relegated to League One. Yet his second season was very different; like *Mission Impossible: Fallout, Mad Max: Road Warrior, Captain America: The Winter Soldier*. You get the gist: all sequels superior to the one that came before it. Pinnock went up another gear.

Having shaken off injury concerns, Pinnock played every single League One game for the Tykes in 2018/19 and helped them to an instant return to the Championship. And as well as ending the campaign with a promotion medal round his neck, he added the supporters' player of the year trophy, a League One Team of the Year inclusion, a place in the PFA League One Team of the Year, and a League One Player of the Month award. Pinnock didn't just impress; he was arguably pound-for-pound the best centre-half in the EFL.

It was no surprise that summer saw him subject to lots of interest from higher-level clubs; he was coming into his prime years at 26 and tall, strong, quick, good on the ball and adept in the air. Thomas Frank of Brentford knocked loudest; Pinnock was the exact type of player they wanted to go for. The Bees had a track record of top recruitment under owner Matthew Benham and Pinnock fitted the bill perfectly. After stabilising in 2018/19, the 2019/20 season was one where Brentford decided to loosen the purse strings and bring in the next wave of talent in a mission to get to the Premier League. Arriving were Christian Norgaard (Fiorentina), David Raya (Blackburn Rovers), Pontus Jansson (Leeds United), Mathias Jensen (Celta Vigo) and Bryan Mbeumo (Troyes).

Pinnock was also on that list, signing for around £3m. It proved to be a successful first season for Pinnock in Brentford colours and once again, he was getting the taste of a promotion campaign. It ended in defeat to Fulham at Wembley in the play-off final, but as he had learned during his time with Dulwich Hamlet, it was time to get up off the canvas and go again. That he did; the Bees bounced back and won promotion at Wembley a year later, beating Swansea City

2-0. Pinnock bagged himself a second PFA Team of the Year inclusion as the pick of the defenders in the Championship.

Pinnock has continued to ply his trade in the Premier League to this day as a regular for Brentford. In 2021, his continued rise saw him rewarded with a call-up to the Jamaica squad, qualifying via his father. At the time of writing he had won 19 caps for the Reggae Boyz, providing a poetic development to his career. Nyron Nosworthy made 14 appearances for Jamaica, and ten years on from joining Dulwich Hamlet as a youngster, Pinnock achieved his aim of following in Nosworthy's footsteps as a Premier League footballer and an international; his cousin would be proud.

* * *

In March 2024, I was lucky enough to make the trip to Llanelli to watch England C against Wales C in their annual fixture. During my trip, I got the opportunity to sit down with assistant manager Mick Payne, who has worked as Paul Fairclough's right-hand man for more than 20 years. He has played a part in coaching some of the very best players to have graced a non-league pitch during that time, overseeing in excess of 300 who have since gone on to play in either the EFL or the Scottish Premier League. Payne kindly offered to discuss his time with England C, some of the players he has had the privilege of coaching, and the importance that the team still has as the pinnacle for non-league players.

How important a platform do you feel England C is for players to showcase what they are about?
'I have been doing this job for over 20 years and I have done in excess of 70 internationals. The number of players

that have come through with us and gone on to have good careers at the top of the game is exceptional. Myself and Paul believe that England C is the rubber stamp of getting players to the next level. There are a number of top scouts who always come to the games, and they see the players playing international football. It sets their careers up for success.'

Do you think that England C is viewed as a badge of honour to differentiate good players from the upper echelon of players in non-league?

'Without a doubt. It is a massive honour for the players to go away with their England cap and shirt. It is something that they can never have taken away from them. The memory will be a little bit sweeter if they manage to get a result when they do represent their country, but just that experience is something that will live with them for ever.'

You have coached so many top players over the years during your time at England C. If you had to pick a standout player – the best you have coached, if you will – then who would it be?

'That is a very difficult question; I can't name just one. I think all of them have been exceptional. As you know, I am officially the assistant manager of this team now; however, I have been primarily the goalkeeping coach for a number of years prior to that. I have had some wonderful goalkeepers, and every one of them has been brilliant. If any of them are reading this, I would like them to know that I have enjoyed every single minute and it was a pleasure to coach them.'

How difficult is it for you to pick a squad when there are no doubt so many players that you want to give an opportunity to?

'It is more than difficult. In terms of the National League and downwards, there is an incredible talent pool and to pick only 16 players is no easy task. Paul has done a fantastic job over the years to pick a team and get them to gel. We have opted to pick one per club, and I think that way we are able to strike the right balance between recognising a whole range of talent rather than just highlighting one or two teams.'

Ryan de Havilland scored the winner for England C in the game at Altrincham in 2023, and he got a move to the EFL off the back of that. Does that highlight the pathway that England C has for players to set up their careers?

'Without a doubt. You've said it there; it is the pathway that it has for players to go and have successful careers in the game. When they play for England C, they are noticed. Ephron Mason-Clark was at Peterborough United and he also played for the England C team. He got a move to Coventry City off the back of that, and so it just goes to show what can be achieved for players that pull on the England C jersey.'

11

Modern-Day Successes

I HAVE trawled back through the archives to look at various players and managers who have graced non-league before graduating to the big time. Such a path continues to be trodden today, with so many of the players currently at the top level of the game citing non-league roots.

Dan Burn

One player whose career has gone full circle via a tour of non-league close to hometown Blyth is Dan Burn. The defender is excelling with Newcastle United at the time of writing, and is perhaps remembered more so for the fact he only has four fingers on one hand than he is as someone who has graced a non-league pitch. Yet he spent time playing in the Conference Premier prior to sealing a big move to Fulham in the Premier League.

In the 2022 January window, Newcastle signed Burn from fellow Premier League side Brighton & Hove Albion, and in the process sealed his return after he'd left the club 19 years previous. As a Magpies supporter from young, he dreamed that he would one day play at St James' Park and emulate his idols; even he would perhaps not expect it to take around 20 years for him to get his first start in the famous black and white stripes. He did so against Aston Villa that February.

Burn's dream would seemingly come crashing down at the age of 11, released by the Magpies and he had to turn to non-league and play academy football. It was with two of Blyth's teams – Town and Spartans – that Burn would spend most of his teens, as well as a short spell with New Hartley, a small village south of Blyth. Burn later worked in a supermarket, and football – while still very much his passion – was a hobby, although he still dreamed that one day he could make it in the game.

In 2009, a chance viewing would give Burn a route in. At the time, he was very much a regular for Asda FC, capable of playing as a centre cashier, but it wasn't his proficiency on the bakery counter or in the milk aisle that earned him his big break. Instead, he caught the attention of a scout while playing for Blyth Spartans, and so convinced were they that he was the real deal that Darlington signed him ahead of the 2009/10 campaign. This was at a time when they were suffering with major financial problems, going into administration three times within nine years as a result of spiralling and unserviceable costs required to finance their new stadium. In 2009 especially, the Quakers very much needed all the help they could get, and while only 16 Burn was hurled straight into the deep end. Would he sink or swim?

After that spell with the Quakers, it is fair to say that he swam. Burn earned a big money move – amid lots of interest from elsewhere – to Fulham in the summer of 2011.

In December 2009, Darlington manager Mark Cooper was quoted as saying, 'If I were a Premier League manager,

I would sign him straight away whatever the cost.' The Cottagers took up that offer and Burn forged a reputation for being versatile enough to play all over the pitch – 'in defence, midfield or in attack' according to Cooper. It was on the left of the defence where he would make his mark, but initially he would have to bide his time and develop in the reserve team. Successful loans with Yeovil Town and Birmingham City would see him earn a move to Wigan Athletic, then on to Brighton. He has since gone on to play for his boyhood club, and remains there to the time of writing.

The 2024/25 season saw Burn immediately establish himself as a regular in the Magpies' side, and in March 2025 the towering defender won his first England cap as part of new boss Thomas Tuchel's first Three Lions squad; his debut came in a World Cup qualifier against Albania, playing the full 90 minutes. Better still, just a matter of days earlier Burn had started – and scored – for Newcastle in the final of the League Cup, helping the Magpies to lift their first major domestic trophy since 1955.

* * *

Mark Cooper has managed several of the players featured in this book and I had the privilege of speaking with him during the 2023/24 campaign about the role that he has played in their development.

You managed Dan Burn at Darlington. What were your first impressions?

'From the moment I saw him, I thought that he'd play in the Premier League. He was a scholar. We quickly put him into the first-team squad. I spoke to a number of Premier

League managers that I knew at the time, and there were a number that were interested, but Fulham were the ones that jumped. They paid about half a million for him.'

Why do you think he has been able to go all the way when some of the other talented players you have managed haven't?

'He had a really good family around him to keep him grounded. He had a brilliant work ethic; he wanted to work hard and wanted to be a top player. Nothing was going to get in the way of that. He is single-minded. When he got in the team, I think I sent him out on loan somewhere to just go and get a few stitches and broken nose to toughen him up, and he gobbled that up. Because he was so tall and didn't have lightning pace, I think that made him concentrate on his defending and ensure he didn't get isolated.'

You signed Ethan Pinnock at Forest Green Rovers. How did that signing come about, and what made you sign him?

'I had a tip-off from Stuart Cash [father of Aston Villa's Matty Cash]. He rang me and said had I seen this kid playing at Dulwich Hamlet; I hadn't. So, I went and saw him play in the play-offs for Dulwich Hamlet against East Thurrock United and I said to the owner of Forest Green Rovers straight away that we had to sign him. To begin with he was very raw. He was skinny and lean. I think we paid £5,000 for him. He was like a sponge; he took to it straight away. Some players at the level you have to tell them things three or four times before they get it; with Ethan, he got it after you told him once.'

Why do you feel Ethan Pinnock has gone on to have the career he has?

'He is athletic. He is 6ft 3in. He can play with the ball, is quick, can defend, and is aggressive; if you put all of those attributes together into a left-footed centre-back then you have got a top player regardless of the level. He only spent one season with us at Rovers, but you knew straight away he was going to leave us to go on to bigger and better things. I think if you asked any of the boys in that team and the staff they'd say that he was the one. I knew after five games that we wouldn't keep him long.'

You have brought through so many good players. Are you always actively looking to try and find the next Ethan Pinnock?

'Absolutely. I had Liam Kitching [at Forest Green]. He is doing really well; he's at Coventry City. I also have Jake Wannell here now [at Yeovil] and he is also a left-footed centre-back that I believe can go on and play in the Championship. The way that I like my teams to play, the left centre-back is really important as they have to be good on the ball, and so naturally it lends itself to me developing top players in that position.'

You had Kieffer Moore at Forest Green Rovers. You sent him out on loan to Torquay United before he got his big move, but did you always know that there was a player there with him or did it surprise you?

'Kieffer Moore came to see me and said he wanted to move to Torquay. His girlfriend wanted to move to Torquay and he wanted to settle in the area. At Rovers, we had four good strikers; Christian Doidge, Rhys Murphy, Matt Tubbs and

Kieffer Moore. They were all battling for places. Kieffer came and saw me saying that he wanted to leave; I didn't want to let him go, but he pleaded. We had agreed a deal of £25,000, and reluctantly let him leave if it was going to make him happy. That afternoon, I got a call from his agent and asked if that asking price was the same for a Championship club. I was a bit confused, as Moore had said to me he wanted to go to Torquay, but yet his agent said that there was an offer from Ipswich Town which was miles away. We then had to do a different deal with them, and we had to negotiate a good fee, and he has since gone on and done well.'

He was close to joining Torquay. Did the fact he decided to change his mind and go to sign for Ipswich Town actually help him in that he put his career first rather than his want to be closer to home with his girlfriend?
'Absolutely. Kieffer was a great lad; he worked hard and had a good family around him. You could say that I got that one wrong, but I had three other strikers that were all scoring goals. I perhaps didn't think he would go on to do as well as he has, but I am so pleased for him.'

You have had lots of good strikers work under you that have perhaps – at the time, or at one stage in their career – been better goalscorers than Kieffer. Why do you think he has been able to go on and play in the Premier League and for his country, when the others haven't?
'His attributes. He's massive, good in the air, rapidly quick and can score goals. I think players – and they are all different – get to an age where the penny drops and they become a good player. For Kieffer, it came slightly later in

his career, but it has certainly clicked and he has since gone on to be an international footballer. When you compare him to Christian Doidge – who is the same age as Kieffer Moore – I think that at the time you would have perhaps put Doidge as the better of the two; he was in great form, scoring goals, aggressive, had decent pace, brilliant in both boxes. Yet, I think Doidge made the wrong move at the wrong time; he moved to Bolton Wanderers for a million, and they went under with Ken Anderson. The move fell apart, and then I think the move to Scotland went wrong. I think Kieffer Moore got the right move, and I think Christian got the wrong move.'

* * *

Jarrod Bowen

When Jarrod Bowen ran through on goal and slotted home past Pietro Terracciano in the last seconds of the 2023 Europa Conference League Final, while there would have no doubt been jubilation back home in West Ham, there would have been even louder cheers from Herefordshire. It was the Hammers' first trophy in 43 years and the third European trophy in their history, and the match-winner was a player who had graduated out of the Hereford United academy only nine years previous. From playing at Edgar Street as a teenager, scoring a winning goal in a European final in Prague was quite the journey.

Bowen would spend just the 2013/14 season in the first team with the Bulls and yet while United struggled, being expelled from the Conference Premier upon its conclusion and going out in the first rounds of the FA Cup and FA Trophy, the fresh-faced forward provided a sole silver lining in an otherwise cloudy campaign. In terms of having to learn quickly, that season was certainly a challenging one and very much character-building for Bowen. United were struggling financially amid ownership problems and so didn't have the benefit of investing in their side; as such, aged 17 he was handed an opportunity in the first team under Peter Beadle. The Bulls realised that Bowen was a future talent who would go far – having been on trial with Aston Villa and Cardiff City – and offered him a three-year deal despite their off-field struggles, but he would depart the club that summer and join Hull City.

A fruitful spell with the Tigers paved the way for a big-money move to West Ham in January 2020. He has since become a Premier League captain, European trophy winner, England international and scorer, gone to a major tournament with the Three Lions, and followed in the footsteps of legendary Hammers Scott Parker, Paolo Di Canio, Julian Dicks, Billy Bonds, Bobby Moore, Geoff Hurst and Martin Peters in winning the club's player of the year award.

Tyrone Mings

If you asked any football fan to name a Premier League player who has played in non-league, if the answer wasn't Jamie Vardy, it might well be Tyrone Mings. Often wheeled out as one of the poster boys for the success of non-league, Mings is a testament to the platform that non-league can provide to aspiring players and how it acts as an oasis for those deemed seemingly not good enough through the Premier League academy route.

It shouldn't have come as a surprise that Mings would end up making a successful career in the game, with his dad Adie having been a non-league player. It is somewhat poetic that Tyrone got his big break – or at least made a name for himself – with Chippenham Town, as that was where Adie started out his career and would go on to be a club legend in playing and managerial capacities. It is widely publicised that Tyrone played for Chippenham in the embryonic years of his career. Perhaps even more publicised is the fact that while playing semi-professionally, he was a mortgage advisor.

However, it wasn't actually with the Bluebirds that he made his bow in senior football – instead it was with Yate Town. There were always hopes – despite having turned to non-league – that he was destined to be a professional. He was in the academy with Southampton, a club with a track record in youth development, and so there was clearly talent; even at the age of 18 he was a towering physical presence. It was with the Bluebells and then the Bluebirds that he was able to overcome the rejection of being turned down by Eastleigh – an unsuccessful trial after leaving Southampton in 2009 – and he was later able to realise his ambitions, and things have worked out for him since.

Mings got his move to the Football League in December 2012 with Ipswich Town, making his Championship debut on the final day of the 2012/13 season. He impressed over the next two years, signing for Bournemouth in the Premier League for £8m in 2015, but injury problems restricted his appearances on the south coast and he joined Aston Villa on loan in January 2019.

Helping Villa win promotion in the Championship play-off final, he joined permanently that summer, playing in the following season's League Cup Final, becoming an England international, playing in the European

Championship of 2021 and establishing himself as a consistent top-flight performer.

In the conversation for the Mount Rushmore of non-league alumni, Mings definitely deserves a mention.

Kellen Fisher

The timing at which I write this almost mandates that I talk about the next player in this chapter – emerging Norwich City prospect Kellen Fisher. Such has been Fisher's meteoric rise to stardom that even by the age of 20, the full-back had developed far beyond simply a 'prospect' and had instead become a staple of a Norwich team competing at the top end of the Championship. So impressive has Fisher been that there are calls for him to gain senior international recognition, with many expecting that he will eclipse the efforts of highly regarded former Canary Max Aarons. Having watched Fisher live several times, I can vouch for the legitimacy of such praise; he's a special talent.

In unearthing the roots of his footballing journey, it once again takes us to Hayes Lane; Fisher came off the Bromley conveyor belt. They have also been responsible for producing Ben Krauhaus, who made the move to Premier League Brentford in the middle of 2023. As such, it is perhaps not a surprise that Fisher has gone on to forge a reputation quickly; youth development is one thing that Bromley get right.

Fisher's early development is deep-rooted in non-league and his first loan spell was with Welling United. However, that could be filed in the category of first-loan-itis as there was not a lot to write home about, and it helped more with character building than anything else. His first real taste of men's football came with Cray Wanderers. Wanderers – who shared a ground with Bromley – took Fisher on loan in late October 2022. He would only spend a month with the Wands, however. You didn't need to tell Bromley twice; they liked what they saw, with many rave reviews over his performances. Loan in October 2022. New contract by February 2023. It's almost as if Bromley boss Andy Woodman – who had been around the game long enough – knew a player when he saw one; Fisher is a proper player.

It was quickly evident that Fisher was a talent, and after his recall from Cray, Woodman immediately integrated him into the first team as the Ravens went on to finish 2022/23 as National League play-off semi-finalists. Fisher became a regular, making a total of 25 appearances. Such was his impact that Norwich came circling for his signature in June 2023. Talk about a rapid rise. A year earlier he had been on the periphery of a sixth-tier winged outfit in Welling, the Wings, yet now he was signing for a second-tier winged fellow in the Canaries.

It has to be said that Fisher's time spent playing in non-league at an early age has played an integral part in developing technical proficiencies that are now very much the hallmark of his playing style. By no means the biggest, Fisher was always going to be up against it when it came to the physical side of the game, especially in the well-documented rough and tumble of non-league. As such, the experience of being plunged into men's football as early as 18 years of age was a godsend in giving him the confidence to play. Fisher was initially a swashbuckling wing-back in Woodman's Bromley side, and then with Norwich City he became a flashy, modern-day, inverted full-back under Johannes Hoff Thorup.

It is perhaps not surprising that Fisher is so proficient with the ball at his feet; he reportedly played as a striker in his youth days, finishing as top scorer for his local amateur side in the London Youth League for four consecutive seasons. In his mid-teens, Fisher was deployed as a midfielder, and it was only upon joining the Bromley academy that he became a right-back. He has always had a tendency to be more proficient with the ball than you would naturally attribute to defenders, yet I do feel that a lot of credit has to go to his time in non-league and the exposure he had in almost forcing his hand to develop that side of his game.

Handed a new four-year contract only 14 appearances into his City career, Fisher has also won England under-20 caps. His current deal is set to run out in 2028. If he continues to develop at the rate he is, chances are he will be added to the list of non-league to Premier League alumni in due course and may well not still be a Canary by then.

Dominic Calvert-Lewin

While his time in non-league may not have been the most exhaustive of spells, it played a key part in Dominic Calvert-Lewin's rise to being a recognised Premier League footballer.

Prior to joining Stalybridge Celtic on loan in December 2014, Calvert-Lewin was actually a midfielder, but the Greater Manchester side made use of his height and played him as a makeshift striker, giving us the birth of the bustling, robust frontman we see today. If his height was the starting point, his obvious proficiency in front of goal to follow would cement his newfound position.

Calvert-Lewin started out in the academy at Sheffield United, joining them aged just eight, and managed to make his way through to the first team; he signed his first professional deal in April 2015 with the Blades already confident that he had the ability to make it.

Very few players start out in an academy and then get into the first team. In 2021, less than 0.5 per cent of young players in an academy would make it as a professional. Previous to that, earlier estimates had suggested that the figure was merely 0.012 per cent, which makes Calvert-Lewin's rise all the more incredible. Nine years of having to prove himself, get new deals, pass fresh intakes, and convince people that he was worth taking forward; the Blades were pretty confident – quite clearly – that Calvert-Lewin was in the 0.012 per cent. They weren't wrong.

In January 2014 he got his first taste of the first-team environment in featuring as an unused substitute in the FA Cup as Sheffield United played Aston Villa. While he didn't get on to the pitch, it marked a real light bulb moment for the youngster; he was within touching distance of his big break. His progress did not go unnoticed, either; in 2014, he was named in League Football Education's 'The 11', a concept – still in place to this day – to highlight some of the best young talent in the game. If he ever needed it, Calvert-Lewin's inclusion was a big tick against his name. Looking back on it, as important as manager Nigel Clough's willingness to throw him in the deep end was key in kick-starting his career, his loan spell in Conference North was equally – if not more so – vital.

While he never had the opportunity to fully establish himself as a regular for the Blades, his displays out on loan with Stalybridge and Northampton Town – plus the 'noise' he was making around the first team at Bramall Lane – were enough for Everton to come calling in August 2016 for an initial £1.5m fee. On 7 August 2015 he'd been embarking on his second professional loan with the Cobblers, yet just over a year later he was a Premier League player.

Calvert-Lewin's time as a Toffee has more recently been blighted by injury – a case of 'what could have been' perhaps – yet the Sheffield-born striker has still gone on to forge a top-flight career that has seen him amass just shy of 300 appearances. He's also received international recognition at under-20 and under-21 level for England, and made his senior international debut in 2020. To date, Calvert-Lewin has scored four goals for the Three Lions, with his first in his maiden appearance against Wales. He remains a Toffee at the time of writing.

Solly March and Ollie Tanner

At the time of writing, Solly March is still plying his trade in the Premier League, with Brighton & Hove Albion. There is poetic irony in March's story as he started out with Crystal Palace from 11 until the age of 13, and yet has gone on to write himself into club legend status with the Eagles' A23 derby neighbours; there is something awfully pleasing about that if you are Albion.

March moved from Palace and signed for local side Eastbourne Borough – the place of his birth – in their youth team soon after. He would spend a year with the Sports, before he would again be on the move to join

Lewes, where he got his big break after just a single game. He made his debut at the age of 17 and was being courted by top sides. Newcastle United and Sunderland were both reportedly in for the youngster, with the former offering him a trial, while Brighton put in an offer for him, as did Millwall. For March, the move to Brighton was always going to be the most appealing, not just because it was local, but his dad Steve had earlier played for the club so it was a chance to follow in family footsteps.

Since then, March has helped the Seagulls to establish themselves as members of the pack chasing European qualification via the Premier League. The winger has had some injury problems in recent campaigns, but his versatility and adaptability to play in different systems and as part of an increasingly swashbuckling and stylish Brighton team has made him a fixture in making just shy of 300 appearances across 13 seasons in their colours. He first joined with Brighton competing in the top six in the Championship, and remains on their books as they challenge for the top six in the Premier League.

March is just one recent example of a player to have come through with Lewes and gone on to play at a higher level; in 2022, winger Ollie Tanner – formerly of Bromley and more prominently the Rooks – got a high-profile transfer to Cardiff City. Tanner's pathway in his still very embryonic career is like so many of the players in this book; early experience of playing in a top-level academy, not making the grade, and having to turn to the solace of non-league to rebuild his career. He has most certainly done that, going from the seventh tier to the second.

While not making the transition from the academy to the first teams with the club(s) he started his career at, it is not surprising that Tanner has ultimately realised the extent of his abilities having started out at Charlton Athletic before going on to play in youth football at Arsenal. The Addicks have a long tradition of developing young players of real calibre: Joe Gomez, Ademola Lookman, Ezri Konsa and Joe Aribo to name just four. Then you've got Arsenal, who've likewise provided a springboard for setting up so many successful careers. As such, despite not being signed on professional terms with either club, there was certainly grounds to suggest that Tanner had talent.

After being released by Arsenal, Tanner joined the Bromley academy and managed to make the transition into the first team while signing professional forms at Hayes Lane in 2019. He would only go on to make a couple of appearances before he departed in 2022 to join Lewes. There the saying that 'you need to take one step back to take two forwards', and in dropping down from the National League to the Isthmian League Premier Division the apparent upturn in fortunes certainly provided evidence of that; it would be a decision that would prove to be transformative.

The manager of Lewes at the time was Tony Russell, someone with a good track record of producing players and in particular those of an attacking nature, and it's fair to say that Tanner remains Russell's proudest alumnus of his coaching tenure; his game would go from strength to strength under Russell's leadership. He developed a reputation quickly for being one of the standout players in the Isthmian Premier Division, hitting double figures in 2021/22, at which point the Dripping Pan was awash with Premier League and EFL scouts all clamouring to get a look at this latest non-league hotshot.

The major light bulb moment for Tanner came in 2022 when he was the subject of a bid from Tottenham Hotspur. For any aspiring young non-league player, you would think that the lure of Tottenham would be too good to turn down. Not for Tanner; he made the brave decision to say no to Spurs, plus other clubs who also came calling, and it was only when Cardiff offered him a trial that he finally decided to spread his wings and make the move away from the Dripping Pan. A smart move if you ask me. Rather than being discarded in the scrapheap of academy football, Tanner became a part of the first team with the Bluebirds.

In 2022 – shortly after signing for Cardiff City – Tony Russell did an interview in which he was hugely glowing of Tanner's abilities. We have already talked about Alfie May earlier in this book, another player Russell worked with earlier in his coaching career. Tanner was – in Russell's own words – 'on another level'. While the winger's playing style earned early comparisons from Bluebirds supporters to legendary Welsh figure Gareth Bale, Russell himself drew comparisons to how the confidence Tanner played with was similar to Rio Ferdinand. Russell was a personal friend of Ferdinand, with the pair playing together at county level when young, and he recalled how Tanner also carried the same sort of composure and unperturbed nature. If Tanner lives up to the hype of being compared to Rio Ferdinand and Gareth Bale, he is going to end up having a half-decent career.

* * *

One of Tanner's coaches during his time at the Dripping Pan was Joe Vines, assistant to Tony Russell. Vines has overseen the development of several talented players, and played a key role in Tanner's development. I sat down with Vines and discussed Tanner's meteoric rise, his first impressions of the youngster, and what he feels sets Tanner apart from the other players that he has coached.

Why do you feel Ollie Tanner has become a part of the Cardiff City first team so quickly when so many perhaps take time to adapt to full-time football and a higher level?

'It's not an "overnight success story". There have been several managers there and he had a loan spell with York City where he was playing in a formation and system that didn't suit him. It has happened quickly, but it hasn't been all roses. Testament to him; his mentality, his work ethic and his character has got him to where he is now. The ability is easy. His strength is the mentality and his single-mindedness. When players transition from non-league to full-time, they often struggle with the workloads, the physicality and the regime. Examples like Garath McLeary and Michail Antonio spring to mind. It takes time to acclimatise to the expectations and the schedule. I think Ollie Tanner is in a good place, but there is more to come.'

You have coached a lot of talented players. Did you know that Ollie Tanner was that little bit special compared to the rest?

'When we brought Ollie Tanner in, we knew after one training session that he was a perfect fit for us and our style. He was released from Bromley and his agent was an old friend of mine and asked if he could come in. Once we had seen him train, we quickly put a deal to him. Working with Tony Russell – who is someone who has developed a catalogue of wide forwards over the years – was only going to end up one way. Ollie's finishing with either foot was the standout technical quality he had. We worked with him to get him in situations where he could use that more often and to greater effect. Ollie didn't always have it his own way and there were examples of poor decisions and uninspiring performances, but he desperately wanted to learn and he appreciated honest feedback and guidance.'

From the point of view of a higher team, what do you feel made Tanner such an attractive proposition to sign?
'Tanner has excellent pace and acceleration. He is comfortable travelling with the ball at speed. Tony used to liken him to Gareth Bale as he was just as quick with the ball as he was without it. Ollie has match-winning attributes and the self-belief to take shots on from all sorts of angles and distances. These are rare qualities especially when modern coaching is diluting the dribblers and the mavericks from our game.'

What do you feel sets Tanner aside from the other good players you have coached that have perhaps not got that big move?
'Ollie and his agent made the decision to join Cardiff City because the pathway to the first team was clearer and I respect that. He had something ridiculous like 27 clubs interested in him. Being at Tottenham Hotspur might have stunted his progress with talents like Son [Heung-min] or [Dejan] Kulusevski ahead of him so I think he's been very

wise to go somewhere he felt he would get opportunities. I know for a fact that there has been further interest from Premier League clubs, but he seems to be happy at Cardiff City currently and wants to do well for the club that took a chance on him. The Championship is a terrific level of football and highly competitive.'

Ollie Tanner had a trial with Tottenham Hotspur. He hasn't been able to get to Premier League level in the time since then, but do you feel he can get there, and how far do you think he can go?

'Ollie is the only player that ever came to me and told me that they had got a job and I actively discouraged them. Working in non-league, I often help youngsters find their first roles outside of the game and I help them find a hybrid of work and football that allows for them to be successful in life. Ollie Tanner was born to play football. I am very proud to have played a tiny part in his journey, but he must take all the credit for being an incredible kid who has worked his socks off to pursue his dream and he deserves everything that comes his way. To add to this, when he is back home from Cardiff he reaches out to some of the old players and staff to catch up. He has never forgotten where he came from and that – for me – is the biggest factor in who he is and who he will be; just a lovely kid who wants to be the best they can.'

* * *

Alex Scott

For those readers of a Bristolian or south coast persuasion, it would be hugely remiss of me to go through the entire book without mentioning one of the most naturally talented in the form of the 'Guernsey Grealish'. Bristol City have, in recent campaigns, shown a tendency to sign from Guernsey, and without a doubt the biggest success story is Alex Scott.

In terms of giving players exposure to men's football as early as possible, Scott is a fitting example of that. The midfielder was plunged into the first team at 16 years of age for Guernsey under the tutelage of Tony Vance. Footballing environments weren't completely alien to Scott at this point, having already stood out in his youth and trialled with south coast neighbours Southampton and Bournemouth prior to signing forms with Guernsey.

His rise was rather rapid to say the least; Scott spent just the single season in Guernsey colours prior to being plucked by Bristol City and the experienced eye of Brian Tinnion. Tinnion has a vast track record of identifying talented young players; he is to academy football what a sommelier is to a vintage French wine. Ahead of the January 2020 transfer window, the Robins brought Scott in, and while he was to begin with part of the youth team, it wasn't long before he was making waves and forced his way into the first-team fold. He signed professional forms in March 2021 and made his first-team debut five months later aged just 18. His first goal was only two months away, too; as first impressions go, Scott had made quite the impact at Ashton Gate.

Despite the Robins having more experienced options in the middle of the park, Scott soon established himself as a regular in the team, so much so that he was almost indispensable despite only being in his late teens. Early in 2021/22 he had become one of the first names on the team sheet and would only miss eight games that season, developing a reputation for being a silky ball player at the base of City's midfield. Even better still, if there were any concerns over whether Scott's slight figure would stand up to the physical rigours of the Championship, City fans needn't hasve worried as he was as tenacious in the tackle as he was proficient in possession; he topped most statistics charts that term, one of which was the yellow card count with 12.

Bristol City have developed their share of talent over recent years, with many having made their way out the door at Ashton Gate for big-money deals elsewhere; striker Antoine Semenyo moved to Bournemouth a few months before Scott took the same journey. Semenyo had also featured in non-league in his early career with a loan spell at Bath City. Lloyd Kelly, Aaron Webster and Josh Brownhill are three more examples.

You often get a sense when a player has perhaps outgrown their environment, and the 2022/23 season displayed all the hallmarks of that. Awash with awards, silverware and accolades coming out of his ears, praise being thrown in every direction; it was a halcyon time for Scott. When you've got the best manager in world football calling you an 'unbelievable player', it gives you confidence that you may well have a bit of a future in the game. Indeed, after excelling for the Robins against Manchester City in an FA Cup tie, the question was now a case of when and not if; Scott was heading for the big time, and it wasn't going to be with Bristol City.

Despite his glowing praise for Scott, it wouldn't be Pep Guardiola who would come calling; instead, Bournemouth made their move. Fortunately for Bristol City, the 2022/23 campaign provided the perfect backboard for Scott's valuation; with every honour that came his way, City could see a couple more noughts added to the price tag. That season he was by far and away the best young player in the division, being named Championship Young Player of the Year and appearing in the PFA Team of the Year in a City side that finished 14th. There was a clean sweep of City's end-of-season awards for good measure. Even better still for the Robins, manager Nigel Pearson had made clear to the media that Scott was at the very least a £25m player. Asking price set; asking price matched and he made his way to the south coast to sign for Bournemouth.

Despite battling injury problems since, Scott has – in glimpses – shown why he is highly regarded as being a star of the future. Silky, technical, tenacious and now an England under-21 international, the Guernsey lad has shown beyond doubt that his career is only heading upwards. The Green Lions to the Three Lions; what a journey.

* * *

The Worthing Revolution

The director of football at Brighton & Hove Albion at the time of Solly March's move to the Seagulls was Martin Hinshelwood, which brings us quite nicely on to another more recent example of players spring-boarding to success off the back of time in non-league: Worthing. Martin's nephew Adam was the manager of the Rebels, and oversaw the development of several top young players who have since gone on to carve out careers in the EFL and beyond.

Indeed, if you scour the Premier League and EFL, there are sprinklings of Worthing stardust all over the place.

Brentford have developed a reputation for signing some of the best young talent in the lower leagues, with their B team acting very much as a rock pool to the ocean of the first team; the chance to roll the dice on some aspiring talents who may one day land them a big return on their investment. Ben Krauhaus sealed a move to Brentford's B team having impressed in the National League with Bromley, and another that has followed the same path is former Worthing man Fin Stevens. Stevens was formerly on the books of Arsenal but was adjudged not up to the grade, and upon his release from the Emirates aged 16 he signed for Worthing. The Rebels are based locally to Brighton, so are very much in the landing net of players with potential who perhaps just miss the mark; Stevens is one of those.

One of the major benefits of joining Worthing was that Stevens would see regular first-team minutes having only recently turned 17. Hinshelwood's willingness to put players in and the acceptance of the youth-based model implemented by the Rebels lends itself to players in their late teens being thrust into the limelight perhaps before they would do elsewhere. Despite joining the youth team initially, Stevens quickly established himself as a regular in the first team.

His form persuaded Brentford to make a move for him in the summer of 2020. While Stevens did not make the impact that he would have liked for the Bees – limited to ten appearances in all competitions at the time of writing – his rise is still mightily impressive. Many players can take years to make the Premier League. Jamie Vardy is heralded as the standard bearer and yet he still took two and a bit seasons to go from non-league to the top tier. Stevens was able to do that in just 676 days.

Fin is one of a handful of players to have forged out successful routes into higher-league football off the back of time with the Rebels, also going on loan to Swansea City in 2022/23 and Oxford United the following season, eventually leaving Brentford in the summer of 2024 for German Bundesliga club St Pauli having also won two caps for Wales. Kwame Poku is often heralded as being a graduate of Colchester United's continually impressive youth conveyor belt, yet it was Worthing where the youngster got his first extended run of first-team football. Poku started out with fellow Isthmian League Premier Division side Cray Wanderers – graduating from their academy, and going on to make just a single appearance – but it was in Worthing colours that he got his big break; signing in February 2019 then heading to the EFL with Colchester three months later.

One of the most high-profile – or at least recognised – of their alumni is Lucas Covolan, the goalkeeper responsible for one of the most exhilarating moments in play-off history when going up for a set piece and scoring an added-time equaliser for Torquay United in the 2021 National League play-off final against Hartlepool United. Covolan didn't graduate from the Rebels' academy; indeed, the goalkeeper started out life in South America playing with the likes of future Brazil internationals Philippe Coutinho and Oscar. From the grandeur of Brazil and Spain, Covolan landed on English shores with Worthing. It was from there – having proven himself with Hinshelwood's side – that he went on to develop a reputation for being the flamboyant yet strong goalkeeper that he is. In the 2023/24 FA Cup third round, Covolan helped Maidstone United to a shock victory away to Championship side Ipswich Town with a heroic display.

* * *

One person instrumental behind the success at Worthing is Nathan Bowen. Bowen's story is rather unique, having spent the entirety of his professional career in either coaching or advisory capacities rather than playing. In recent years, having spent time with Brighton & Hove Albion's academy, Bowen was appointed as football director for Worthing, a position he still held at the time of writing. I sat down with Nathan to discuss the secret behind Worthing's success, and got an insight into why he feels they have such a strong reputation within the game for player development.

You have worked in and around Brighton & Hove Albion's academy before, as well as with Worthing. What do you think playing in non-league gives players that they perhaps don't get in academy football?
'I feel that the difference between academy football and non-league is variety. If you watch Category One football, you've got the pick of all the best players in the area and at that age level. They are all athletic and technically strong, supported by the best coaches and with modern philosophies; as such, quite a lot of games cancel each other out. At non-league, you get more variety in terms of style and shapes to teams, and I feel that can benefit teams. In academy football, the styles of play are all the same, by and large. In non-league, you've got different styles; some that go short, some that go long, some that play quickly, some that are patient. That variety is so useful. Furthermore, I think that in non-league

there is often greater freedom to go and express yourself and show what you are about, whereas in some academies philosophy comes first above anything else.'

You've seen so many players from Worthing go on to play at a higher level. What do you think is the key to that success?

'There are a few different reasons. The main one – I feel – is the staff involvement; players such as Hinsh [Adam Hinshelwood], Gary Elphick, Dean Hammond and now Aggy [Chris Agutter]. They are all good coaches with strong reputations in the game. As such, players don't look at us as a non-league side, but a good insight into the professional game. When they come in, they are learning from ex-players that have played at a higher level. You look at the likes of Hinshelwood [who went on to play for England at under-21 level and in the Championship] or Dean Hammond [who played in the Premier League]; that first-hand knowledge is so important. I think that also helps our ex-players that do go on to play higher be successful, as with us they have already had the principles of the professional game instilled into them; they are working every day with people who have been and done that.'

What is the one trait – or traits – that you look for in a young player who you think can go on to play at a higher level?

'We look for a number of traits, but the main ones are technical ability and the willingness to learn. Technical ability gets a player through the door at under-14 level for trials. Once they are in the door, we look for players who implement what they are being taught. We put them in scenarios whereby what we are teaching them may actually lose us the game, but in the long run we know that it is going to be beneficial for their development as they learn. Being able to problem-solve is also key; the ability to learn and retain information, and perhaps come up with solutions themselves independently of input from the coaches, too.'

From the perspective of Premier League and EFL teams, what benefit do you think there is in signing good players purely from non-league?
'I think in non-league there is a sense of urgency. At Worthing, we are fortunate to plan very much in the long term; there is no pressure to win everything at youth level. However, at a lot of non-league clubs, there is pressure that they *have* to win. As a result, players play with a sense of urgency. A lot of players are dependent on their individual success to provide them with finance; ultimately, doing well in non-league will earn them more, perhaps with double pay and bonuses. It teaches players the urgency and importance of every minute, and to make the most of every opportunity you get. That is why the loan system works so well; players come from an environment where there is that high pressure that they have to win. It gives players that steel and drive that you perhaps don't get in a comfortable environment of non-league.'

When Fin Stevens made his Premier League debut, what was that feeling like, to know that you and Worthing had played such a key part in his development?
'Amazing. We have had a lot of players over the years that have come through and done well, and we are proud of their efforts and individual journeys to have got where

they have. However, for Stevens to have come through with us and made his Premier League debut and play for St Pauli in the Bundesliga shows us that there is a fine line between being a professional player and one playing in non-league; one minute he was playing for Worthing against Hornchurch, and the next minute he is playing for Brentford against Manchester United [a pre-season friendly in July 2021; Stevens' Premier League debut came in a game at Southampton in January 2022]. Fin is a fantastic role model for the young players in our community and academy, as it gives them the belief that they can follow a similar path. I have no doubt that the success Fin has had drove Brad Dolaghan on to get the move he did to West Ham United. It makes that pathway tangible.

* * *

The Emergence of B Teams

While non-league is becoming increasingly well-financed, for clubs at EFL level looking towards signing from non-league it still – in the most part – remains a cost-effective avenue for securing high-potential, low-risk, often younger players who represent more sensible long-term investments. Going down the route of favouring recruitment from non-league over using the loan market on some emerging youngster out of a Premier League academy is fast becoming the norm, especially for League One and League Two clubs. As emphasis of this, in the 2024/25 summer transfer window alone, there were 54 players signed by clubs in League One and League Two directly out of non-league, and this is purely a drop in the ocean given the amount of players in recent years to have taken such a leap.

When you take into account the Championship, this number rises to 63; including the Premier League this is as high as 68. This is purely in one transfer window. Of course, a small portion of these 68 players is accounted for with your 'household' non-league names, the likes of Chris Conn-Clarke (Altrincham to Peterborough United) and Ed Francis (Gateshead to Exeter City). The large majority of this number is accounted for by players who are lesser-known and are still relatively unknown quantities even at non-league level: Zac Jeanes (Worthing to Swansea City), Jerome Richards (Enfield to Derby County), Aston Ellard (Conquest Academy to Coventry City), Rafiq Lamptey (Harrow Borough to Millwall), Aidon Shehu (Southend United to Hull City), Ethan Mann (Mickleover FC to Stockport County), Jack Matton (Binfield to Wycombe Wanderers), K'Marni Miller (Guiseley to Wigan Athletic) and Frankie Phillips (Paulton Rovers to Exeter).

All of these players have by no means been signed with an immediate role within the first 11 in mind; it will likely be years before they are breaking through and even beginning to establish themselves in the EFL and higher. This underlines the level of interest that teams have now in the pool of players at the very base of the pyramid; so akin to the goldmine of non-league now are the top-level clubs in this country that quite a few players will be signed purely, for starters, anyway, to form part of academy setups and an ever-increasing trend of B teams. These transfers provide a cash cow for non-league sides; in most cases they only need one of those young players to force their way into the first team and go on to be sold for profit to stay afloat and be financially healthy.

One club with joy out of investing in a B team, or development squad, is Wycombe Wanderers. The Chairboys have not been by any means big spenders in the market over recent years; it was only a takeover by the Wycombe Wanderers Trust in 2012 that took them out of an imposed transfer embargo amid a landscape of financial instability. The option to invest in a second-string side working in conjunction with the first team in which they could locate young, up-and-coming talents to invest in for the long term seemed – certainly on paper, at least – an attractive proposition; it would allow the club to be more sustainable and self-sufficient than they had been prior to 2012.

In 2020, they announced the launch of a new B team, under the guidance of UEFA A-licensed coach Sam Grace working under then first-team boss Gareth Ainsworth. Upon its inception, while simultaneously citing the B team as a useful avenue for providing an environment for Ainsworth to give his injured or out-of-favour first-team players a chance of regular football, then chairman Rob Couhig championed the move as a major step forward for the club in terms of being able to develop the careers of many young players. They have remained loyal to that commitment to this day.

Anis Mehmeti

The major success story of the still fledgling Wycombe B team is Anis Mehmeti. The Albanian midfielder's career path has been well-trodden by others; formerly of a top-level academy, let go at a young age, and turning to non-league to rebuild and reignite his aspirations of being a professional. Mehmeti signed for the Chairboys at the same time as striker Malachi Linton, winger Andron

Georgiou and defender Andre Burley. The latter trio have certainly not established themselves as far as the EFL is concerned – all three having since forged out careers in non-league following their exit from Adams Park – but such is the nature of investing in young players for B teams, you only need one of the yearly intake to go on to good things to make the whole thing a success. Anis Mehmeti was that player for Wycombe.

Originally from Islington, Mehmeti spent much of his schoolboy days floating around London academies, starting out with Fulham before going on to feature for Tottenham Hotspur. At the age of 16 and upon transition into academy football, Mehmeti would sign for Norwich City and spend two years at Carrow Road, departing to join non-league outfit Woodford Town; they were competing at Step 9 of the pyramid. It was a far cry from playing in academy football, but it would ultimately prove to be a hugely beneficial period as even amid Covid-19 disruptions he was able to amass enough minutes to convince Wycombe to take him on.

Mehmeti would go on to spend three years with Wycombe before being sold to Championship side Bristol City, for a record Wanderers incoming fee. He had flourished in the first team at Adams Park under Gareth Ainsworth to the tune of generating the Chairboys their biggest windfall of any player in their history; not a bad return on their investment. From having fallen through the trapdoor of academy football, Mehmeti has – as a result of his rebound of non-league – gone on to be a Championship star, and even better still a full international, winning his first cap for Albania in March 2023, just four years after his spell at Woodford Town.

Richard Kone

Perhaps the proudest find that the Chairboys have managed to sign from the lower leagues, a player with arguably the most inspiring story of any in this book, is striker Richard Kone. Signing for Wanderers in January 2024, Kone has made a positive impression and all of the signs are pointing towards him going on to be a player who, in the long term, they will look back on and classify as their most successful signing from non-league.

While Kone can now proudly call himself a professional, it could have quite easily worked out differently. In terms of upbringing and the challenges that he has had to face to get to where he has, there is no doubting that Kone's journey is unique given the magnitude of the struggle and toil that he has had to overcome. Theodore Roosevelt once said that 'nothing in the world is worth having or worth doing unless it means effort, pain and difficulty'; there couldn't be any truer sentiment to encapsulate Kone's route from the streets of Ivory Coast to the streets of Buckinghamshire.

Kone was born in Abidjan in 2003. I certainly see a synergy – in terms of the route into football and the profile of striker that he is – with arguably the greatest African striker of all time, Didier Drogba. The former Chelsea man was also born in Abidjan, albeit 25 years earlier; if you told Kone that he would achieve even half of what Drogba did then he would be a happy man.

Kone spent the early days of his footballing career playing on the streets of Abidjan. At the age of 16, he decided to leave his native country and moved to Cardiff. Despite his age, he was classified as homeless after being ostracised by his family, and arrived in the Welsh capital to compete in the Homeless World Cup. That tournament at Bute Park would be the start of his footballing career almost out of the blue; it's amazing how things can fall into place.

Kone impressed and had interest from clubs across the UK; Lopes Tavares London handed him a deal. The club had only been founded in 2015, so Kone joined while it was very much in its infancy, and looking back on his time with the Kings, 'King Kone' is hugely synonymous with them. If you ask anyone in the non-league scene to choose someone who epitomises Lopes Tavares, or Athletic Newham as they are now called, then apart from their founder Ulisses Felipe Lopes Tavares, Kone is the one who stands out. His success is such that he is very much viewed as the figurehead of the club since its inception. He was so prolific that in terms of the best strikers in non-league over recent years, you'd be hard pushed not to include him as a contender for the Mount Rushmore of non-league football. In his first campaign after making the move over from Abidjan, Kone announced himself with 20 goals to his name; that was a sign of things to come.

He moved to Wycombe in January 2024 on a permanent deal after an extended trial, and one of his proudest achievements to date came in September 2024 as the Chairboys lost 2-1 to Aston Villa in the League Cup. Despite their exit, it was a night that provided a timely and poignant reminder as to why Wanderers had embarked on the journey of investing time in signing from non-league. Aston Villa's starting 11 included Champions League finalist Ian Maatsen, Europa League and FA Cup winner Ross Barkley, £50m Belgian international Amadou Onana and two-time Championship winner Emi Buendía.

Wycombe, meanwhile, included Declan Skura and Franco Ravizzoli, with Kone among their substitutes, all three having started out in non-league. On a night where Matt Bloomfield's men won many plaudits with their display, in stoppage time Kone managed to get himself on the scoresheet. It was the crowning moment to announce himself on the big stage; a goal that epitomises all that he was about. A proud moment. Since then, he has gone on to get his first professional hat-trick, in a 3-1 win against Peterborough United in October 2024, and hit double figures in his first full season with the Chairboys, enhancing his glowing – and indeed growing – reputation for being one of the best young forwards in the country while being the headline act in a Chairboys side pushing for promotion from League One.

* * *

I spoke to Richard Kone about his rise from non-league, the journey to making it as a professional footballer, and how he has adapted to life in League One.

You had interest from Colchester United in 2021. Despite that deal not being completed, did the fact you had that interest from an EFL side give you the hunger to be a professional footballer?
'It wasn't just the interest from a higher club that motivated me to try and be a professional footballer. I had that fire in me to make it in the professional league, because I knew I had the ability and the hunger to push myself towards getting a professional contract. So, it wasn't just about the interest from the bigger clubs; I was ready to put in the work to get there.'

Your rise from Athletic Newham to Wycombe Wanderers has been rather fast. What do you put it down to?

'One of the reasons why I was able to make such a swift rise was because of my willingness to keep learning and improving my game on top of what I already knew. I was constantly trying to get better by learning from the top professionals around me. It was five years of learning, ups and downs, challenges and stresses on and off the pitch, and not knowing if I'd ever succeed or if a professional club would ever look at me. But, I had the support of everyone at Athletic Newham; the manager, the chairman and obviously the players. So, I couldn't give up easily. I learned a lot. My ability to adapt so quickly to League One came from playing in non-league football, playing against men at the age of 16 and experiencing the pressure of needing to get three points. I know that it is minor compared to league football, but it is still something you are willing to fight for. It helped me mature quickly and be ready for anything.'

What was the feeling like becoming a Wycombe Wanderers player; was it a dream come true?

'Being unveiled as a Wycombe Wanderers player was a dream that I never thought would come true. God was by my side in everything I have been through, and so I was really happy to finally get that move sorted. It is a feeling that you cannot express unless you experience it yourself. It was immense for me. To then score on my debut, that was the cherry on top. I couldn't have imagined scoring on my debut, but I did have a feeling that I would score and it happened. I was really happy, but in my mind it was a case of "this is just the start". I knew I had to keep working.'

Your record of 125 goals in 148 appearances for Athletic Newham is hugely impressive, and one of the best records we have seen at non-league level. What do you put that down to?

'Like I said, when you have the ability and believe in yourself, nothing can stop you. This journey has been hard work. I wasn't always a goalscorer; I had to adapt my game to be a goal machine. It's taken a lot of work, and it hasn't always been easy. There were times when I couldn't score a goal, but it was all part of the learning process. I am glad I went through that as it has made me the man and the player I am now.'

Wycombe have signed a lot of players from non-league. Did their track record of helping young players influence your decision on who to sign for, in that you could potentially follow a similar path to success?

'Everyone wants to play for a big club. I hadn't heard of Wycombe Wanderers before I first went there for a trial, so I didn't know about all the non-league players that they had signed before. But, I can say for a fact that they were there for me when I needed them. I had interest from other clubs, but Wycombe Wanderers showed the most interest in me. I was with them for a long period before I signed. With the project and what the manager wanted from me, I can say that signing for Wycombe Wanderers is one of the best decisions I have ever made in my life. It became clear that Wycombe Wanderers were the club I wanted to sign for more than anyone else, and I am glad that I did.'

For any other young forward coming through from non-league, what advice would you give to them?

'Be patient, work hard, stay quiet and work two or three times harder than anyone else. Surround yourself with a good environment, and most importantly believe in God and yourself. Don't let anyone tell you that you can't do something, and the results will come.'

* * *

Jasper Pattenden

Earlier in this chapter, I talked about the players produced by Worthing who have forged opportunities in the EFL. In this segment, the perfect intersection for both strands is Jasper Pattenden, who started out his career in the Rebels' academy before he was plucked by Wycombe in 2022. Originally for the B team, Pattenden has now made his transition into the first team setup at Adams Park and is proving every bit the investment that Wanderers were confident they were making. I was lucky enough to sit down (well, virtually) with Pattenden just one day after that League Cup defeat to Aston Villa back in September 2024. We discussed his journey in the game, his early days in youth football with Worthing and breaking through into the first team, early experiences of men's football, landing the move to Wycombe and his experiences since arriving at Adams Park.

What did first-team football at the age of 16 with Worthing give you over and above playing academy football?

'I played first-team football at 16, and went into a first-team dressing room at 15; that was invaluable. The experiences you have and the lessons that you learn – not just on the pitch – were so important. Being around adults, you learn so many life lessons. Anyone that is released from top academies or youth teams that asks me what they should do in their careers, I say the same thing every time; just go and play men's football as early as you can. I am so grateful for being in that position so early on in my development.'

Having been in academy football and also in non-league, can you see why so many who chose to go down the non-league route have since gone on to have success?
'Absolutely. I joined Brighton & Hove Albion's academy at the age of seven or eight, and transitioned into non-league at 15. You have seen so many players make that jump out of non-league. There is success out of academy football – absolutely – but I definitely think that playing men's football in non-league is so beneficial in improving players and giving them a pathway and platform to go on and be successful. You see some players drop out of academies later on and then go into non-league and it is a bit of a struggle; that's why early exposure to men's football is so paramount.'

Having been at the club, why do you think Worthing have such a good track record of producing top players?
'Worthing is a special club. I will always be indebted to the club, George [Dowell], Adam Hinshelwood; there are so many special people there. They have a clear system and pathway from the youth team into the first team, and that is the reason why so many boys go on to have the success that they have. They have good young managers – Adam Hinshelwood when I was there, and now Chris Agutter – that know the game, and play an attractive brand of football; players want to come and play for Worthing. Bar the National League, it is the most attractive club in non-

league. It is no coincidence as to why there have been so many players – in my time at the club, and since I've left – that have since come through and got moves. It's credit to all the hard work that goes on behind the scenes.'

What influence has Adam Hinshelwood had on your career, and why do you feel he is able to produce so many talented young players?

'Hinsh has had such a massive impact on my career; I still speak to him to this day. He was the one that gave me the text when I was 15 years old and released by Brighton & Hove Albion to come in and train at Worthing and gave me my opportunity; I will always be grateful for that. He gave me my debut in the first team at 16 years of age. He is a brilliant coach; the technical and tactical sides of his game are superb. He's also a great man-manager, and he got the best out of me as both a player and a person. It wasn't just me; there were so many that came through in that Worthing side when I was there. He just has a brilliant way of working with young players. He's a fantastic individual; that man-management side of the game is what makes him so special, and what gives him that edge as a coach to get the best out of players. I will always be grateful for the work he did with me to make me the player I am today.'

Do you feel that the early introduction to men's football has given you an advantage over other players your age that have perhaps gone down the academy route?

'I think it has definitely helped me. There are a lot of players that have stayed in academy football that are in indifferent positions in their careers now. I have had so much experience at a young age of playing men's football;

with Worthing in non-league, and then even now with Wycombe Wanderers. It makes you mature so quickly, and you learn so much about the game. It's what you perhaps don't get in academy football, and I wonder how some of my friends may have benefitted from going the route I have in terms of getting that early exposure to men's football.'

The move to Wycombe – what was it like, and how did it feel to get that opportunity?
'The move to Wycombe Wanderers was crazy. I had a couple of different offers prior to that, but I turned them down as I was so happy at Worthing; I wasn't sure if I wanted to be a professional footballer at the time as I had just set up a coaching business and was enjoying my football where I was. When the move to Wycombe Wanderers came about, I went in and trained with them for three days; I was so nervous. At the end of those three days, they wanted to offer me something; it was the realisation that I was going to be a professional footballer. That was just the foot in the door; I had to go and kick on.'

Wycombe have a B team. How does that compare – in terms of providing development for young players – to academy football and being thrust into first-team football at an early age, like in non-league?
'The B team at Wycombe Wanderers is brilliant; it's a hybrid. It gives you the opportunity to go and train with the first team. From week one, you are working with so many Football League players. The manager at the time was Gareth Ainsworth, and I learned so much in that initial three to six months. There have been a lot of players who come through with Wycombe Wanderers from the

B team, and it is a fantastic system. It helps the younger players to kick on and learn from the senior professionals.'

How refreshing is it to see so many players from non-league get chances in the first team at Wycombe?

'It's brilliant to see so many young players come through with Wycombe Wanderers. You don't just come to Wycombe Wanderers to sit in the B team. The whole objective is that if you are signed for Wycombe Wanderers, it is with the aim to push through and get an opportunity in the first team. Being at a football club where you know you are going to get opportunities is extremely rewarding. You know that if you work hard, train well and stay professional that you are going to get opportunities. You know that the manager is willing to throw young players into the team; that is the model that both Wycombe Wanderers and Worthing have.'

Your first game in the EFL – what was that like? Tell us about the game and the feeling of finally being an EFL player.

'My debut was in the Carabao Cup against Northampton Town [on 9 August 2022] and that was my first professional start; it was an incredible feeling. I made my Football League debut in League One away at Exeter City [seven days later], coming on for the last ten minutes. Coming off the pitch, you almost have to pinch yourself; I had come from the Isthmian League to playing in League One in the space of six months. It just shows how quickly things can change. However, that was just the start; it was the stepping stone to go on and achieve bigger and better things. Wanderers are a special football club, and you want to go and achieve for the club and the community.'

12

Scouting for Greatness

SO FAR, I've looked at players from various decades who have all started out in non-league and then gone on to play in the Football League, the Premier League or even beyond that on the European and international stage. Every club in the English pyramid – especially those money-makers at the top – strive to be able to find their own gems in non-league, some of whom they can sell on for big fees and in the process yield large profits on their investments.

Yet they aren't all fortunate enough to show that eye for spotting talent. Peterborough United have based their success since the turn of the millennium in identifying lower-division and non-league talent and being self-sufficient with a buy cheap, sell high model. Brighton & Hove Albion and Brentford are likewise showing an increasing willingness to delve into the non-league markets and find young talent for smaller fees. So how does one go about trying to predict a player's potential and identify a gem while they are still merely minerals?

Max Kilman

I thought I would take a look at that exact process by shining a light on Englishman Max Kilman, on the books of West Ham United at the time of writing. He started out with Welling United then moved on to Maidenhead United, and in August 2018 Wolverhampton Wanderers made a move for the National League defender. It is fair to say he has not looked back since, establishing himself as a regular in the Premier League. Kilman grew up as a youngster in West Ham, so it is perhaps apt that he would go on to sign for the Hammers for £40m in July 2024. There is something even more poetic about Kilman's journey that he got his major break at first-team level thanks to a West Ham legend in Alan Devonshire.

Despite joining Maidenhead in 2015, it wasn't until 2017/18 that Kilman would get his chance in the first team and he took to that like a duck to water. Having made over 30 appearances in Magpies colours that season, it was one game into the following campaign that Wolves came in. At this point he'd enjoyed a brief taste of non-league football but had majorly impressed as part of Maidenhead's youth team. Kilman first started out his journey at junior level by playing futsal for Genesis Futsal Club, so he developed an early tendency to be proficient in possession; such skills saw him deployed in midfield on occasions for the Magpies. For a defender to be so comfortable with the ball, it would take little time for the centre-back to spark interest.

That technical quality – coupled with his size – made him the perfect option for top-level clubs, particularly for the intensity of the Premier League, and that resulted in Wolves getting the deal done. So sure of his quality and potential were they that they handed him a two-year contract, and this off the back of a fairly limited sample size of minutes. They'd had only a very brief insight into Kilman's credentials, but there was clearly sufficient evidence to suggest that he was a future top-flight defender. It provides further evidence of the sheer importance – regardless of the quantity – of getting out and playing first-team games. By the time of his move to Molineux, Kilman had just 33 National League appearances to his name, along with 30 in Southern League Division One Central for Marlow, and a handful of appearances in youth and minor competitions.

The scout that was responsible for identifying Kilman was Joe Monks. He may not be a household name to the readers, but he has held various roles at different levels – including head of recruitment at Barnet and Colchester United, as well as heading up an emerging talent programme with Stockport County, and more recently as head of football operations with Hartlepool United. It is fair to say that in terms of finding players, Monks knows his stuff. Kilman making in excess of 100 Premier League appearances for Wolves before his move to West Ham suggests that Monks was on to something. Without a doubt, Kilman is the proudest find of Monks' career and is testament to his eye for talent.

* * *

I spoke with Joe Monks about how he went about scouting Kilman, what made him stand out from the crowd, and in general what Monks looks for when trying to scout players.

What is the one thing that you look for in particular when it comes to scouting players?
'Two things really: physical attributes and a willingness to learn. The professional game is so quick and physical nowadays, and players need to be athletically outstanding

to compete. That is a cornerstone for me. If I've identified that, I want to see if the youngster has a desire to improve, a passion for the game and an eagerness to take on board information. They don't have to apply all the information instantly – part of being a young player is making mistakes – but they have to want to try the right things. That makes it more likely they will improve as they get older.'

How did you first get into scouting?

'I loved football, but I was a bang-average player. My local club was Brentford who were in League One at the time, and as a 16-year-old I tried a bit of coaching but didn't really take to it. I fell under the mentorship of Shaun O'Connor, head of academy recruitment at Brentford. My dad used to be the opposition scout for Bath City when they were in the National League, and he used to take me along to games. I volunteered at Brentford to see if I could find any players. My first ever game was Lancaster Diamonds vs Hayes & Yeading on Wormwood Scrubs. Hayes & Yeading had a lad who scored three or four and got countless assists. They won comfortably – like by double figures – and this lad was clearly the best player on the pitch. I called Shaun after the game and he said Brentford already knew about him through their scouting network. Within a few days, they had brought him in on trial and signed him. I thought to myself, "This is easy, I've cracked it," and the rest is history. The lad was called Reece Cole, and he is now doing well at Exeter City.

Tell us a little bit about your scouting expertise.

'I wouldn't necessarily call it expertise; the key is hard work. Scouting is simple. You need to understand what the club wants, and what profile they need. Your opinion as a scout is irrelevant. Joe Monks' opinion does not matter – I work for the club. Your employer's opinion matters and so you have to think, "Right, Club X wants a really athletic, leggy, powerful central midfielder for the first team. They aren't too bothered about what they're like on the ball as they have good ball players; they want a destroyer." You just watch as many games as possible where that type of player might be playing, and watch the games with that in mind. If you see a clever number ten, you make a note for yourself, but there is no point feeding that back to the club; it doesn't help them.

'At academy level, it is even simpler. In the pre-academy and foundation phase [ages six to 12], you are just looking for "can they run?" and "can they learn?" as the basis. As the kids get older, the technical level needs to increase. It's about athleticism and whether they can take information on board. Academies now have excellent coaching, so those youngsters will get better technically when they go there. At YDP [Youth Development Phase, ages 12 to 16], the kids need a technical base which enables them to compete at academy level, plus they still need to be able to run and learn; that is three of the four corners of the FA model. At PDP [Professional Development Phase, ages 16 to 21], they need to be technically capable of playing in elite football, physically good and tactically aware. At that stage, the focus on their ability to learn shifts more towards mindset and work ethic. By that point, you are looking for all corners of the FA model.'

How do you ensure that what you see from a player in a trial match is a true reflection of a player's ability?

'You can't. You scout a player based on their USP. You need them to show their USP in the game. Let's take a winger. He's rapid, but his end product is inconsistent. He's only 17. You've seen him playing at Step 4. Sometimes, he has an absolute worldie and scores a hat-trick, but you've also seen him have really quiet games and miss open goals. In the trial game, even if he generally has a terrible time, as long as he shows what he is good at, you might take him for a further look. The USP is what will get him opportunities higher up the pyramid. A great example is Harry Smith, now playing for Swindon Town and formerly of Northampton Town and Sutton United. I saw him playing for Chatham Town as a 16-year-old, all 6ft 5in of him. He came on against Waltham Forest, used his body really well, his movement was good, but he missed an open goal in the last minute. He didn't perform to the level he wanted, but you could see there was potential. We still brought him in on trial, and he's gone on and had a good career.'

When did you first find out about Max Kilman and what were your first impressions?

'The story of Max Kilman is a funny one. I saw him playing for Maidenhead United after he had previously been on loan at Marlow. At Maidenhead, Max was in a direct and physical team – he was a good header of the ball and a steady defender, but you didn't get the chance to see how good he was technically. He never really had enough possession of the ball to show how good he was with his feet. We monitored him at Wanderers for a season while he was still young. We had some reservations about his ability with his feet. Then, when the summer came, I was taking part in a Grenfell charity football tournament as I am from west London. The best players from the area took part, plus there were a couple of ringers there to make up the numbers. Our team was arranged by a lad called Tayshan Hayden-Smith; he is the bloke who got Max his Wolverhampton Wanderers move.

'We played for the day and I was impressed by Kilman's use of the ball in tight areas. I'd been expecting him to struggle in the small spaces based on what we had seen at Maidenhead United, but he was actually one of the best players there on the day, even with multiple older EFL players playing. After the tournament, I asked Kilman if he fancied a trial at Wanderers. I don't think he believed me, but come Monday he was in the building trialling with the under-21s. The key difference between elite Premier League players and most footballers is their mindset. Kilman's application is exceptional. Lots of players have great shape and size like him, but they can't apply themselves in the same way on a daily basis. He has all the ingredients; technically excellent, reads the game well, and good athleticism. Matt Hobbs – now sporting director – was in charge of Wolverhampton Wanderers' under-21 recruitment while my remit was the schoolboy academy. Matt successfully negotiated a permanent deal with Maidenhead United, and the rest is history.'

Kilman is the standout name that you have scouted; tell us about some of the others that you have scouted that have gone on to do well.
'As a scout, you identify a lot of players. There were plenty of players that were signed to clubs – Junior Tchamadeu, Kwame Poku, Samson Tovide at Colchester United,

Dexter Lembikisa at Wolverhampton Wanderers, Ronnie Edwards at Barnet – and many others who have gone on to make a living out of the game in the EFL and the National League.

'At Barnet, we had a lad called Rob Atkinson who I felt we should sign, yet the coaches didn't agree. Alongside my role at Barnet, I was managing [Southern Combination club] St Francis Rangers. I played him in the men's team at 16 as the youth team didn't pick him. He went on to play for Bristol City in the Championship [joining from Oxford United in 2021]. Keenan Davis came into Barnet and was told no before Aston Villa signed him. One of my favourites is we had Inih Effiong and Nicke Kabamba both on trial at Barnet about a week apart. Inih was at Biggleswade and Nicke from Hampton. Both were deemed not technically of the level and now are both proven National League strikers. It is funny how much bias coaches put on technical ability, and how many of them dismiss the actual impact players can have in a game.'

How much pride does it give you to see what Max Kilman has gone on to do?

'Max took the opportunity with both hands, and players like him will rise to the top. That is less of an achievement than taking someone maybe from a difficult background or tough environment and helping them get opportunities through football that mean their quality of life might improve. Some young players have no support outside the game. You can use football to give them opportunities they may not otherwise have – whether that be as a professional, as a scholar at an American or English university, or pursuing a career in football after not quite making it.

Sometimes it is about having the influence of academy football, or non-league football. That can give a person real focus in their life, and that might prevent them from going off the rails. The player I'm proudest of scouting no longer plays football. He was released at the end of his scholarship, and never actually played a professional game. But, football gave him a grounding that enabled him to leave behind very difficult circumstances, to become a proud parent to his children, and hold down a career.'

Why do you think so many young players in non-league go on to do well at a higher level?
'The gap between League Two and the National League now is minimal. When you've got full-time teams in the National League North and South, where do you draw the line in terms of non-league in its "true form"? – it's difficult. I think young players from the non-league pyramid go on to do well because they get the opportunity to play men's football from a younger age. Those minutes are the most important development tool for young players. The more exposure that they get to that, the better their chance of playing at a higher level. It is "real football". The difference between League Two and the Isthmian Premier League is minimal in terms of actual ability. Attitude will be the main difference, plus small amounts of technical, tactical and physical capability. It's mainly the mentality. Exposing players to that is far better for their development than playing academy matches. Playing in front of hundreds of fans on a cold Tuesday night in Matlock is far closer to playing in the EFL than – let's say – playing on a carpet of a training ground pitch on a Saturday morning in the Under-18 Premier League.'

* * *

Josh Stokes

Regular readers of my blog will know that it would be somewhat remiss of me to write a whole book about the best talent out of non-league and not mention Josh Stokes – a player I was singing the praises of from his time at AFC Sudbury. It would be an oversight if I didn't give some airtime to without a doubt the player who, in all the time I have been covering and watching non-league, is the most natural talent I have had the pleasure of watching. While the likes of Jamie Vardy remain the standard-bearers for the success of former non-league talent, I have no doubt in years to come we will be talking about Josh Stokes as one of the best young English players that his country has to offer.

Stokes's journey is like many of the players in this book, having turned to non-league after the rejection of being released by an academy, in his case Ipswich Town, which led to him signing for AFC Sudbury.

The Suds are blessed with one of the best academies outside of the Football League, with Tyler French (later of Bradford City, Wrexham, Dundee and Sutton United), Barış Altıntop (King's Lynn Town, Braintree Town, Larne and Portadown), Reuben Swann (Portsmouth and Havant & Waterlooville) and Liam Bennett (Cambridge United and Walsall) having all graduated. Josh Stokes is another of what will no doubt eventually be an exhaustive list of talented AFC Sudbury alumni.

Signing at the age of just 16, Stokes played an integral part in AFC Sudbury's Isthmian League North title-winning campaign in 2022/23 with 16 goals to his name. Off the back of those efforts, clubs would unsurprisingly come calling in the summer. Aldershot Town, through manager Tommy Widdrington and head of recruitment Jamie Hedges, swooped to sign Josh Stokes as their marquee capture that summer.

For all of the hype that the youngster had upon arriving at the Recreation Ground, Stokes lived up to it and more in taking the National League by storm as the jewel in the fifth tier's crown. His 16 goals in 29 appearances helped the Shots transform themselves from National League relegation fodder to play-off possibilities, also knocking out Stockport County and Swindon Town in the FA Cup. It was no surprise, therefore, that clubs in the EFL came circling for the youngster, and Bristol City were the lucky beneficiaries in landing his services for a reported paltry fee of just £250,000 up front. I'd have been pushing for at least that just for one of his shin pads. But to Bristol City he went.

At the time of writing Stokes had yet to make his Championship debut for the Robins, appearing in an EFL Cup tie in August 2024 before going on loan to League One side Cambridge United for the season.

Stokes would enjoy a successful loan spell at the Abbey Stadium, reaching five goals and impressing despite the team's overall struggles.

* * *

I spoke to Jamie Hedges about the process he went through to scout and sign Josh Stokes, what makes him such a generational talent, and discuss what his potential in the game is.

You have scouted some top players in your time. Would you say Josh Stokes has been the pick of those?

'Absolutely; I'd say he is definitely *the* pick of those that I have signed. It is purely down to the level of outlay on him and the rewards we got; he certainly lived up to and exceeded our expectations. For us to put in as little as we did to secure his services and then go on to have the season he had; it was quite the story. To sign a player from Step 4 of non-league and take him into Step 1, and then to sell him on to the Championship with Bristol City, all within the space of six months; he's by far the best.'

You have worked with some top players over the years. Would you say that Stokes is the most talented?
'I have been at Bristol Rovers in League One, King's Lynn Town in the National League North and now at Aldershot Town in the National League. If I am being honest, in terms of just general footballing talent then the best I have worked with would be Josh Barrett. Some of the things he does on the training pitch are mesmerising. His vision and technical ability are the likes of which I haven't seen before. I'd put Jonson Clarke-Harris, Josh Stokes and Lorent Tolaj in the mix as being some of the best I've worked with, but I will always stick my neck on the line and say that in terms of just footballing ability, Barrett takes top spot.'

There was a lot of hype about Stokes as being one of the top non-league prospects at the time of his signature for Aldershot Town; did he surprise you with just how good he was?
'I will be honest; did I think he would go and produce the numbers that he has so quickly? I didn't. Did I think he would be sold on at some point in the future? Absolutely;

that's why I recommended the club sign Josh. When he came in, the general consensus for the average punter was that he'd go out on loan and take a couple of years to find his feet. Our view to begin with was for him to just go into training and try to prove himself; we didn't have any expectations or pressure on him. I remember the first training session and he impressed so much that we knew he wasn't going out on loan and that he could handle the step-up to going straight into the first team. From there, he has flourished. He forced everybody's hand with his application and attitude.'

Despite being highly rated, what background work did you do on Josh prior to him signing for Aldershot?
'He was flagged up to me a number of times, and he was someone that I had tracked from afar. I followed his progress for a couple of weeks, and I said to Tommy Widdrington that we needed to go and see him play. We both agreed that he was a good player, but it was more so the physicality that impressed us.

'When you get sent to watch an 18-year-old as he was at the time, you expect a wiry winger, but he was fully developed and handled everything that was thrown at him.'

There is always that one player who comes through and goes on to be a generational talent. Do you feel Josh Stokes can be that, or indeed is already that?
'I think that Josh is without a doubt one of the best players to come out of non-league, and in many respects he is a bit of an outlier. There are lots of good players at Step 3 and Step 4 that have gone on to do well and will go on to

do well, but very few will be able to climb the leagues as quickly as Josh has done. He is a unique player – his all-round profile is like nothing else we have seen before – and so he is certainly a generational talent. There are lots of good players at a lower level. Because of the low success rate of Premier League academies and influx of foreign players, that leaves British-based players as being pushed out of academies at an early age.'

You have signed lots of good young players at Aldershot. Does it just underline the platform that non-league gives to players?
'I have just got it in my thinking as a recruiter that I want to be able to sign a player for X and sell them on for Y at a profit; that – for me – is the ideal. I don't want to pay fees or big money for players who are going to depreciate in value; I want to sign players who are always going to get better and improve the football club. I am always big on young talent and likewise the manager is too. As soon as I was given the opportunity of being in charge of recruitment at King's Lynn Town, and then at Aldershot Town, the one thing that I was big on was pushing for bringing in younger talent. If I see a young player go to another club in our division and do well then I am always thinking, "I haven't done my job properly."'

* * *

Josh Stokes is just one of a handful of players who have gone on to seal big moves and forge successful careers off the back of time at the Recreation Ground; Aldershot have played their part in the development of quite a few sterling examples of non-league alumni.

The Shots have flitted between the Football League and non-league's top table during their existence, spending five years in League Two between 2008 and 2013 before their eventual relegation back into the Conference Premier under Dean Holdsworth. In the 11 years and counting since then they have – barring a fifth-placed finish under Gary Waddock in 2017/18 and a memorable campaign in 2023/24 under Tommy Widdrington – spent much of their time treading, successfully, I must add, against the National League trap door: 15th twice, 18th three times, and 19th, 20th and 21st once each. Couple that with not being far from the financial heavyweights, and their requirement, therefore, to constantly try and take a gamble on a young hotshot from the lower leagues means that it is hardly surprising that they have during this time been able to unearth the odd talent that has since gone on to higher pastures.

I have trawled back through the archives and picked out some of the very best players to have used their time at Aldershot as the springboard for launching their careers. Someone who has had the privilege first-hand of watching all of the Aldershot players featured in this chapter is Rob Worrall. A long-standing supporter and matchday commentator at the Recreation Ground, and follower of the Shots up and down the country, Rob has both enjoyed and endured the joys that come with being a fan of a lower-league club and spoken on so many players in Shots colours. I sat down and spoke with Rob about his memories of each player from their time at the Recreation Ground. Those views are in the pages that follow.

* * *

Ethan Chislett

Another of the brightest stars in the sky of Aldershot alumni is Ethan Chislett. Chislett's stay with the Shots was rather short-lived, making his meteoric rise all the more impressive; he went from being a seventh-tier player with Metropolitan Police to playing in League One within the space of roughly a calendar year, moving to the Recreation Ground in the summer of 2019. Chislett's journey as a whole is the perfect epithet for the springboard that non-league gives players, with his departure from Aldershot in August 2020 for the EFL coming seven years after he had first left the Shots as a released schoolboy, underlined the opportunities that come in football with taking one step backwards to potentially take two forward. In many ways, Chislett's journey – and in particular the move into non-league – is like so many of the others that I have profiled in this book, from rejection to a story of a second chance.

Rob Worrall's view: 'Ethan Chislett stepped up two levels to play for Aldershot Town in 2019, joining from Metropolitan Police. It was evident within the first month of watching him that he would be stepping up again in the not too distant future after that, as he – in the end – did; he went up two more levels to sign for AFC Wimbledon. Technically he was sound, physically he wasn't the biggest, and so therefore had to gain an advantage with his skill, movement and positioning. He was a surprisingly natural goalscorer despite playing in midfield, and he scored a lovely array of goals for Aldershot Town. My favourite memory was a goal at the EBB where he danced past a couple of players and lifted it into the back of the net.'

Danny Hylton

For supporters who have followed an EFL club, Danny Hylton's name is one that will be familiar – he has more than likely scored against your team at some point. One of the true goalscoring greats of the lower levels, Hylton's trajectory since leaving the Recreation Ground takes on an even greater sense of pride given that he is one of Aldershot's own, having come through the academy and since gone on to forge out an 11-year-long association with the Football League.

Hylton never got to enjoy the grandeur of the Premier League, but that matters little as he begins to wind down his career and make the transition into coaching at the time of writing; he has achieved what so many dream of and never get the chance to do. The failure to feast at English football's top table certainly doesn't diminish his achievements; not least the high regard with which the Shots hold their former Conference Premier winner and academy graduate. If you cut him open, he will bleed Aldershot red.

Rob Worrall's view: 'Danny Hylton is the most successful academy graduate that Aldershot Town have ever produced. He broke into the first team in 2006 and he had something different about him. He was totally unorthodox. He was ironically a player that wasn't prolific – and hasn't been prolific – at the start or the end of his career; he played around 170 games in Shots colours and only scored around 35 goals. He was the top goalscorer in the FA Cup one year, and was invited to Wembley for scoring seven goals in that campaign. He didn't do the basics right all the time, but he was a little bit unorthodox and difficult to defend against. If I watched three Danny Hylton moments, it would probably go something like, "Oh, Danny ... oh, Danny ... YES, DANNY." He became a little more prolific towards the maturer end of his career.'

Idris Kanu

On the topic of Shots attacking alumni, that brings me on nicely to another product: the tricky and twinkle-toed Idris Kanu, who still holds the record for being the youngest player to pull on the Aldershot Town colours at the age of 16 in October 2016. His destination after Aldershot will come as little surprise to the readers and indeed observers of non-league; if I had to give you a free £1 bet to put on where a precocious, young, non-league talent would end up, you wouldn't need many guesses until you correctly landed on Peterborough United.

Kanu's route into first-team football and going to non-league is similar to that of Pelly Ruddock Mpanzu in that he also left West Ham in favour of making the brave – yet sensible – decision to grasp the opportunity of action at a lower level when signing for Aldershot. Kanu's decision was even more brave given that his displays in the academy at Upton Park were winning more than just admiring glances from afar. As very much one of the high performers, the speedster was fast becoming one of the brightest prospects at youth level at the time; they often talk about good players being 'tried' in a level up at youth level, but how about playing under-21s football at just 15? The hype around him was so great that Manchester United were even interested.

Despite that, Kanu made the decision to move on to pastures new and it was a former coach of his at West

Ham, the future AFC Fylde and Chesterfield boss James Rowe, that was instrumental in working his move to the Recreation Ground, where Rowe was by now the assistant manager. The youngster rekindled his relationship with Rowe, and that proved to be an inspired decision. At just 16 years of age, Kanu was hurled straight into men's football almost as quickly as he had signed; he completed his forms on the Friday, and by 4.41pm the next day he was a National League player.

His impact under Gary Waddock as the Shots chased the play-offs was enough to lead Town to take the steps to extend his stay and tie down his future; he signed a long-term contract merely three months after joining. He'd made quite the impression, and despite Aldershot's own ambitions of reaching the EFL falling short, Kanu would be heading there anyway – not through the play-offs and a win at Wembley, but via a transfer to Peterborough, the perennial moths to the non-league flame.

Ultimately, Kanu's EFL exploits would be blighted by Posh's change in management. Signed under Grant McCann and under the leadership of Steve Evans within the space of seven months, Kanu's journey was almost over before it started. The next five years on Posh's books would see him largely in the colours of other teams, with three separate loan spells and only making 69 appearances for the Cambridgeshire club. That time at London Road would not see him reinforce his EFL reputation, but would see him secure international recognition for Sierra Leone, qualifying through his parental lineage. Having started in non-league, Kanu's career then saw him return to the National League and excel for Barnet, chasing promotion to League Two at the time of writing.

Rob Worrall's view: 'Idris Kanu made his debut at the age of just 16. He had an opportunity – following a trial – to sign for Manchester United, but he turned it down to play for Aldershot Town; quite possibly the only player ever to do that. He was so exciting to watch from the word go. He was incredibly skilful, but when he left for Peterborough United he did so without great numbers or assists and that is something that dogged him during his time at London Road. He has good recovery pace and strong qualities on the ball, and had to adapt to playing in a right-back role at times. He hasn't quite hit the heights of his potential with Barnet, but he is still someone with so many skills and trickery, and a real asset to Barnet at this time.'

13

Closing Words

SO, THERE we have it.

Hopefully, this book has served as an etymological exploration into the wonders of non-league and the role that it has played in kick-starting the careers of so many players who have since gone on to play at the top level of the game. Be it only a couple of appearances in a first loan away from their parent club, or years of consistent performance rewarded with a marquee move into the EFL, non-league has provided the foundations for an endless list of talent to find their feet in first-team football, accelerate their development and realise their potential.

Indeed, there have been numerous players who even during the writing of this book have spent time playing in non-league football and then gone on to get their big breaks at a higher level. Look at Maxi Oyedele as the prime example. Prior to signing for Altrincham in early 2023, Oyedele's only prior experience of playing first-team football was limited to a couple of EFL Trophy appearances for Manchester United under-21s. No real prospects of a first-team breakthrough. No signs of being in the big time anytime soon. He was merely an aspiring 18-year-old and, after signing for Phil Parkinson's Altrincham in 2023 in his first loan, the midfielder would go on to get invaluable minutes at first-team level and quickly establish himself. He would only play a dozen games for the Robins, but looking back at that spell at Moss Lane, it is fair to say that spell has been immeasurably transformative for his prospects. He is now playing in the top league in Poland with Legia Warsaw, also appearing in the UEFA Europa Conference League, and in October 2024 he became a fully fledged Polish international – although born in Salford, he qualifies through his Polish mother. If you ever needed a testimony to the value of early development in non-league, this is it.

While I covered 82 players during this book, I could have quite easily included many more, and the omission of so many talented names does not diminish the journey that they have gone on. Such is the strength of non-league, I have no doubt that even between sending this book for publication and the time you are now reading it in print there will have been players that have got their breaks with big-money moves up the pyramid. Non-league has such a wealth of future stars, and if you begin to look beneath the surface you will find endless talent waiting to be unearthed and given a platform to shine.

Bibliography

Books:

Book, T. & Clayton, D., *Maine Man: The Tony Book Story* (Edinburgh: Mainstream Publishing, 2004)

Canoville, P., *Black and Blue: How Racism, Drugs and Cancer Almost Destroyed Me* (London: Headline, 2008)

Cashmore, E., *Black Sportsmen* (London: Routledge, 2013)

Ferdinand, L., *Sir Les: The Autobiography of Les Ferdinand* (London: Headline Book Publishing, 1997)

Hugman, B.J., *The PFA Footballers' Who's Who 2010/11* (Edinburgh: Mainstream Publishing, 2010)

Jacobs, N., *Vivian Woodward: Football's Gentleman* (Cheltenham: The History Press Ltd, 2005)

Meynell, J., *Halifax Town: The Complete Record* (Derby: DB Publishing, 2011)

Rollin, J., *Rothmans Football Yearbook: 1980/81* (London: Queen Anne Press, 1981)

Smith, D. & Ward, A., *The Official West Ham Dream Team* (London: Hamlyn, 2003)

Welch, J., *Chapter 5 – The Human Chain of Lightning* (Kingston Upon Thames: Vision Sports Publishing, 2015)

Websites:

barryhugmansfootballers.com
skysports.com
bbc.co.uk

tribalfootball.com
borehamwoodfootballclub.co.uk
hulldailymail.co.uk
londonnewsonline.co.uk
cnwl.ac.uk
thenonleaguefootballpaper.com
inews.co.uk
dailyrecord.uk
chroniclelive.co.uk
guardian.co.uk
ilkestonadvertiser.co.uk
theguardian.com
chrisplatts.co.uk
encyclopedia.com
telegraph.co.uk
footballandthefirstworldwar.org
timesonline.co.uk
buzzsprout.com
theargus.co.uk
independent.co.uk
dailyecho.co.uk
walthamforest-fc.co.uk
kentlive.news
kentishfootball.co.uk
leamingtoncourier.co.uk
maidstoneunited.co.uk
manutd.com
hertfordshiremercury.co.uk
markblundellpartners.com
coventrytelegraph.net
thestar.co.uk
romfordrecorder.co.uk
wikipedia.org
outsports.com

outsideoftheboot.com
scoutedftbl.com
gazettelive.co.uk
menmedia.co.uk
watfordobserver.co.uk
theathletic.co.uk
shieldsgazette.com
stocksbridgeps.co.uk
stocksbridgeparksteels.co.uk
national-football-teams.com
stretfordend.co.uk
thefreelibrary.com
nytimes.com
birminghammail.co.uk
vitalfootball.co.uk
theathletic.com
highbeam.com
thetimes.co.uk
tottenhamhotpsur.com
walesonline.co.uk
wfchistory.com
come-to-wealdstonefc.co.uk
wwfc.com
yahoo.com
yallashoot7.com
nytimes.com